Frew's Daily Archive

Frew's Daily Archive

A Calendar of Commemorations

Compiled by
Andrew W. Frew

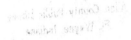

McFarland & Company, Inc., Publishers
Jefferson, North Carolina, and London

Library of Congress Cataloging in Publication Data

Frew, Andrew W., 1944–
Frew's Daily archive.

Includes indexes.
1. Calendars. 2. Chronology, Historical. I. Title.
II. Title: Daily archive.
D11.5.F7 1984   902'.02   84-42612

ISBN 0-89950-127-3

Printed in the United States of America

McFarland Box 611 Jefferson NC 28640

To Sandy and Amy

Also, with special thanks to John Green
for his unwavering zeal

Contents

Preface

This calendar of commemorations consists of a listing of encapsulated events, birthdays and commemorations which are intended to illustrate the significant affairs, the fascinating vagaries, the humor, the ironies of our planet. It is hoped that this collection of facts will become a point of departure for a reader's own personal investigation into whatever may be of interest for whatever reason.

There are a minimum of ten events, two birthdays and one holiday or commemoration for every day in the year, including February 29th. In this compilation, there are over 4,500 events cited, over 2,300 births noted and over 1,300 commemorations enumerated. The entries range from the dawn of the archeozoic era to the birth of an 1890's baseball player to the Independence Day celebration of the new nation of Zimbabwe. Some of the data contained in this chronology involve a degree of conjecture, but every effort has been made to guarantee the accuracy of each item according to available historical and prehistorical records. Some of the commemorations may no longer be observed (e.g., the Shah's birthday in Iran) but may still be of interest.

Aside from this element of conjecture, the occurrences were taken from the historical record at face value. For example, no attempts were made to verify stories about UFO's, monsters, or anything else beyond normal human experience.

All variable holidays, commemorations and feasts are listed on the earliest date on which they can possibly fall. For example, Labour Day is celebrated on the fourth Monday in October in New Zealand. That holiday will be found listed on the twenty-second although it could fall as late as the twenty-eighth.

January

The first day of January marks the following commemorations:

Anniversary of the Revolution (Cuba)
(St.) Basil's Day
Cameroon Independence Day
Feast of the Circumcision
Founding of the Republic of China (Taiwan)
Guen Nyidhok, or Winter Solstice (Bhutan)
Haiti Independence Day
Mummers' Day
New Year's Day
Sudan Independence Day

> Beginning of the Black Nazarene Fiesta (thru the 9th)
> Save the Pun Week
> "Weeks" Week

> National Blood Donor Month
> National Egg Month
> Wheat Bread Month

January 1

153 B.C., the Romans established January 1 as the first day of the
    year, supplanting March 15.
379 A.D., St. Basil the Great died.
1519 the Swiss Reformation, led by Huldreich Zwingli, began.
1801 the minor planet Ceres was discovered.
1804 Haitian independence was proclaimed by Jean Jacques Dessalines.
1840 the first recorded bowling match took place.
1863 Daniel Freeman's homestead at Beatrice, Nebraska was the
    first to be obtained under the Homestead Act.
1863 the Emancipation Proclamation was formally issued by President
    Abraham Lincoln.
1876 Bass' Pale Ale registered their trademark.
1877 the Royal Titles Bill proclaimed Queen Victoria the Empress
    of India.

1

1889 the first Tournament of Roses was held in Pasadena, California.
1901 the Commonwealth of Australia came into being.
1901 the 140 mile Tamatave-Antananarivo Road opened.
1902 the first Rose Bowl football game was played. The final score
        was: University of Michigan 49, Stanford 0.
1914 the St. Petersburg-Tampa Airboat Line became the first airline
        to offer scheduled passenger service.
1939 the University of California opened the first flea laboratory.
1942 Durham, North Carolina provided the site for the only Rose
        Bowl football game not played on the west coast.
1956 Sudan became an independent nation.
1959 Fidel Castro overthrew Fulgencio Batista and took control of
        the Cuban government.
1960 Cameroon proclaimed itself an independent republic.
1962 Western Samoa became an independent state.
1964 Belize (British Honduras) was granted the right of self rule.
2001 marks the first day of the twenty-first century.

The following people were born on January 1:

Huldreich Zwingli in 1484.
Paul Revere in 1735.
General "Mad" Anthony Wayne in 1745.
Betsy Ross in 1752.
Tim Keefe in 1856.
E.M. Forster and William Fox in 1879.
J. Edgar Hoover in 1895.
Xavier Cugat in 1900.
Dana Andrews and Barry Goldwater in 1909.
Hank Greenburg in 1911.
J.D. Salinger in 1919.

January 2   Ancestors' Day (Haiti)
                                        Berchtoldstag (Switzerland)
                                        The Day After (Scotland)
                                        Georgia Ratification Day

1492 Spain recaptured Grenada from the Moors.
1521 Martin Luther was excommunicated.
1788 Georgia ratified the constitution of the United States.
1839 Louis Daguerre took the first photograph of the moon.
1893 the U.S. Post Office issued its first commemorative stamps.
1910 America's first junior high schools were opened in Berkeley,
        California.
1922 the Hadley Correspondence School for the Blind, offering instruc-
        tion in the Braille system, was incorporated.
1925 the American Psychological Association was instituted.

1935 the trial of Bruno Hauptmann began. He was accused of the kidnap-murder of Charles A. Lindbergh, Jr.
1942 Japan occupied Manila and General MacArthur withdrew to Bataan.
1942 the United Nations Pact was signed.
1959 Lunik I, a Soviet rocket, flew by the moon and on into orbit around the sun.
1961 Haleakala, Hawaii registered a temperature of 14° F.
1965 Joe Namath signed a contract with the New York Jets, reportedly for $400,000.

The following people were born on January 2:

General James Wolfe in 1727.
Robert Nathan in 1894.
Isaac Asimov in 1920.
Julius La Rosa in 1930.
Roger Miller in 1936.

January 3   Alaska Admission Day
                                 Upper Voltan Revolution Day

1871 Oleomargarine was patented by Henry W. Bradley.
1876 a group in Florence, Massachusetts opened the first free kindergarten.
1888 Marvin C. Stone patented the artificial drinking straw.
1890 the Univ. of Wisconsin opened the first college level dairy school.
1915 Germany used tear gas against Russian troops and introduced chemical warfare to the world.
1924 the London Evening Standard reported that thousands of red worms fell in a snow storm over Halmstad, Sweden.
1938 the March of Dimes was established.
1947 Congress' opening session was televised for the first time.
1948 the first color newsreel was released.
1959 Alaska was admitted to the Union.
1961 the United States broke off diplomatic relations with Cuba.
1980 Joy Adamson, author of Born Free, was killed in Africa.

The following people were born on January 3:

Cicero in 106 B.C.
Lucretia Mott in 1793.
Earl Clement Attlee in 1883.
Victor Borge in 1909.
Bobby Hull in 1939.
Stephen Stills in 1945.

January 4   Burma Independence Day
                                     Feast of St. Elizabeth Bayley Seton
                                     Utah Admission Day
                                     Zaire Martyrs of Independence Day

1493 Christopher Columbus posted a party of men on Santo Domingo and returned to Portugal.
1869 the State School for the Blind and the Deaf opened in Raleigh, North Carolina.
1885 Dr. W.W. Grant performed the first appendectomy in Davenport, Iowa.
1887 Thomas Stevens completed the first round the world bicycle trip.
1896 the Actors' National Protective Union was chartered.
1896 Utah was admitted to the Union.
1915 Moses Alexander was sworn in in Idaho. He was the first Jewish governor to be elected for a full term in one of the United States.
1939 Frieda Wunderlich became the first woman to be elected dean of a graduate school.
1944 Dr. Ralph J. Bunche was appointed to the State Department's Division of Political Studies.
1948 Burma became an independent republic.

The following people were born on January 4:

Jacob Grimm in 1785.
Louis Braille in 1809.
Sir Isaac Pitman in 1813.
General Tom Thumb (Charles S. Stratton) in 1838.
J.R.R. Tolkien in 1892.
Floyd Patterson in 1935.

January 5   Epiphany Eve
                                     Feast of St. John Nepomucene Neu-
                                     mann
                                     George Washington Carver Day

1,510,428 B.C. the Günz (Nebraskan) period of glaciation began.
1863 Anna Callender Brackett of St. Louis, Missouri became the first woman principal of a normal school.
1903 the first trans-Pacific cable was opened to public use.
1904 Rivervale, New Jersey registered a temperature of -34° F.
1904 Smethport, Pennsylvania registered a temperature of -42° F.
1913 Strawberry Tunnel, Utah registered a temperature of -50° F.
1914 Henry Ford began offering a $5.00 wage for an eight hour day.
1919 Anton Drexler founded the Nazi Party in Munich.

1925 Nellie Ross assumed office in Wyoming and became the first woman governor of one of the United States.
1933 construction of the Golden Gate Bridge began.
1943 George Washington Carver died at seventy-nine years of age.
1970 Joseph Yablonski, United Mine Workers official, was found murdered.
1973 the Baer quintuplets were born.

The following people were born on January 5:

Stephen Decatur in 1779.
Konrad Adenauer in 1876.
Walter Mondale in 1928.
Diane Keaton in 1946.
Don Gullett in 1951.

January 6   Children's Day (Uruguay)
                                 Coptic Christmas
                                 Epiphany
                                 Greek Cross Day
                                 Iraqi Army Day
                                 New Mexico Admission Day
                                 Haym Salomon Day
                                 Three Kings Day

1540 Henry VIII married his fourth wife, Anne of Cleves.
1639 the Virginia tobacco crop surplus was ordered destroyed to ensure a good price for the normal harvest.
1759 George and Martha Washington were married.
1844 S. Broadmeadow patented a process "to obtain malleable iron direct from iron ore."
1857 Samuel Wetherill was granted a patent for a zinc ore reducing process.
1870 the Noble Order of the Knights of Labor became the first U.S. labor union to accept members other than craft workers.
1898 a telephone message from a submerged submarine was received for the first time.
1912 New Mexico was admitted to the Union.
1925 Ahmed Zogu became the head of state in Albania.
1942 a commercial airline made a round the world flight for the first time.
1950 Great Britain announced its recognition of the Chinese People's Republic.

The following people were born on January 6:

Joan of Arc in 1412.

Captain John Smith in 1579.
Carl Sandburg in 1878.
Tom Mix in 1880.
Sam Rayburn in 1882.
Khalil Gibran in 1883.
Loretta Young in 1913.
Danny Thomas in 1914.
Sun Myung Moon and Early Wynn in 1920.
Cary Middlecoff in 1921.
Wilbert Harrison in 1929.

January 7

Bieuwa, the Traditional Day of Of-
fering (Bhutan)
Pioneer's Day (Liberia)
Plough Monday (1st Monday after
Epiphany in England)
Usokae or Bullfinch Exchange Fes-
tival (Japan)

550,720,010 B.C. the first trilobite was hatched off the coast of
present day Australia.
1830 Mount Clare Station in Baltimore, Maryland, the first American
railway station, began operations.
1890 the minelayer U.S.S. Baltimore was commissioned.
1896 Fannie Farmer's first cookbook was published.
1897 the first national amateur handball championship was held in
Jersey City, New Jersey.
1940 "Gene Autry's Melody Ranch" began its broadcasting run.
1941 the "Inner Sanctum Mysteries" debuted on the radio.
1949 Drs. Daniel Chapin Pease and Richard Freligh Baker announced
that they had photographed genes (120,000X magnification).
1955 Marian Anderson first performed with the Metropolitan Opera.
1968 Surveyor VII landed on the moon.
1971 Hawley Lake, Arizona registered a temperature of -40° F.

The following people were born on January 7:

Millard Fillmore in 1800.
St. Bernadette in 1844.
Adolph Zukor in 1873.
Kitty Bransfield in 1875.
Charles Addams in 1912.
Alvin Dark in 1922.

January 8   Battle of New Orleans Day (Louisi-
                                           ana)
                                           St. Gudula's Feast Day
                                           Meitlisunntig (2nd Sunday in Swit-
                                           zerland)
                                           Man Watchers' Week (begins the
                                           second Sunday)

 712 St. Gudula, patron saint of Brussels, died.
1815 the Battle of New Orleans took place.
1833 The Boston Academy of Music was founded.
1878 Crazy Horse was assassinated.
1889 Dr. Herman Hollerith patented a data processing computer.
1901 the American Bowling Congress began its first tournament.
1918 Mississippi became the first state to ratify the prohibition amend-
     ment.
1926 Ibn Saud was proclaimed King of the Hejaz and Sultan of Nejd
     (Saudi Arabia).
1935 Arthur Cobb Hardy patented the spectrophotometer.
1959 Fidel Castro made his triumphal entry into Havana.
1974 Frank Searle sighted and photographed the Loch Ness monster.
     The Glasgow University Zoology Department examined the
     photo and said it "resembles a reptile of the Plesiosaur class."
1976 Chou En-lai died at the age of seventy-eight.

The following people were born on January 8:

Harry "Bud" Weiser in 1891.
Carl Rogers in 1902.
Larry Storch in 1925.
Elvis A. Presley in 1935.
Shirley Bassey in 1937.
Yvette Mimieux in 1942.
David Bowie (David R. Hayward-Jones) in 1947.

January 9   Connecticut Ratification Day
                                           Panama's Day of National Mourning

1788 Connecticut ratified the constitution of the United States.
1792 the Treaty of Jassy ended the second Russo-Turkish War.
1811 the first women's golf tournament was organized by the Mussel-
     burgh Golf Club (Scotland) for the town fishwives.
1861 the S.S. Star of the West, attempting to deliver supplies and
     reinforcements to Fort Sumter, was fired upon. It thereupon
     turned back.
1861 Mississippi seceded from the Union.
1899 Norway House, Manitoba registered a temperature of -53° C.
1929 "The Seeing Eye" dog training school was incorporated.

1936 the U.S. Army adopted the M1 semi-automatic rifle.
1937 San Jacinto, Nevada registered a temperature of –50° F.
1945 General Douglas MacArthur "returned" to invade the Philippines.
1962 it was reported to President John F. Kennedy that the U.S. had 2,646 troops plus combat support personnel in South Vietnam.
1967 Julian Bond took his seat in the Georgia legislature after the U.S. Supreme Court ruled that his criticism of the Vietnam War did not disqualify him as a member of that legislature.

The following people were born on January 9:

Carrie Chapman Catt in 1859.
John B. Watson in 1878.
George Balanchine in 1904.
Richard Nixon in 1913.
Bart Starr in 1934.
Joan Baez and Susannah York in 1941.
Crystal Gayle in 1951.

January 10   Prithivi Jayanti (Nepal)

  49 B.C., Caesar led a legion of his troops across the Rubicon into Italy.
1861 Florida seceded from the Union.
1863 London's Metropolitan (underground) Railway opened.
1901 the first U.S. gusher blew in, spouting a column of oil 200 feet high at Beaumont, Texas.
1910 the first American aviation meet opened in Los Angeles.
1911 a photograph was taken from an airplane for the first time in the sky over San Diego.
1920 the League of Nations opened in Geneva.
1920 Great Britain took control of German East Africa. Its name was changed to Tanganyika.
1925 Mrs. Miriam A. Ferguson was inaugurated as the Governor of Texas.
1928 Leon Trotsky was exiled to Turkestan.
1943 President Franklin D. Roosevelt sailed from Miami to Trinidad to become the first U.S. president to visit a foreign country in wartime.
1946 the first United Nations General Assembly opened.
1956 the U.S. Interstate Commerce Commission ordered an end to segregated seating on interstate buses and trains.

The following people were born on January 10:

Ethan Allen in 1738.

Frank James in 1843.
Francis X. Bushman and Florence Reed in 1883.
Gisele MacKenzie and Johnny Ray in 1927.
Sal Mineo in 1939.
Jim Croce in 1943.
Rod Stewart in 1945.

January 11   Albanian Republic Proclamation Day
                                   DeHosto's Birthday (Puerto Rico)
                                   Feast of the Baptism of the Lord

1589 Sir John Harrington had the first water-closet installed at his
     residence near Bath, England.
1759 the first American life insurance company was incorporated
     in Philadelphia.
1861 Alabama seceded from the Union.
1879 Echo Farms Dairy milkmen became the first to deliver milk
     in glass bottles.
1897 Martha Hughes Cannon of Utah, the first woman state senator,
     was sworn in.
1911 Fort Vermillion, Alberta registered a temperature of -61° C.
1930 Drs. Fred Allison and Edgar J. Murphy announced their discovery
     of francium.
1935 Amelia Earhart took off on a solo flight from Honolulu to Oak-
     land, California.
1942 Japan invaded the Netherlands East Indies.
1942 Kingston, Rhode Island registered a temperature of -23° F.
1945 civil war in Greece (The Battle of Athens) came to an end after
     more than a month of hostilities.
1946 the People's Republic of Albania was proclaimed.
1964 the Surgeon General released his report in which it was deter-
     mined that "cigarette smoking may be hazardous to your
     health."
1974 Sue Rosenkowitz of Cape Town, South Africa, gave birth to
     the first sextuplets with all six surviving.

The following people were born on January 11:

Alexander Hamilton in 1757.
Ezra Cornell in 1807.
William James in 1842.
Elmer Flick in 1876.
Alice Paul in 1885.
Max Carey in 1890.

January 12   Zanzibar Revolution Day (Tanzania)

1853 Williamette University in Salem, Oregon was incorporated.
1876 the Minnesota Forestry Association was organized.
1896 Dr. Henry Louis Smith took the first X-ray photograph.
1909 Canada and the United States signed the Arbitration Treaty.
1912 Washta, Iowa registered a temperature of -47° F.
1932 Hattie Ophelia Wyatt Caraway, who later became the first
      woman to preside over the U.S. Senate, was elected Senator
      from Arkansas.
1932 the "Ed Sullivan Show" premiered on CBS radio.
1937 the submarine cable plow was patented.
1953 Yugoslavia adopted a new constitution.
1964 a revolutionary coup overthrew the sultan of Zanzibar.
1970 Biafra surrendered and the Nigerian civil war ended.

The following people were born on January 12:

John Singer Sargent in 1856.
Jack London in 1876.
Hermann Göring in 1893.
Woodward M. "Tex" Ritter in 1906.
James Farmer in 1920.

January 13   Stephen Foster Memorial Day
                                              Togo Liberation Day
                                              Cuckoo Dancing Week (Sault Ste.
                                              Marie, Michigan)

1794 the United States added two stars to its flag representing Vermont
      and Kentucky.
1854 Anthony Faas patented the accordian.
1863 William Canter patented a chenille manufacturing machine.
1912 Oakland, Maryland registered a temperature of -40° F.
1929 the Humanist Society was established in Hollywood, California.
1935 Germany annexed the Saar.
1942 Henry Ford patented plastic automobile construction.
1942 an aircraft ejection seat was used in an actual emergency for
      the first time.
1952 K.J.W. Hackett caught an 83 pound barracuda off the coast
      of Nigeria.
1956 South Africa disenfranchised 60,000 "Coloreds" in Cape Province.
1966 Robert C. Weaver was appointed Secretary of Housing and Urban
      Development. He was the first black man to hold that position.

The following people were born on January 13:

Salmon P. Chase in 1808.
Horatio Alger in 1834.
Sophie Tucker in 1884.
Frank J. "Cactus" Keck in 1899.
Robert Stack in 1919.
Gwen Verdon in 1925.
Charles Nelson Reilly in 1931.

January 14   Eastern Orthodox New Year's Day
                                         Tha Tamil Thai-Pongal Day (Sri
                                           Lanka)
                                         United States' Ratification Day

347 B.C., Plato died in Athens at the age of 80.
1761 the Battle of Panipat seriously disrupted the political stability
     of India.
1784 the American Revolution officially came to an end when the
     Continental Congress ratified the Treaty of Paris.
1794 Dr. Jessee Bennett of Edom, Virginia, performed the first success-
     ful Cesarean operation.
1846 the Magnetic Telegraph Company was formed.
1893 United States Marines landed on Hawaii.
1929 the first delivery of international mail by dog sled was made
     in Montreal.
1938 the National Society for the Legalization of Euthanasia was
     formed.
1952 "The Today Show" debuted, with Dave Garroway as host, on
     NBC television.
1953 Marshal (Josip Broz) Tito became president of Yugoslavia.
1977 Phillip Bryers caught a 417 pound striped marlin off the coast
     of New Zealand.

The following people were born on January 14:

Benedict Arnold in 1741.
Albert Schweitzer in 1875.
John Dos Passos in 1896.
William Bendix in 1906.
Loretta Lynn in 1932.
Jack Jones in 1938.
Julian Bond in 1940.
Faye Dunaway in 1941.

January 15   Adults' Day (Japan)
                                         Arbor Day (Jordan)

Martin Luther King's Birthday
Lee-Jackson Day (3rd Monday in
   Virginia)
Moliere Day (France)
Jaycee Week (begins the 3rd Sunday)

1559   Queen Elizabeth I was crowned.
1609   the first newspaper was printed: the <u>Aviso Relation oder Zeitung</u> of Wolfenbüttel, Germany.
1777   Vermont declared itself an independent state; a status that was maintained until 1791.
1797   John Hetherington became the first person to wear a top hat.
1831   Mr. and Mrs. Pierson made the first railroad honeymoon trip on record.
1833   the "Georgia Infirmary, for the relief and protection of aged and afflicted Negroes" was organized.
1870   the Democratic Party was first represented by a donkey.
1882   the Nansen Ski Club was formed in Berlin, New Hampshire.
1892   the first basketball rule book was published.
1906   Willie Hoppe won his first world billiard championship and began a career during which he remained a world champion for 46 years.
1908   the Alpha Kappa Alpha Sorority was founded.
1941   British troops landed in Ethiopia.
1955   Raymond Whitcomb Bliss built a solar-heated/radiation-cooled house in Tucson, Arizona.

The following people were born on January 15:

Cole Younger in 1844.
Aristotle Onassis in 1906.
Edward Teller in 1908.
Gene Krupa in 1909.
Lloyd Bridges in 1913.
Gamel Abdel Nasser in 1918.
Charles "Chuck" Berry in 1926.
Rev. Dr. Martin Luther King, Jr. in 1929.

January 16   Benín Martyrs' Day
                                 National Nothing Day

1840   a United States government expedition arrived in the Antarctic.
1866   Everett Hosmer Barney patented the all-metal screw clamp skate.
1877   Bainbridge Bishop patented the color organ.
1877   Halcyon Skinner patented a power loom to weave Axminster carpets for Alexander Smith & Sons of Yonkers, New York.

1919 the prohibition amendment to the U.S. constitution was ratified.
1920 the prohibition amendment to the U.S. constitution took effect.
1936 Hialeah Racetrack installed an electric eye camera to record photo finishes.
1943 Island Park Dam, Idaho registered a temperature of -60° F.
1944 General Dwight D. Eisenhower took over the Allied Command.
1957 the first round-the-world non-stop jet flight took off from Merced, California.

The following people were born on January 16:

Jimmy Collins in 1870.
Robert Service in 1874.
Jay Hanna "Dizzy" Dean in 1911.
A.J. Foyt in 1935.

January 17   The Blessing of the Animals at the
                                  Cathedral or St. Anthony's Day
                                  (Mexico)
                                  Thomas Crapper Day (England)
                                  Mali's National Holiday

 356 A.D., St. Anthony the Abbot, patron saint of animals, died in Egypt.
1806 James M. Randolph became the first child to be born in the White House.
1871 Andrew S. Hallidie patented his cable car design for the city of San Francisco. It became the first such design to actually be implemented.
1887 the Army and Navy Hospital in Hot Springs opened.
1893 Millsboro, Delaware registered a temperature of -17° F.
1899 the United States took possession of Wake Island.
1905 Charles A. Brewer patented the punchboard.
1917 the United States purchased the Virgin Islands from Denmark.
1928 Anatol M. Josepho patented a fully automatic film developing machine.
1934 the Electric Home and Farm Authority was incorporated.
1943 Winston Churchill and Franklin Roosevelt met at Casablanca.
1950 Brink's headquarters in Boston was robbed of $2,800,000, of which $1,200,000 was in cash.
1963 Katanga was reunited with the Republic of the Congo (Leopoldville).
1966 a U.S. Air Force plane accidentally dropped four unarmed H-bombs near the coast of Spain. Recovery took months.

The following people were born on January 17:

Benjamin Franklin in 1706.
Anton Chekhov in 1860.
David Lloyd George in 1863.
Mack Sennett in 1884.
Al Capone in 1899.
James Earl Jones in 1931.
Shari Lewis in 1934.

January 18   Tunisian Revolution Day

1535 Francisco Pizarro founded Lima, Peru.
1733 a polar bear was exhibited in Boston for the first time.
1778 Captain James Cook landed in Hawaii (Sandwich Islands).
1788 the first load of British convicts was landed at Botany Bay,
      Australia. Britain claimed all of Australia east of 135° East
      Longitude.
1826 the New York Drawing Association was formed.
1871 Prince Bismarck's negotiations led to the unification of Germany
      and the founding of the German empire.
1911 aircraft landed on a shipboard flightdeck for the first time.
1930 Watts, Oklahoma registered a temperature of -27° F.
1934 the United States Information Service was organized.
1957 Birch Hill Dam, Massachusetts registered a temperature of
      -34° F.
1977 Caesar's Head, South Carolina registered a temperature of
      -20° F.

The following people were born January 18:

Peter M. Roget in 1779.
Daniel Webster in 1782.
Alan Alexander Milne in 1882.
Oliver Hardy in 1892.
Cary Grant in 1904.
Danny Kaye in 1913.
Bobby Goldsboro and David Ruffin in 1941.
Muhammad Ali in 1942.

January 19   Confederate Heroes Day (Texas)
                                      Robert E. Lee's Birthday (Southern
                                      U.S.)

1825 Ezra Daggett and Thomas Kensett patented the tin can.
1861 Georgia seceded from the Union.

1861 the Fort Jefferson military prison was garrisoned.
1883 the German steamer <u>Cambria</u> hit an iceberg and sank: 389 lives were lost.
1886 the Aurora Ski Club was organized in Red Wing, Minnesota.
1915 a patent was issued to George Claude for a neon tube advertising sign.
1925 Van Buren, Maine registered a temperature of -48° F.
1928 Eleanora R. Sears won the first U.S.A. Women's Squash Racquets Singles championship.
1945 Soviet troops succeeded in capturing Warsaw, Tarnow, Cracow and Lodz in Poland.
1966 Jawaharlal Nehru's daughter, Mrs. Indira Gandhi, became Prime Minister of India.

The following people were born on January 19:

James Watt in 1736.
Robert E. Lee in 1807.
Edgar Allan Poe in 1809.
Sir Henry Bessemer in 1813.
Paul Cézanne in 1839.
Victor Mature in 1916.
Jean Stapleton in 1923.
Phil Everly in 1938.
Janis Joplin in 1943.
Dolly Parton in 1946.

January 20

Guinea-Bissau National Heroes Day
Cape Verde National Heroes Day
Nosso Senhor do Bonfim Festival (Brazil)
Rio de Janeiro Foundation Day (Brazil)
San Sebastion's Day (Brazil)
United States Presidential Inauguration Day

the sun enters the house of Aquarius.
4521 B.C., Abu-Banad of Sumer announced his invention of the first effective copper smelting technique.
1783 hostilities between Great Britain and the United States came to an end and peace negotiations began.
1795 a French horse cavalry unit captured a Dutch naval fleet off the coast of the island of Texel.
1846 a telegraph line opened between New York and Philadelphia.
1887 the United States obtained Pearl Harbor from Hawaii for the purpose of building a naval station.

1937 Boca, California registered a temperature of –45° F.
1945 Hungary signed an armistice with the Allies.
1954 the National Negro Network was formed.
1954 Rogers Pass, Montana registered a temperature of –70° F.
1981 after being held for ransom in Iran for fourteen and a half months, fifty-two American hostages were released.

The following people were born on January 20:

George Burns in 1898.
Federico Fellini in 1920.
Patricial Neal in 1926.
Edwin "Buzz" Aldrin, Jr. in 1930.
Arte Johnson in 1934.
Paul Stanley in 1952.

January 21   Feast of Our Lady of Altagracia
                                          (Dominican Republic)
                                          Feast of St. Agnes
                                          Lenin Memorial Day (U.S.S.R.)

1488 Bartolomeu Dias rounded the Cape of Good Hope.
1793 Louis XVI was guillotined after a short trial.
1853 Russell L. Hawes patented an envelope folding machine.
1880 Memphis, Tennessee began construction on the first independent municipal sewage system in the United States.
1911 the National Progressive Republican League was organized.
1915 Kiwanis International was founded in Detroit, Michigan.
1919 fighting broke out between British and Irish nationalist forces when the Irish Parliament (Sinn Fein) declared Ireland an independent republic.
1924 the first Kuomintang national congress was held at Canton with Sun Yat-sen as president.
1924 the death of V.I. Lenin set off a power struggle between Stalin and Trotsky.
1941 commercial magnesium production began in Freeport, Texas.
1950 Alger Hiss was convicted of perjury.
1952 F. Dowley caught a 40 pound skipjack tuna in the Bahamas.
1954 the U.S.S. Nautilus, the world's first nuclear powered submarine was launched at Groton, Connecticut.
1964 Kenneth Kaunda became Zambia's first Prime Minister.

The following people were born January 21:

John C. Breckinridge in 1821.
Thomas J. "Stonewall" Jackson in 1824.
John W. "Snake" Deal in 1879.

J. Carrol Naish in 1900.
Telly Savalas in 1927.
Jack Nicklaus in 1940.
Richie Havens in 1941.
Mac Davis in 1942.

January 22   Discovery Day (St. Vincent)
                                   Feast of St. Vincent
                                   Wellington Provincial Anniversary
                                   (New Zealand)

426,422 B.C., fire was first deliberately used by a caveman. Boodge-Gah
    of the Boodge band built a fire in his cave to warm himself.
1517 the Turks, under Selim, captured and sacked Cairo.
1673 postal service began between Boston and New York.
1814 the Knights Templar Grand Encampment was held in New York
    City.
1840 the first British colonists landed in New Zealand.
1881 Cleopatra's Needle was placed in Central Park in New York
    City.
1895 the National Association of Manufacturers was organized.
1905 "Bloody Sunday" in Russia inspired a national rebellion.
1930 Mount Carroll, Illinois registered a temperature of -30° F.
1944 Allied troops landed at Anzio.
1972 Great Britain, Denmark, Ireland and Norway were granted admis-
    sion to the European Common Market.

The following people were born on January 22:

Francis Bacon in 1561.
Andre Ampere in 1775.
Lord Byron in 1788.
Ann Southern and U Thant in 1909.
Birch Bayh in 1928.
Piper Laurie in 1932.
Bill Bixby in 1934.
Sam Cooke in 1935.
Linda Blair in 1959.

January 23   Feast of St. John the Almsgiver

426,422 B.C., Boodge-Dolel, Boodge-Gah's wife, invented a first aid
    technique for treating burned fingers.
1789 Georgetown College was established.

1793 the Humane Society of Philadelphia (the first "First Aid" emergency organization) was incorporated.
1845 election day for the United States was established as "The Tuesday next after the first Monday in the month of November of the year in which they are to be appointed."
1849 Dr. Elizabeth Blackwell received her M.D. from the Medical Institution of Geneva, New York and became the first American-trained woman physician.
1907 Charles Curtis began serving as the United States Senator from Kansas. He was the first American Indian to hold such office.
1935 Iroquois Falls, Ontario registered a temperature of -58° C.
1943 the British captured Tripoli.
1960 the bathyscaphe Trieste dove to the bottom of the Mariana Trench.
1968 North Korea captured the U.S.S. Pueblo.
1971 Prospect Creek Camp, Alaska registered a temperature of -79.8° F.
1973 the volcano Eldfell, on the island of Heimaey, erupted, posing a serious threat to the people of Vestmannaeyjar.

The following people were born on January 23:

John Hancock in 1737.
Edouard Manet in 1832.
Humphrey Bogart in 1899.
Randolph Scott in 1903.
Dan Duryea and Hideki Yukawa in 1907.
Ernie Kovacs in 1919.

January 24   Alacitis Fair (Bolivia)
                                   Economic Liberation Day (Togo)
                                   Union Day (Romania)

  41 A.D., the Roman emperor Gaius Caligula was assassinated.
1556 an earthquake in Shaanxi, China killed 830,000 people.
1848 gold was discovered at Sutter's Mill in California.
1899 Humphrey O'Sullivan patented the rubber heel.
1903 the boundary between the United States and Canada was fixed.
1908 the first boy scout troop was organized in England by Lord Robert Baden-Powell.
1922 Christian K. Nelson patented the Eskimo Pie.
1922 Danbury, Wisconsin registered a temperature of -54° F.
1925 a moving picture was taken of a solar eclipse for the first time.
1935 beer was offered for sale in cans in Richmond, Virginia for the first time.

The following people were born on January 24:

Hadrian in 76 A.D.
Cornelius "Mickey" Finn in 1902.
Ernest Borgnine in 1917.
Oral Roberts in 1918.
Maria Tallchief in 1925.
Neil Diamond in 1941.
John Belushi in 1951.

January 25   Robert Burns Day
                                          Feast of the Conversion of St. Paul
                                          São Paulo Foundation Day (Brazil)
                                          Up Helly Aa' (last Tuesday in Scot-
                                              land)

1533 Henry VIII married his second wife, Anne Boleyn.
1787 participants in Shays' Rebellion attempted to capture the Conti-
        nental Arsenal at Springfield, Massachusetts but were repulsed.
1799 Eliakim Spooner of Vermont patented a seeding machine.
1825 Rensselaer Polytechnic Institute opened.
1890 Nellie Bly returned to New York City from her round the world
        tour.
1905 the Cullinan Diamond was found.
1915 the transcontinental telephone was demonstrated for the first
        time.
1924 the first winter Olympics opened at Chamonix, France.
1942 Siam declared war on Great Britain and the United States.
1945 Audie Murphy was awarded the U.S. Medal of Honor for his
        exploits in France.
1945 Grand Rapids, Michigan began fluoridating its water.

The following people were born on January 25:

Robert Boyle in 1627.
Robert Burns in 1759.
Charles Curtis in 1860.
William Somerset Maugham in 1874.
Edwin Newman in 1919.
Dean Jones in 1935.

January 26   Basant Panchimi or Indian Republic
                                              Day
                                          Duarte's Day (Dominican Republic)
                                          Michigan Admission Day

1695 Captain William Kidd made the first workman's compensation agreement by promising to compensate his crew for any physical harm that befell them.
1776 Reverend Louis E. Lotbiniere was appointed as the first U.S. Army chaplain.
1778 a British settlement was established at Sydney, Australia.
1837 Michigan was admitted to the Union.
1855 Sardinia declared war on Russia and joined the Crimean War.
1861 Louisiana seceded from the Union.
1870 Virginia was readmitted to the Union.
1875 George F. Green patented an electric (battery powered) dental drill.
1884 Kilmahumaig, Prince Edward Island registered a temperature of -37° C.
1885 General Charles Gordon and the British garrison at Khartoum were killed by Sudanese rebels.
1907 the United States enacted a corrupt election practices law.
1939 General Francisco Franco's forces triumphed in the Spanish civil war.
1950 India became an independent republic.

The following people were born on January 26:

Douglas MacArthur in 1880.
Virginia Woolf in 1882.
Paul Newman in 1925.
Eartha Kitt and Roger Vadim in 1928.
Jules Feiffer in 1929.
Bob Uecker in 1935.
Angela Davis in 1944.
Wayne Gretzky in 1961.

January 27   Feast of St. Julian of LeMans
                                   St. Devote (Monaco)

1785 the University of Georgia was chartered.
1870 Kappa Alpha Theta was founded.
1880 Thomas Edison patented the electric light.
1888 the National Geographic Society was founded in Washington, D.C.
1900 the Social Democrat Party held its first convention in Rochester, New York.
1940 C.C.C. Camp F-16 in Georgia registered a temperature of -17° F.
1944 Soviet forces began to drive German troops from Leningrad.
1948 the first locomotive to carry the weight of 1,000,000 pounds pulled out of Norfolk, Virginia.

1950 the development of terramycin was announced to the public.
1964 France established diplomatic relations with the People's Republic of China.
1967 Virgil Grissom, Edward H. White and Roger B. Chaffee were killed in a fire during an Apollo I launch simulation.
1973 formal peace accords were signed by North Vietnam, the National Liberation Front, South Vietnam and the United States.
1982 Minoru Honda discovered a new nova in the constellation Aquila.

The following people were born on January 27:

Wolfgang Amadeus Mozart in 1756.
Charles Dodgson (Lewis Carroll) in 1832.
Samuel Gompers in 1850.
Jerome Kern in 1885.
Hyman Rickover in 1900.
Skitch Henderson in 1918.
Donna Reed in 1921.
Bobby "Blue" Bland in 1930.
Troy Donahue in 1936.

January 28   Australia Day
                                        Democracy Day (Rwanda)
                                        International Clergy Appreciation
                                            Week (begins the Sunday before
                                            February 3)

1596 Sir Francis Drake, notorious buccaneer, died at the age of 51.
1882 the first "cable street railway" opened in Chicago.
1899 the American Social Science Association was incorporated.
1915 the U.S.S. William P. Frye became the first U.S. ship to be sunk in World War I.
1915 the United States Coast Guard was created.
1925 Pittsburg, New Hampshire registered a temperature of -46° F.
1934 the first rope ski tow went into operation in Woodstock, Vermont.
1942 the Merchant Marine Academy at Kings Point, New York received its first class.
1958 construction began at Buchanan, New York on the first privately owned thorium-uranium nuclear reactor.
1963 Cynthiana, Kentucky registered a temperature of -34° F.

The following people were born on January 28:

George Wright in 1847.
Artur Rubinstein in 1887.
Jackson Pollock in 1912.

Alan Alda in 1936.
Mikhail Baryshnikov in 1948.

January 29   Auckland Provincial Anniversary
                                    (New Zealand)
                                    Kansas Day
                                    Nepal Martyr's Day
                                    Northland Provincial Anniversary
                                    (New Zealand)

1802 John Beckley was appointed as the first Librarian of Congress.
1819 Sir Stamford Raffles founded Singapore.
1861 Kansas was admitted to the Union.
1900 the American League of Baseball Clubs was formed.
1919 the prohibition amendment officially became a part of the consti-
     tution.
1924 Carl Rutherford Taylor patented an ice cream cone rolling
     machine.
1936 the first players were elected to the baseball Hall of Fame.
1940 the first known tetraploid flower went on public display.
1943 Ruth C. Streeter was promoted to the rank of major in the
     U.S. Marine Corps, becoming the first woman to hold that
     rank.
1949 the U.S.S. Newport News was commissioned and the U.S. Navy
     obtained its first air conditioned ship.
1974 U.C.L.A. won its eighty-eighth consecutive basketball game.

The following people were born on January 29:

Daniel Bernoulli in 1700.
Thomas Paine in 1737.
Henry "Light Horse Harry" Lee in 1756.
William McKinley in 1843.
John D. Rockefeller, Jr. in 1874.
Berner E. "Barney" Oldfield in 1878.
W.C. Fields (William C. Dukenfield) in 1880.
Claudine Longet in 1942.

January 30   Franklin D. Roosevelt Day (Ken-
                                    tucky)

1647 the Scots sent Charles I back to Parliament in return for their
     back pay.
1649 after continuing at odds with Parliament, and a second civil
     war, Charles I was beheaded at Whitehall.

1798 the U.S. House of Representatives had its first brawl.
1835 an attempt was made to assassinate President Andrew Jackson.
1838 the great Seminole leader, Osceola, died.
1894 Charles Brady King patented the pneumatic hammer.
1902 England and Japan recognized the independence of China and Korea.
1922 the International Court at The Hague held its first meeting.
1933 "The Lone Ranger" was first heard on Detroit radio station WXYZ.
1933 Adolf Hitler became chancellor of Germany.
1948 Mahatma Gandhi was assassinated in New Delhi.
1966 New Market, Alabama registered a temperature of -27° F.
1966 Corinth, Mississippi registered a temperature of -19° F.
1966 Mt. Mitchell, North Carolina registered a temperature of -29° F.
1968 North Vietnamese forces began their Tet offensive.
1972 James M. Hussey caught a 31 pound, 12 ounce bluefish off the coast of North Carolina.

The following people were born on January 30:

Muhammad in 570.
Franklin D. Roosevelt in 1882.
Gene Hackman in 1931.
Tammy Grimes in 1936.
Vanessa Redgrave and Boris Spassky in 1937.

January 31   Nauru Independence Day

1606 Guy Fawkes was executed for his part in the "Gunpowder Plot."
1709 Alexander Selkirk was rescued after being marooned for four years on Juan Fernandez Island.
1747 London Lock Hospital opened a venereal disease clinic.
1863 the First Regiment South Carolina Volunteers was mustered into federal service.
1905 a Napier driven by Arthur MacDonald became the first automobile to exceed 100 miles per hour.
1920 Upper Stewiacke, Nova Scotia registered a temperature of -41° C.
1928 the 3M Company began marketing Scotch Tape.
1936 "The Green Hornet" was first heard on Detroit radio station WXYZ.
1943 German Field Marshal Paulus surrendered at Stalingrad.
1947 Smith River, British Columbia registered a temperature of -59° C.
1950 the Atomic Energy Commission began production of the H-Bomb.
1958 the United States launched "Explorer I."

1968 Nauru became an independent nation.

The following people were born January 31:

Franz Schubert in 1797.
Zane Grey in 1875.
Eddie Cantor in 1892.
Tallulah Bankhead in 1903.
Jackie Robinson in 1919.
Stewart Udall in 1920.
Mario Lanza in 1921.
Carol Channing, Joanne Dru and Norman Mailer in 1923.
Ernie Banks in 1931.
Suzanne Pleshette in 1937.
Nolan Ryan in 1947.

February

The first day of February marks the following commemorations:

St. Brigid's Day
Robinson Crusoe Day
Homstrom (first Sunday in Switzerland)
National Freedom Day
Nelson Provincial Anniversary (New Zealand)

National Children's Dental Health Week (first Sunday)
National Pay Your Bills Week (first Monday)

Afro-American History Month
American History Month
American Music Month
Boy Scouts of American Anniversary Month
National Cherry Month

February 1

1411 Poland, following its victory at Tannenberg, concluded the First Peace of Thorn with the Teutonic Knights.
1861 Texas seceded from the Union.
1862 Julia Ward Howe's "Battle Hymn of the Republic" was published in The Atlantic Monthly.
1865 Congress' proposed thirteenth amendment to the Constitution was approved by President Abraham Lincoln, and slavery was abolished in the United States.
1893 Prince Albert, Saskatchewan registered a temperature of -57° C.
1906 construction of the federal penitentiary at Leavenworth, Kansas was completed.
1917 Germany began unrestricted submarine warfare.
1937 the port of Stapleton, on Staten Island, was opened as a free port.
1940 Captain Marvel first appeared in Whiz Comics.
1946 the Hungarian People's Republic was proclaimed.

1946 Trygve Lie became the first Secretary General of the United Nations.
1951 a United Nations vote declared the People's Republic of China to be the aggressor in Korea.
1951 Taylor Park, Colorado registered a temperature of -60° F.
1951 Gavilan, New Mexico registered a temperature of -50° F.
1954 "The Secret Storm" debuted on CBS television.
1955 Sisson Dam, New Brunswick registered a temperature of -47° C.
1958 the United Arab Republic was established.
1960 America's first segregated lunch counter sit-in took place in Greensboro, North Carolina.

The following people were born on February 1:

Conn Smythe in 1895.
Clark Gable in 1901.
Langston Hughes in 1902.
S.J. Perelman in 1904.
Don Everly and Ray "Dr. Hook" Sawyer in 1937.

February 2   Candlemas or Feast of the Presen-
                                        tation of the Lord
                                        Día de la Candelaria (Mexico)
                                        Ground Hog Day
                                        Porto Alegre (Brazil)

1509 Francisco de Almeida established Portuguese naval supremacy around India by defeating the Moslem fleet in the Battle of Diu.
1653 the city of New Amsterdam was incorporated.
1808 French forces occupied Rome and captured the pope.
1848 according to provisions in the Treaty of Guadalupe Hidalgo, Mexico ceded California and New Mexico to the United States.
1858 Thomas Crane Wales patented "Arctics" waterproof boots.
1876 the National League of Baseball Clubs was formed.
1912 Frederick Rodman Law performed the first movie stunt by parachuting from the Statue of Liberty.
1914 Peter Baden-Powell founded the Cub Scouts in Sussex, England.
1923 ethyl gasoline was first marketed in Dayton, Ohio.
1943 the last German troops surrendered to Soviet forces and the Battle of Stalingrad came to an end.
1951 Greensburg, Indiana registered a temperature of -35° F.
1962 John Uelses became the first person to pole vault over sixteen feet.
1975 Anne Cochain caught a twenty-three and a half pound Pacific bonito near Seychelles.

The following people were born on February 2:

Fritz Kreisler in 1875.
Orval Overall in 1881.
James Joyce in 1882.
Charles Correll in 1890.
Jascha Heifetz in 1901.
Ayn Rand in 1905.
Red Schoendienst in 1923.
Tom Smothers in 1937.
Graham Nash in 1942.
Farrah Fawcett in 1947.

February 3   Four Chaplains Memorial Day
                                  Mozambique Heroes Day
                                  San Blas Day (Paraguay)
                                  São Tomé and Príncipe Heroes Day
                                  Setsubun or Bean Throwing Festival
                                  (Japan)

287,398,666 B.C., a Thunder Bay, Ontario tree became the first ever
    to produce a pine cone.
1690 Massachusetts issued paper money.
1836 the Whig Party held its first state convention in Albany, New
    York.
1865 a secret peace conference was held between President Abraham
    Lincoln and Confederate Vice-President Alexander H. Stephens.
1894 the first American steel sailing vessel, the Dirigo, was launched
    from Bath, Maine.
1933 the American Legislators' Association held its inaugural meeting.
1943 four chaplains aboard the U.S.S. Dorchester gave their lifejackets
    to some regular army soldiers and consequently went down
    with the ship.
1947 a black news correspondent was admitted to the United States
    Congressional news gallery for the first time.
1947 Snag, Yukon Territory registered a temperature of -63° C.
1949 for the first time, enlisted men sat as members of the court
    in a U.S. military court martial.
1959 Buddy Holly, J.P. Richardson (The Big Bopper) and Richie Valens
    were killed in an airplane crash.
1964 negro and Puerto Rican parents and children boycotted New
    York City public schools.

The following people were born on February 3:

Felix Mendelssohn in 1809.
Horace Greeley in 1811.

Gertrude Stein in 1874.
Norman Rockwell in 1894.
Nelson L. "Chicken" Hawks in 1896.
James Michener in 1907.
Joey Bishop in 1918.
Fran Tarkenton in 1940.
Melanie in 1947.

February 4   Commencement of the Angolan
                                   Armed Struggle
                                   Sri Lanka Independence Day

1847 the Magnetic Telegraph Company was incorporated.
1861 the Congress of the Confederate States of America opened
     its first session.
1887 the Interstate Commerce Act was passed.
1899 a revolt against United States governance began in the Philip-
     pines.
1913 the demountable tire carrying rim was patented.
1932 the winter Olympic Games opened at Lake Placid, New York.
1941 the United Service Organizations (the U.S.O.) was founded.
1945 the Yalta Conference opened.
1948 Ceylon (Sri Lanka) became a self governing state within the
     British Commonwealth.
1974 Patty Hearst was kidnapped.
1976 an earthquake measuring 7.5 on the Richter scale hit Guatemala.
     It left 23,000 dead, 77,000 injured and 1,000,000-plus homeless.

The following people were born on February 4:

George B. "Possum" Whitted in 1890.
Raymond Dart in 1893.
Charles Lindbergh in 1902.
Byron Nelson in 1912.
Ida Lupino in 1918.
Betty Friedan in 1921.
Alice Cooper (Vincent Furnier) in 1948.

February 5   Anniversary of Chama cha Mapinduzi
                                   (CCM) and Arusha Declaration
                                   (Tanzania)
                                   Charro Days Fiesta (Brownsville,
                                   Texas and Matamoros, Tamaulipas)
                                   Feast of St. Agatha, patron saint of

San Marino
Mexican Constitution Day
Weatherman's Day

3,012,461,223 B.C., the Archeozoic era began.

1531 Roger Williams arrived in America.

1777 Georgia abolished both entail and primogeniture.

1778 South Carolina ratified the Articles of Confederation.

1817 the Gas Light Company of Baltimore was incorporated.

1846 the Oregon Spectator, the first newspaper to be published on the Pacific coast of America, began publication.

1850 DuBois D. Parmelee patented an adding machine that employed depressible keys.

1861 Samuel D. Goodale patented the peep show machine.

1901 Edwin Prescott patented the loop the loop "centrifugal railway."

1923 Doucet, Quebec registered a temperature of –54° C.

1948 Richard Button won a gold medal in figure skating in the Olympic Games.

The following people were born on February 5:

Belle Starr in 1848.
Adlai E. Stevenson in 1900.
John Carradine in 1906.
Red Buttons (Aaron Chwatt) in 1919.
Hank Aaron in 1934.
Roger Staubach in 1942.

February 6   Massachusetts Ratification Day
                                    Mid-Winter's Day
                                    Waitangi Day (New Zealand)
                                    National Crime Prevention Week
                                    (begins Sunday of the week with
                                    Lincoln's birthday)

1693 William and Mary College received its charter and was incorporated at Williamsburg, Virginia.

1778 according to the Treaties of Commerce and Alliance, France recognized the independence of the United States of America and gave assistance to the new country which included the services of Generals Lafayette and deKalb.

1788 Massachusetts ratified the constitution of the United States.

1902 the Young Women's Hebrew Association was organized.

1932 a dog sled race was included in an Olympic demonstration program.

1944 U.S. forces invaded the Kwajalein Islands.

1952 King George VI of England died.

1956 Autherine B. Lucy, the first black student at the University of Alabama, was stoned by a mob of whites on her third day of classes.

1957 Dudley Allen Buck reported that he had developed the cryotron.

1966 the Tukutese quintuplets were born.

The following people were born on February 6:

Queen Anne of England in 1665.
Aaron Burr in 1756.
George Herman "Babe" Ruth in 1895.
Ronald Reagan in 1911.
Zsa Zsa Gabor in 1919.
Rip Torn in 1931.
Mamie Van Doren in 1933.
Tom Brokaw in 1940.
Fabian (Fabiano Forte) in 1943.
Natalie Cole in 1950.

February 7   Grenada Independence Day

1818 the first successful American education magazine, The Academ-
     ician, began publication in New York City.
1827 Madame Francisquy Hutin introduced ballet to America at the
     Bowery Theatre in New York City.
1877 eleven men from five states met in New York City to organize
     the American Guernsey Cattle Club.
1893 Elisha Gray patented the telautograph.
1904 a disastrous fire started in Baltimore that lasted thirty hours
     and destroyed 2,600 buildings.
1934 a contract went into effect which provided for Tupelo, Mississippi
     to purchase its municipal electricity from T.V.A.
1935 Gene Sarazen refused to play in the Caliente (Mexico) golf
     tournament because of the provision for pari-mutuel betting
     cn the golfers.
1936 the United States' Vice-President's flag was adopted by executive
     crder.
1942 Cornelius Warmerdam became the first person to pole vault
     over fifteen feet indoors.
1969 at Hialeah Racetrack, Diane Crump became the first woman
     jockey to race at a U.S. pari-mutuel race track.
1973 the United States Senate established a committee to investigate
     the electronic surveillance device incident at Watergate.
1974 Grenada became an independent nation.

The following people were born on February 7:

Sir Thomas More in 1477.

Charles Dickens in 1812.
Dmitri Mendeleev in 1834.
Eubie Blake in 1883.
Sinclair Lewis in 1885.
Buster Crabbe in 1908.
Oscar Brand in 1920.

February 8   Arbor Day (Arizona)
                                    Founding of the People's Army
                                       (North Korea)
                                    Iraqi Eighth of February Revolution

1587 Mary Queen of Scots (Mary Stuart) was executed at Fotheringay.
1887 the Dawes Act was passed.
1898 John Ames Sherman patented an envelope folding and gumming
         machine.
1904 war broke out between Russia and Japan over the issue of domina-
         tion in Korea.
1910 the Boy Scouts of America was incorporated.
1915 Birth of a Nation premiered in Los Angeles. It portrayed freed
         slaves as predatory in character and Ku Klux Klansmen as
         heroes. Woodrow Wilson called it "like history in lightning,
         and all too true."
1924 America's first gas chamber execution took place at Nevada
         State Prison.
1928 the first trans-oceanic television image was received in Hartsdale,
         New York.
1933 Seminole, Texas registered a temperature of -23° F.
1944 a black news correspondent received accreditation from the
         White House for the first time.
1952 the reign of Elizabeth II of England began.
1955 Nikolai Bulganin became Premier of the Union of Soviet Socialist
         Republics.

The following people were born on February 8:

William Tecumseh Sherman in 1820.
Jules Verne in 1828.
Lana Turner in 1920.
Jack Lemmon in 1925.
Gary Coleman in 1968.

February 9   Feast of St. Maron (Lebanon)
                                    Shree Panchami (Nepal)

1822 the American Indian Society was organized.
1861 Jefferson Davis was elected President of the Confederate States of America.
1870 the United States authorized its first weather bureau.
1871 a federal fish protection office was authorized.
1909 the Davey Tree Expert Company was incorporated in Ohio. It was the first forestry school to offer scientific instruction on the care and preservation of trees.
1909 Congress passed an act prohibiting the importation of opium.
1913 sightings of groups of UFO's were reported in Canada, Bermuda, Brazil and Africa.
1932 two man bobsled competition was initiated as an Olympic event.
1933 Moran, Wyoming registered a temperature of -63° F.
1934 Vanderbilt, Michigan registered a temperature of -51° F.
1934 Stillwater Reservoir, New York registered a temperature of -52° F.
1943 Japanese troops evacuated Guadalcanal.

The following people were born on February 9:

William H. Harrison in 1773.
Dean Rusk in 1909.
Gypsy Rose Lee, Carmen Miranda, Ernest Tubb and Bill Veeck in 1914.
Ford P. "Moon" Mullen in 1917.
Carole King in 1941.
Bill Bergey and Mia Farrow in 1945.

February 10   Feast of St. Paul's Shipwreck (Malta)
                                    Oruro (Bolivia)

  60 A.D., St. Paul was shipwrecked on the north coast of Malta.
1763 the Treaty of Paris ended the French and Indian War in America.
1840 Queen Victoria of England married Prince Albert of Saxe-Coburg-Gotha.
1855 Woman's Hospital was founded in New York City. It was the world's first hospital founded by women for women.
1863 Alanson Crane's fire extinguisher became the first to receive a patent in the U.S.
1899 Milligan, Ohio registered ᶠ temperature of -39° F.
1899 Monterey, Virginia registered a temperature of -29° F.
1899 a treaty was signed ending the Spanish-American War.
1933 the singing telegram was introduced in New York City.
1933 Seneca, Oregon registered a temperature of -54° F.
1936 the Nazi secret police in Germany, the Gestapo, were authorized to arrest and imprison without trial.
1942 Glen Miller received a gold record for "Chattanooga Choo Choo."

1949 Arthur Miller's <u>Death of a Salesman</u> opened at the Morosco
     Theater in New York.

The following people were born on February 10:

Jimmy Durante and Bill Tilden in 1893.
Harold Macmillan and Herb Pennock in 1894.
John Enders in 1897.
Bertolt Brecht in 1898.
Leontyne Price in 1927.
Robert Wagner in 1930.
Roberta Flack in 1940.
Mark Spitz in 1950.

February 11   Anniversary of the Lateranensi
                                     Pacts (The Vatican)
                                   Day of Conciliation (Italy)
                                   Empire Day or Founding of the Na-
                                     tion (Japan)
                                   Feast of the Appearance of Our
                                     Lady at Lourdes
                                   Iranian Revolution Day
                                   Liberian Armed Forces Day
                                   White Shirt Day
                                   Youth Day (Cameroon)

1828 B.C., the iron age began in Kush.
 660 B.C., emperor Jimmu Tenno founded the nation of Japan.
1808 Judge Jesse Fell demonstrated in Wilkes Barre, Pennsylvania
     that anthracite coal could be burned.
1836 Mount Holyoke Seminary, the first women's college in America,
     was chartered.
1878 the Boston Bicycle Club was formed.
1889 Japan's new constitution was promulgated.
1899 Washington, D.C. registered a temperature of -15° F.
1929 Italy signed an agreement recognizing the Vatican as an indepen-
     dent state.
1944 Lt. Paul Liske Collins joined his father as a member of the
     Caterpillar Club. They were the first father and son combina-
     tion to become members.
1945 the first gas turbine propeller driven airplane was tested at
     Muroc, California.
1958 Ruth Carol Taylor became the first black airline stewardess.

The following people were born on February 11:

Thomas Alva Edison in 1847.

Leo Szilard in 1898.
King Farouk of Egypt in 1920.
Eva Gabor and Virginia E. Johnson in 1925.
Tina Louise and Mary Quant in 1934.
Burt Reynolds in 1936.
Sergio Mendes in 1941.

February 12   Burmese Union Day
                                    Georgia Day or Oglethorpe Day
                                    Kościuszko Day
                                    Abraham Lincoln's Birthday

1,382,169 B.C., the Günz glaciation period ended and the first intergla-
    cial period began.
1793 the fugitive slave law was enacted.
1873 the First Spanish Republic was proclaimed.
1878 Frederick W. Thayer patented the baseball catcher's mask.
1880 the National Croquet League was organized.
1899 Camp Clarke, Nebraska registered a temperature of -47° F.
1908 the first round the world automobile race was flagged off the
    starting line.
1912 a provisional Chinese republic was established when the last
    of the Manchu emperors abdicated.
1924 Paul Whiteman and George Gershwin introduced "Rhapsody
    in Blue."
1925 a federal arbitration law was enacted.
1940 the "Superman" serial debuted on the radio.
1947 C.W. Stewart caught a 221 pound Pacific sailfish off the coast
    of Ecuador.
1953 Egypt and Great Britain sanctioned a general referendum in
    Sudan which established the wish of the Sudanese people
    to form an independent nation as of January 1, 1956.
1961 Patrice Lumumba was killed in Katanga.

The following people were born on February 12:

Cotton Mather in 1663.
Thaddeus Kościuszko in 1746.
Charles Darwin and Abraham Lincoln in 1809.
Omar Bradley in 1893.
Lorne Greene in 1915.
Forrest Tucker in 1919.
Joe Garagiola in 1926.
Bill Russell in 1934.

February 13   Feast of St. Martinian the Hermit

1542 Catherine Howard was beheaded and on every subsequent Febru-
     ary 13, her spirit is said to have haunted Hampton Court
     Palace and Eythorne Manor.
1635 the Boston Public Latin School was established.
1689 Parliament proclaimed William and Mary to be King and Queen
     of England.
1795 the University of North Carolina opened.
1854 Commodore Matthew C. Perry secured the Treaty of Kanagawa
     with Japan which opened two ports to trade with the United
     States.
1877 the first long distance phone call was made from Salem to Boston.
1899 Tallahassee, Florida registered a temperature of -2° F.
1899 Minden, Louisiana registered a temperature of -16° F.
1905 Pond, Arkansas registered a temperature of -29° F.
1905 Lebanon, Kansas registered a temperature of -40° F.
1905 Warsaw, Missouri registered a temperature of -40° F.
1929 Dr. Alexander Fleming announced his discovery of penicillin.
1935 Dr. Claude Schaeffer Beck performed the first heart operation
     to relieve angina pectoris.
1960 France tested its first nuclear bomb in the Sahara Desert.

The following people were born on February 13:

Talleyrand in 1754.
Elizabeth "Bess" Truman in 1885.
Grant Wood in 1892.
William Shockley in 1910.
"Tennessee" Ernie Ford in 1919.
George Segal in 1934.
Carol Lynley in 1942.
Sal Bando and Peter Tork in 1944.

February 14   Arizona Admission Day
                                        Literacy Day (Liberia)
                                        Oregon Admission Day
                                        Trifon Zarezan or Viticulturists'
                                            Day (Bulgaria)
                                        St. Valentine's Day

1780 James Watt patented the duplicating machine.
1803 Moses Coats patented the apple parer.
1859 Oregon was admitted to the Union.
1862 the first sea-going iron-clad warship, the Galena, was launched
     from Mystic, Connecticut.
1872 the Lake Merritt bird refuge was established by the state of
     California.

1883 New Jersey legalized labor union organizing activities.
1907 the Masters of Fox Hounds Association was formed in New York City.
1912 Arizona was admitted to the Union.
1929 the "St. Valentine's Day Massacre" took place in Chicago.
1940 a porpoise was born in captivity for the first time at Marineland, Florida.
1950 China and the Soviet Union agreed to a thirty year alliance.
1961 the discovery of lawrencium was announced.

The following people were born on February 14:

Thomas R. Malthus in 1766.
Frederick Douglass in 1817.
John Barrymore in 1882.
Jack Benny in 1894.
Mel Allen, Woody Hayes and Jimmy Hoffa in 1913.
Hugh Downs and Skeezix Wallet in 1921.
Florence Henderson in 1934.
Mickey Wright in 1935.
Carl Bernstein in 1944.

February 15   Susan B. Anthony Day
                                       U.S.S. Maine Memorial Day
                                       Menendez Day (St. Augustine, Florida)
                                       Presidents' Day (third Monday)

3117 B.C., Dar-Homah introduced an improved writing technique called cuneiform at the Society of Sumerian Scribes convention in Baghdad.
1763 the Treaty of Hubertusberg ended the Seven Years' War.
1764 Auguste Chouteau established a settlement near the confluence of the Missouri and Mississippi Rivers which he called St. Louis.
1768 Benjamin Jackson began manufacturing mustard in Philadelphia.
1898 the U.S.S. Maine mysteriously exploded in Havana's harbor.
1924 Alexandra Kollantai became the world's first woman ambassador.
1932 marked the first regular radio broadcast of "Burns and Allen" on CBS.
1936 Parshall, North Dakota registered a temperature of -60° F.
1942 Singapore surrendered to the Japanese.
1961 thirty-four members of the United States figure skating team were killed in an airline crash near Brussels, Belgium.
1970 Judge Julius Hoffman accused, tried, convicted and sentenced the "Chicago Seven" for contempt of court.
1978 Wayne Sommers caught a forty-one and a half pound pompano near Fort Lauderdale.

The following people were born on February 15:

Philipp Melanchthon in 1497.
Galilee Galilei in 1564.
Cyrus Hall McCormick in 1809.
Susan B. Anthony in 1820.
Elihu Root in 1845.
Alfred North Whitehead in 1861.
George J. "Candy" LaChance in 1870.
Cesar Romero in 1907.
Harvey Korman in 1927.
Claire Bloom in 1931.
Melissa Manchester in 1951.

February 16   Lithuanian Independence Day
                                    National Future Farmer of America
                                       Week (begins the Saturday before
                                       the twenty-second)

1804 Stephen Decatur led a Naval attack on the pirate stronghold
        at Tripoli.
1857 the National Deaf Mute College was incorporated.
1868 the Benevolent Protective Order of Elks was organized.
1880 the American Society of Mechanical Engineers was founded.
1900 the treaty establishing American Samoa was ratified.
1903 Pokegama Dam, Minnesota registered a temperature of -59° F.
1905 the Esperanto Association was organized.
1918 Lithuania issued a formal declaration of independence.
1932 Manchukuo (Manchuria) became a puppet state of the Japanese.
1932 James Markham patented a new strain of peach tree.
1937 DuPont patented nylon.
1943 Falls Village, Connecticut registered a temperature of -32° F.
1976 Norton Thomton caught a ninety pound mackerel off Key West.

The following people were born on February 16:

Henry Wilson in 1812.
"Sliding Billy" Hamilton in 1866.
Edgar Bergen in 1903.
Frank "Creepy" Crespi in 1918.
Salvatore "Sonny" Bono in 1940.

February 17   Lossar or New Year's Day (Bhutan)
                                    P.T.A. Founders Day

Frances E. Willard Memorial Day
National Engineers Week (begins
Sunday of the last full week of
the month)

1405 Tamerlane died.
1776 the United States Marines saw action for the first time in the
Bahamas.
1863 the International Red Cross was founded in Geneva.
1864 the Confederate submarine Hunley torpedoed and sank the Union
warship Housatonic.
1890 the British steamer Duburg was wrecked. Four hundred lives
were lost.
1897 the National Congress of Mothers (later the P.T.A.) was organized
in Washington, D.C.
1913 modern art was introduced in the United States at the New
York Armory Show.
1932 "Baby Face" Nelson escaped from Joliet Prison.
1936 McIntosh, South Dakota registered a temperature of -58° F.
1957 Brian Galvin caught a 739 pound thresher shark off New Zealand.
1959 the U.S. Navy launched the "Vanguard II" weather satellite.
1961 Baxley McQuaig, Jr. caught a nine pound, six ounce pickerel
in Georgia.
1970 James Penwarden caught a 1,061 pound mako shark near New
Zealand.

The following people were born on February 17:

Alfred Adler in 1870.
Marian Anderson in 1902.
Walter L. "Red" Barber in 1908.
Hal Holbrook in 1925.
Jim Brown in 1936.
Gene Pitney in 1941.

February 18   Gambia Independence Day
Tribhuvan Jayanti (King Tribhuvan's
Birthday) or Democracy Day (Ne-
pal)

1688 the German Friends staged a protest against slavery in German-
town, Pennsylvania.
1834 The Man began publication in New York City.
1856 the American Party held its first convention in Philadelphia.
1861 Jefferson Davis was inaugurated as President of the Confederate
States of America.
1908 postage stamps were first issued in coils.

1915 the German Navy set up a submarine blockade of Great Britain.
1930 Elm Farm Ollie became the first cow to fly in an airplane.
1930 Pluto was discovered by Clyde W. Tombaugh.
1951 Nepal officially adopted a constitutional form of government.
1953 the first "3-D" movie, Bwana Devil, opened in New York City.
1965 Gambia became an independent nation.
1970 the "Chicago Seven" were acquitted of conspiracy to incite riots during the 1968 Democratic Convention. Five were convicted of other offenses.

The following people were born on February 18:

Count Alessandro Volta in 1745.
Ernst Mach in 1838.
Wendell Willkie in 1892.
Andres Segovia in 1894.
Bill Cullen and Jack Palance in 1920.
Helen Gurley Brown in 1922.
Sherman A. Strickhouser in 1932.
Kim Novak in 1933.
John Travolta in 1954.

February 19   Makha Bucha Day (Thailand)

1794 the Massachusetts Historical Society was incorporated.
1831 Phineas Davis tested the first practical American made coal burning locomotive.
1856 Hamilton Lamphere Smith patented the tin-type camera.
1862 construction of the U.S.S. Monitor was completed.
1864 the fraternal society of the Knights of Pythias was founded in Washington, D.C.
1878 Thomas Alva Edison patented the phonograph.
1929 doctors made the first use of a diathermy machine.
1945 the U.S. Marines landed and the Battle of Iwo Jima began.
1953 the State of Georgia approved a state board of censorship on literature.
1957 the S.S. Tropicana, the first ship to carry a cargo of fresh orange juice in stainless steel tanks, arrived in Whitestone, New York.

The following people were born on February 19:

Nicolaus Copernicus in 1473.
Stan Kenton in 1912.
Eddie Arcaro in 1916.
Lee Marvin in 1924.
William "Smokey" Robinson in 1940.

February 20   Frederick Douglass Day
                                         John Glenn Day

the sun enters the house of Pisces.
1725 ten New Hampshire Indians were scalped by a party of whites
     for a bounty of 100 pounds each.
1768 the first American fire insurance company received its charter.
1865 the Massachusetts Institute of Technology was established.
1872 Silas Noble and James P. Cooley patented a toothpick manufac-
     turing machine.
1872 Cyrus W. Baldwin patented his version of the elevator.
1895 Frederick Douglass died at the age of seventy-eight.
1920 the dog racing track at Emeryville, California was opened.
1937 the first combination automobile-airplane was ready for testing.
1944 U.S. planes began bombing German industrial cities.
1962 John Glenn became the first U.S. astronaut to orbit the earth.
1978 William G. Foster caught a 116 pound giant trevally near Pago
     Pago.

The following people were born on February 20:

Harry H. Truman in 1866.
Sam Rice in 1890.
Ansel Adams in 1902.
Alexei Kosygin in 1904.
Sidney Poitier in 1927.
Nancy Wilson in 1937.
Buffy Sainte-Marie in 1941.
Phil Esposito in 1942.
Sandy Duncan and J. Geils in 1946.
Jennifer O'Neill in 1949.
Patty Hearst in 1954.

February 21   Shaheed Day (Bangladesh)

 950 A.D., Harald Bluetooth acceded to the throne of Denmark.
1828 the Cherokee Phoenix began publication in New Echota, Georgia.
1842 John James Greenough patented his sewing machine.
1848 Karl Marx and Friedrich Engels published The Communist Mani-
     festo.
1878 New Haven, Connecticut issued the first telephone book.
1885 the Washington Monument was dedicated.
1904 the National Ski Association was formed at Ishpeming, Michigan.
1916 the Battle of Verdun began which eventually resulted in over
     1,000,000 casualties.
1921 William Devoe Coney made the first one day trans-United States
     flight from San Diego to Jacksonville.

1925 The New Yorker magazine began publication.
1944 U.S. troops invaded Eniwetok Island.
1947 Edwin Herbert Land demonstrated that his Land camera was
      capable of developing and printing photographs on the spot.
1972 President Nixon arrived in the People's Republic of China.

The following people were born on February 21:

W.H. Auden in 1907.
Sam Peckinpah in 1925.
Erma Bombeck in 1927.
Tricia Nixon Cox in 1946.

February 22   George Washington's Birthday

1630 popcorn was introduced to the English colonists by Quadequina,
      brother of Massasoit.
1770 eleven year old Christopher Snider was killed in Boston by Ebene-
      zer Richardson.
1819 Spain sold Florida to the United States for $5,000,000.
1854 the Republican Party originated in Michigan.
1872 the Labor Reform Party held its first convention.
1872 the Prohibition Party held its first national convention.
1878 the Greenback Labor Party was organized in Toledo, Ohio.
1878 the first Bulgarian Constitutional Assembly convened.
1879 F.W. Woolworth opened the original five and ten cent store.
1886 the London Times began printing its "personal column."
1909 the "Great White Fleet" completed its circumnavigation of
      the earth.
1923 America's first chinchilla farm was established in Los Angeles.
1973 China and the United States exchanged liaison offices.
1979 St. Lucia attained independence.

The following people were born on February 22:

George Washington in 1732.
Arthur Schopenhauer in 1788.
Frederic Chopin in 1810.
James Russell Lowell in 1819.
Edna St. Vincent Millay in 1892.
Robert Young in 1907.
Edward M. Kennedy in 1932.
George "Sparky" Anderson in 1934.

February 23   Guyanese Republic Day

303 A.D., Galerius persuaded Diocletian to declare a general persecu-
     tion of the Christians.
1813 the first cotton mill in the world to process cotton completely
     by power from spinning to weaving went into operation in
     Waltham, Massachusetts.
1836 the siege of the Alamo began in San Antonio, Texas.
1870 Mississippi was readmitted to the Union.
1883 the American Anti-Vivisection Society was organized.
1883 Alabama enacted America's first anti-trust law. It was aimed
     specifically at "monopolies in the transportation of freight."
1886 Charles Martin Hall invented a process for the commercial
     production of aluminum.
1892 the Bryn Mawr Self-Government Association was chartered.
1905 the Rotary Club was founded in Chicago.
1917 the American Society of Orthodontists was incorporated.
1921 the Kronstadt Mutiny began as Russian sailors revolted against
     the new government.

The following people were born on February 23:

George Frederick Handel in 1685.
W.E.B. DuBois in 1868.
Peter Fonda in 1939.
Johnny Winter in 1944.

February 24   Feast of St. Matthias (Protestant)
                                       Flag Day (Mexico)
                                       Proclamation of Baire (Cuba)

1582 Pope Gregory XIII issued a papal bull establishing the Gregorian
     calender, effective October 4, 1582.
1821 Mexico announced the Plan of Iguala which proclaimed its inde-
     pendence from Spain.
1839 William S. Otis patented the steam shovel.
1868 the House of Representatives voted to impeach Andrew Johnson.
1925 thermite was used for the first time in breaking up an ice jam.
1933 Japan withdrew from the League of Nations.
1938 DuPont began producing nylon toothbrush bristles.
1946 Juan Peron became president of Argentina.
1949 the first multi-stage rocket was fired at White Sands Proving
     Ground in New Mexico.
1953 the South African government assumed dictatorial powers aimed
     at the suppression of Negro and Indian rights movements.
1970 the Kienast quintuplets were born.
1980 the United States' Olympic hockey team won the gold medal
     at Lake Placid, New York.

The following people were born on January 24:

Wilhelm Karl Grimm in 1786.
Winslow Homer in 1836.
Honus Wagner in 1874.
Abe Vigoda in 1921.

February 25   Feast of St. Walpurgis
                                    Kuwait's National Day

483 B.C., Siddhartha Gautama (Buddha) died at the age of eighty.
779 A.D., the abbess, St. Walpurgis, died at the Heidenheim monastery.
1795 Union College was incorporated in Schenectady, New York.
1836 Samuel Colt patented his revolving barrel pistol.
1837 Thomas Davenport of Rutland, Vermont patented the electric printing press.
1908 the Hudson and Manhattan railroad tunnel under the Hudson River was opened.
1913 the sixteenth (income tax) amendment to the U.S. constitution became law.
1933 the United States' first aircraft carrier, the U.S.S. Ranger, was launched from Newport News, Virginia.
1940 the New York Rangers and the Montreal Canadians were the teams involved in the first telecast of a professional hockey game.
1964 Cassius Clay (later Muhammad Ali) knocked out Sonny Liston in the seventh round.
1974 Richard Nixon's lawyer, Herbert Kalmbach, entered a guilty plea in respose to the charge of campaign fund impropriety.

The following people were born on February 25:

Pierre Auguste Renoir in 1841.
Jim Backus in 1913.
Jack W. "Lucky" Lohrke in 1924.
George Harrison in 1943.

February 26   Feast of St. Alexander of Alexandria

1876 Japan became the first nation to establish trade relations with Korea.
1895 Michael Joseph Owens patented a glass blowing machine.
1914 the Museum of Peaceful Arts (now the New York Museum of Science and Industry) was established.

1915 Germany began using flame throwers in battle against the French.
1916 the French cruiser _Provence_ sank in the Mediterranean Sea; 3,100 lives were lost.
1919 the Grand Canyon became a national park.
1944 Sue Sophia Dauser became the first woman to attain the rank of captain in the U.S. Navy.
1949 the first non-stop round the world airplane flight began.
1952 Winston Churchill announced the production of a nuclear bomb by Great Britain.
1955 George Franklin Smith became the first pilot to bail out of an airplane at supersonic speed.
1980 an accident at the Crystal River, Florida nuclear reactor forced partial evacuation and an emergency shutdown.

The following people were born on February 26:

Victor Hugo in 1802.
"Buffalo Bill" Cody in 1845.
Grover Alexander in 1887.
Preacher Roe in 1915.
Jackie Gleason in 1916.
Tony Randall in 1920.
Antoine "Fats" Domino in 1928.
Johnny Cash in 1932.

February 27   Dominican Republic Independence
                                    Day
                                    Feast of St. Gabriel Possenti
                                    Statehood Day (West Indies Asso-
                                    ciated States)

1410 B.C., Joshua fought the Battle of Jericho and the walls came tumbling down.
1189 Richard the Lion Hearted ascended the throne of England.
1813 steamboat mail delivery was authorized by the U.S. government.
1879 Constantine Fahlberg and Ira Remsen announced the discovery of saccharin.
1883 Oscar Hammerstein patented a cigar rolling machine.
1919 the American Association for the Hard of Hearing was formed.
1933 Nazi party members burned the German Reichstag. Adolf Hitler blamed communists and suspended freedom of speech and freedom of the press.
1935 vectolite was first manufactured at West Lynn, Massachusetts.
1939 the United States Supreme Court ruled sit-down strikes to be illegal.
1973 A.I.M. members occupied the trading post and church at Wounded Knee, South Dakota.

The following people were born on February 27:

Henry Wadsworth Longfellow in 1807.
Enrico Caruso in 1873.
Gene Sarazen in 1901.
John Steinbeck in 1902.
Lawrence Durrell in 1912.
John Connally in 1917.
Elizabeth Taylor in 1932.
Ralph Nader in 1934.

February 28   Action Line Day
                                Bachelors Day (in non-leap years)

1810 the American Fire Insurance Company of Philadelphia was organized.
1822 Farmer's Fire Insurance and Loan Company was incorporated in New York City.
1827 the Baltimore and Ohio Railroad Company was incorporated.
1849 the first regular steamboat service arrived in San Francisco, California via Cape Horn.
1882 the Harvard Co-Operative Society was constituted.
1893 Edward Goodrich Acheson received a patent for carborundum.
1921 the Soviet Union and Afghanistan concluded a treaty of friendship which resulted in substantial Bolshevik support for the Afghan regime in its resistance to the British.
1922 Egypt was declared an independent nation.
1940 Fordham University and the University of Pittsburgh were involved in the first telecast of a basketball game.
1954 the phase-contrast cinemicrography film, The Birth of a Plant, was televised by KPIX in San Francisco.

The following people were born on February 28:

Michel de Montaigne in 1533.
Waslaw Nijinsky in 1890.
Linus Pauling in 1901.
Zero Mostel in 1915.
Mario Andretti in 1940.
Bernadette Peters in 1948.

February 29   Bachelors Day (in leap years)
                                Leap Year Day

3,887,492,104 B.C., the first blue-green algae produced seventeen
    oxygen molecules.
 992 A.D., St. Oswald, Bishop of Worcester, died.
1704 a French and Indian detachment from Canada overran the colonial
    garrison at Deerfield, Massachusetts.
1744 Benjamin Franklin published James Logan's translation of the
    classic The Cato Major.
1804 the Democratic-Republican Party held the first open congression-
    al caucus in Washington, D.C. and nominated Thomas Jefferson
    for president of the United States.
1892 Great Britain and the United States concluded a treaty on seal
    hunting in the Bering Sea.
1932 an unsuccessful coup was attempted in Finland by a group of
    right wing rebels.
1940 Hattie McDaniel was presented an Oscar for her performance
    in Gone with the Wind.
1944 Dorothy E. Vredenburgh was appointed secretary of the Democra-
    tic National Committee.
1956 Pakistan proclaimed itself an Islamic republic effective March
    twenty-third.
1968 the President's Commission on Civil Disorders issued a report
    that found white racism to be the major cause of black violence
    in the United States.

The following people were born on February 29:

Marquis de Montcalm in 1712.
Ann Lee in 1736.
Gioacchino Antonio Rossini in 1792.
Ed Appleton in 1892.
Ralph Miller in 1896.
Jimmy Dorsey and Johnny "Pepper" Martin in 1904.
Arthur Franz, James Mitchell and Michelle Morgan in 1920.

March

The first day of March marks the following commemorations:

Chalandra Marz (Engadine, Switzerland)
Commemoration of the Arrival of Martín Pinzón (Bayona, Spain)
St. David's Day (Wales)
Eight Hour Day (Tasmania)
Korea Independence Movement Day (South Korea)
Nebraska State Day
Ohio Admission Day
Panamanian Constitution Day
Paraguay Heroes Day
Vermont Town Meeting Day (first Tuesday)

American Camping Week (begins the first Sunday)
National Aardvark Week (begins the first Sunday)
National Procrastination Week (begins the first Sunday)
Omizutori or Water-Drawing Festival (first to the fourteenth Japan)
Return the Borrowed Book Week
Save Your Vision Week (begins the first Sunday)

Month of Civilized and Polite Behavior Among Citizens (China, People's Republic of)
National Nutrition Month
National Peanut Month
Philatelic Literature Month
Red Cross Month
Youth Art Month

March 1

293 A.D., Diocletian chose Galerius, and Maximian selected Constantius as their respective successors.
1642 Georgeana, Maine became the first city to be incorporated in North America.
1780 Pennsylvania abolished slavery.

47

1780 the United States issued its first bank charter to the Bank of Philadelphia.
1803 Ohio was admitted to the Union.
1845 the United States Annexed Texas.
1847 the abolition of capital punishment went into effect in Michigan.
1867 Nebraska was admitted to the Union.
1872 Yellowstone National Park was authorized.
1883 the National Woman's Christian Temperance Union was organized.
1932 twenty month old Charles A. Lindbergh, Jr. was kidnapped.
1941 "Captain America" first appeared in a comic book.
1941 Bulgaria joined the Axis.
1950 Chiang Kai-shek resumed the presidency of Nationalist China (on Formosa).
1954 the United States detonated a hydrogen bomb in the Marshall Islands.
1954 Puerto Rican nationalists shot and wounded five members of Congress in the United States House of Representatives.
1961 President John F. Kennedy created the Peace Corps.
1962 Uganda became a self governing country.

The following people were born on March 1:

Glenn Miller in 1904.
David Niven in 1910.
Dinah Shore in 1918.
Harry Belafonte in 1927.
Robert Conrad in 1935.
Ron Howard in 1954.

March 2   Guam Discovery Day
                                     Morocco Independence Day
                                     Old Stuff Day
                                     Peasants Day (Burma)
                                     Texas Independence Day
                                     Victory of Adwa Commemoration
                                          Day (Ethiopia)

1331 Nicaea (Iznik) was taken by the Turks.
1476 the Battle of Grandson took place.
1717 the first ballet to rely strictly on mime was presented.
1829 the New England Asylum for the Blind was incorporated in Boston.
1836 Texas declared itself independent of Mexico.
1858 Frederick Cook patented the cotton-bale metallic tie.
1866 the Excelsior Needle Company was incorporated.
1867 Howard University was incorporated.
1917 the Jones Act made Puerto Rico a U.S. territory and granted its inhabitants U.S. citizenship.

1923 Time magazine was first published.
1925 the United States adopted a national road numbering system.
1940 an intercollegiate track meet was telecast for the first time.
1956 Morocco became an independent nation and France recognized it as such.
1958 Sir Vivian Fuchs' expedition completed the first land crossing of Antarctica.
1962 Wilt Chamberlain scored 100 points in one game.

The following people were born on March 2:

Juvenal in 60 A.D.
Sam Houston in 1793.
Pope Pius XII (Eugenio Pacelli) in 1876.
Dr. Seuss (Theodor S. Geisel) in 1904.
Mel Ott in 1909.
Desi Arnaz in 1917.
Karen Carpenter in 1950.

March 3   Feast of the Throne (Morocco)
                                     Florida Admission Day
                                     Hinamatsuri or Doll Festival (Japan)
                                     Malawi Martyr's Day
                                     National Anthem Day
                                     Sudanese Unity Day

1791 Congress passed the Internal Revenue Act.
1801 David Emanuel of Georgia became the first Jewish governor in the United States when Governor James Jackson resigned.
1842 Massachusetts passed a law stating that no child under twelve years of age could work more than ten hours a day.
1845 Florida was admitted to the Union.
1847 the United States approved the use of postage stamps.
1861 Alexander II of Russia issued the Emancipation Edict.
1863 the National Academy of Sciences was incorporated.
1863 Congress approved the drafting of men into the U.S. armed forces.
1875 the first organized ice hockey match took place in Montreal.
1878 the Treaty of San Stefano ended the third Russo-Turkish War.
1918 the Treaty of Brest-Litovsk was dictated to Russia by Germany.
1931 the "Star Spangled Banner" was designated the United States' national anthem.
1936 "Renfrew of the Mounted" premiered on CBS radio.
1945 Finland declared war on Germany.
1953 a Canadian Pacific Comet jet crashed at Karachi, Pakistan, becoming the first commercial jet to be involved in a crash resulting in fatalities.

1961 King Hassan II ascended the throne of Morocco.

The following people were born on March 3:

George M. Pullman in 1831.
Alexander Graham Bell in 1847.
Monte Ward in 1860.
Willie Keeler in 1872.
Jean Harlow in 1911.
Julius Boros in 1920.
Lee Radziwill in 1933.

March 4   Maha Sivarathri Day (Sri Lanka)
                               Mahashiva Ratri (Nepal)
                               Vermont Admission Day

338,271 B.C., the Riss glaciation period ended and the third inter-gla-
        cial period began.
1681 William Penn received the charter for Pennsylvania from Charles II.
1789 the first Congress of the United States convened in New York City.
1791 Vermont was admitted to the Union.
1826 the Granite Railway of Massachusetts was incorporated. It
        was the first American railroad to remain in operation 100
        years.
1829 Andrew Jackson began a "spoils system" in filling civil service
        appointments.
1861 the Confederate States of America adopted the "stars and bars"
        as its flag.
1868 Jessie Chisholm, who established the Chisholm Trail, died from
        an acute case of ptomaine poisoning.
1881 James Garfield became the first president to use a telephone.
1921 Hot Springs Park was designated a national park after having
        been under reservation status since 1832.
1961 "Freedom Riders" began touring the South.

The following people were born on March 4:

Henry the Navigator in 1394.
Antonio Vivaldi in 1678.
Casimir Pulaski in 1748.
Charles "Piano Legs" Hickman in 1876.
Knute Rockne in 1888.
Clarence "Dazzy" Vance in 1891.
Jim Clark in 1936.
Paula Prentiss in 1939.

March 5
                                        Crispus Attucks Day
                                        Equatorial Guinean National Holiday
                                        Gospel Arrival in Polynesia
                                        Labour Day (Western Australia)

1623 Virginia enacted North America's first temperance law.
1770 Crispus Attucks and four others died in the "Boston Massacre."
1868 the stapler was patented in Birmingham, England by C.H. Gould.
1872 George Westinghouse patented the triple air brake.
1923 Montana and Nevada enacted old age pension law.
1924 Frank Carauana rolled two "300" games in succession in Buffalo,
       New York.
1927 1,000 Marines landed in China to protect U.S. property during
       the civil war.
1953 Josef Stalin died and was succeeded by Georgi Malenkov.
1963 Patsy Cline, Cowboy Copas and Hawkshaw Hawkins were killed
       in an airplane crash.
1966 a BOAC Boeing 707 crashed on Mount Fuji killing 124.
1970 the nuclear non-proliferation treaty took effect.
1980 the largest burst of gamma rays ever recorded by earth satellites
       was detected coming from the remnant of supernova N-49
       in the Large Magellanic Cloud.

The following people were born on March 5:

Gerhardus Mercator in 1512.
James M. Ives in 1824.
Rex Harrison in 1908.
Paul Bohannan in 1920.
Samantha Eggar in 1939.
Robert "Rocky" Bleier in 1946.
Andy Gibb in 1958.

March 6
                                        Alamo Day (Texas)
                                        Ghana Independence Day
                                        King's Birthday (Cambodia or Kam-
                                            puchea)
                                        Magellan Day (Guam)
                                        Girl Scout Week (the week that in-
                                            cludes the twelfth)

1480 the Treaty of Alcacovas settled the possession of the islands
       off the coast of Africa.
1775 Prince Hall, the first negro Mason, entered Army Lodge #441.
1831 Edgar Allan Poe was expelled from West Point for "gross neglect
       of duty" and "disobedience of orders."
1836 the Alamo fell.

1853 "La Traviata" was performed for the first time.
1857 the Dred Scott decision upheld the legality of slavery.
1869 the first international cycle race was held in England.
1886 America's first alternating current power plant went into operation in Great Barrington, Massachusetts.
1930 Clarence Birdseye marketed the first frozen foods.
1931 "The March of Time" was first heard on CBS radio.
1940 a telecast was made from an airplane for the first time.
1957 Ghana became an independent nation with Kwame Nkrumah
as prime minister.
1981 Walter Cronkite made his farewell newscast.

The following people were born on March 6:

Michelangelo Buonarroti in 1475.
Hector S. Cyrano de Bergerac in 1619.
Elizabeth Barret Browning in 1806.
Robert "Lefty" Grove in 1900.
Lou Costello in 1908.
Ed McMahon in 1923.
Willie Stargell in 1940.
Rob Reiner in 1945.

March 7   Luther Burbank Day
                                     Feast of St. Thomas Aquinas

 322 B.C., Aristotle died on the island of Euboea at the age of 62.
 161 A.D., Marcus Aurelius became emperor of Rome.
1274 St. Thomas Aquinas died at Fossanova at the age of 49.
1644 Massachusetts established the first bicameral legislature in
North America.
1854 Charles Miller patented a sewing machine that made button
holes.
1855 the first field-service telegraph went into operation at Kadikoi,
Russia.
1876 Alexander Graham Bell received a patent for the telephone.
1911 Willis S. Farnsworth patented the coin operated locker.
1936 Germany violated the Locarno Pact by reoccupying the Rhineland.
1945 the United States Army crossed the Rhine River.
1968 Twin Falls, Newfoundland registered a temperature of -49° C.

The following people were born on March 7:

Luther Burbank in 1849.
Thomas Masaryk in 1850.
Piet Mondrian in 1872.
Clarence "Soup" Campbell in 1915.

March 8   Be Nast-y Day
                                               International Women's Day
                                               Syrian Revolution Day

1550 St. John of God, Spanish patron saint of nurses, died at Grenada.
1855 the Niagara Falls railroad suspension bridge opened.
1887 Everett Horton patented the telescoping steel tube fishing rod.
1894 a dog license law was enacted for New York City.
1917 the United States Senate adopted a measure permitting cloture.
1917 riots in St. Petersburg marked the onset of the revolution against
        the Russian monarchy.
1933 the Franklin Chamber of Commerce of Franklin, Indiana issued
        $2,400 worth of self-liquidating scrip money.
1945 Phyllis M. Daley became the first black nurse to be sworn in
        as an ensign in the U.S. Navy.
1954 the United States and Japan signed a mutual defense agreement.
1957 Ghana joined the United Nations.
1963 the Revolutionary National Council took control of the govern-
        ment of the Syrian Arab Republic.
1968 black students and police clashed in Orangeburg, South Carolina.
        Three students were killed and the National Guard was called
        in to restore order.
1972 Norman W. Mize caught a five pound, five ounce white bass
        in California.

The following people were born on March 8:

Oliver Wendell Holmes, Jr. in 1841.
Otto Hahn in 1879.
"Mississippi" John Hurt in 1892.
Cyd Charisse in 1923.
James Bouton in 1939.
Richie Allen in 1942.
Lynn Redgrave in 1943.

March 9   Baron Bliss Day (Belize)
                                               Commonwealth Day (British Virgin
                                                  Islands)
                                               Feast of St. Frances of Rome
                                               Amerigo Vespucci Day

 432 B.C., the Parthenon in Athens was consecrated.
1500 Pedro Cabral led a fleet of thirteen ships out of Lisbon on a
        six month voyage to India.
1799 the first United States pistol contract was made with Simeon
        North of Berlin, Connecticut.
1822 C.M. Graham was granted a patent for artificial teeth.

1841 the Baltimore College of Dental Surgery conferred its first
     two degrees.
1858 Albert Potts patented the mail box.
1862 the U.S.S. Monitor and the C.S.S. Merrimac did battle.
1889 Kansas passed the first state anti-trust law that was generally
     applicable to all areas of commerce.
1907 sterilization legislation was enacted by Indiana for eugenic,
     punitive and therapeutic reasons.
1916 "Pancho" Villa's Mexican irregulars killed fifteen in a raid on
     Columbus, New Mexico.
1916 Germany declared war on Portugal.
1945 heavy U.S. bombing of Tokyo destroyed sixteen square miles
     of the city and killed 85,000.
1979 Linda Morabito discovered volcanic activity on Io.

The following people were born on March 9:

Amerigo Vespucci in 1451.
Vyacheslav A. Molotov in 1890.
George Lincoln Rockwell and Mickey Spillane in 1918.
Yuri Gagarin in 1934.
Keeley Smith in 1935.
Bobby Fischer in 1943.
Mickey Dolenz in 1945.

March 10   Commonwealth Day (Swaziland)
                                     Harriet Tubman Day

1791 John Stone patented the pile driver.
1839 Lin Tse-hsü confiscated 30,000 chests of opium in Canton and
     burned it. This direct affront to British interests led to hostili-
     ties between Britain and China.
1862 the United States first issued paper money.
1876 the first distinguishable telephone message was transmitted
     by Alexander Graham Bell.
1880 the Salvation Army got its start in the United States.
1898 the Guildford Badminton Tournament opened.
1903 Harry Christian Gammeter patented the multigraph.
1909 Arizona approved America's first "Home for the Aged and Infirm
     Arizona Pioneers" in Prescott.
1912 after decades of humiliation and exploitation, China began
     to organize itself by establishing a constitution.
1913 Harriet Tubman died in Auburn, New York.
1922 Mahatma Gandhi was arrested and imprisoned.
1933 Nevada became the first state to adopt narcotics regulations
     of its own.
1952 Fulgencio Batista overthrew the Cuban government, proclaiming
     himself "Chief of State."

The following people were born on March 10:

Marcello Malpighi in 1628.
James Earl Ray in 1928.
Prince Edward of England in 1964.

March 11   Decoration Day (Liberia)

1779 the Army Corps of Engineers was established.
1823 the Concord (Vermont) Academy for teachers was opened.
1861 the constitution of the Confederate States of America was adopted.
1882 the Intercollegiate Lacrosse Association was organized.
1888 the four day blizzard of '88 brought a record snowfall to the northeastern United States.
1895 after years of friction, the Pamir boundary between Russia and Afghanistan was settled.
1896 the National Commandery of the Military Order of Foreign Wars was instituted.
1917 Baghdad was occupied by the British.
1927 the "Flatheads" gang pulled the first armored car hold-up by dynamiting a car near Pittsburgh, Pennsylvania.
1940 the first color cystoscopic photographs were shown to the public in Birmingham, Alabama.
1941 the United States Congress passed the Lend-Lease Act.
1966 Indonesian President Achmed Sukarno was overthrown by a military coup.

The following people were born on March 11:

Sir Malcolm Campbell in 1885.
Lawrence Welk in 1903.
Harold Wilson in 1916.
Ralph Abernathy in 1926.

March 12   Anniversary of Renewal (Gabon Republic)
                                     Jane Delano Day
                                     King's Birthday (Libya)
                                     Mauritius Independence Day
                                     Moshoeshoe's Day (Lesotho)

1804 federal judge John Pickering was impeached.
1832 the ballet tutu was presented for the first time.

1849 the Pacific Railroad became the first railroad to run west of the Mississippi River.
1894 Coca-Cola was first sold in bottles.
1904 the Carnegie Hero Fund Commission was established.
1912 Albert Berry became the first person to parachute from an airplane.
1912 the Girl Scouts of the U.S.A. was founded in Savannah, Georgia.
1930 Mahatma Gandhi began another civil disobedience campaign in India in response to the British salt tax.
1933 President Franklin D. Roosevelt broadcast his first fireside chat.
1947 the pronouncement of the Truman Doctrine placed the United States in active opposition to communism.
1966 General Suharto assumed control of Indonesia.
1968 Mauritius became an independent nation.
1979 Linda Morabito's Jet Propulsion Lab imaging team reported that they had discovered six erupting volcanoes on Io.

The following people were born on March 12:

Colonel Charles Young in 1864.
Kemal Ataturk in 1881.
Andrew Young and Jack Kerouac in 1922.
Barbara Feldon in 1941.
Liza Minelli in 1946.
James Taylor in 1948.

March 13   Grenadian Revolution Day

415,231 B.C., the Shell band of homo erectus was the first group to use wood in the construction of a shelter. They lived in the area known today as the south of France.
850 A.D., Al-Khwarizmi, an Arabian mathemetician from Uzbek, died at the age of 70.
1638 the Ancient and Honorable Artillery Company was chartered, becoming the first organized military association in North America.
1852 the first "Uncle Sam" cartoon was published by Frank H.T. Bellew. "Uncle Sam" was said to have been modeled after Samuel Wilson of New Hampshire.
1868 impeachment proceedings were begun against President Andrew Johnson.
1877 Chester Greenwood patented earmuffs.
1881 Czar Alexander II of Russia was assassinated.
1894 the "strip tease" was introduced in Paris.
1913 Kansas approved the creation of the first state motion picture censorship board.

1930 the discovery of Pluto was announced.
1938 Arthur Seyss-Inquart proclaimed Austrian unification with Germany.
1942 Japanese troops landed in the Solomon Islands.
1954 the beginning of the Siege of Dienbienphu marked North Vietnamese independence.

The following people were born on March 13:

Joseph Priestley in 1733.
Percival Lowell in 1855.
L. Ron Hubbard in 1911.
Joe Rossi in 1923.
Neil Sedaka in 1939.

March 14   Feast of St. Matilda

923 A.D., Rhazes, a Persian physician and alchemist, died in Rai, a town near Tehran, at the age of seventy-three.
1794 Eli Whitney received a patent for his cotton gin.
1812 the United States first authorized the sale of war bonds.
1813 the first U.S. flagship to round Cape Horn arrived in Valparaiso, Chile.
1826 the first conference of the American Republics was assembled at Panama.
1900 the United States Congress approved the adoption of the gold standard.
1903 Theodore Roosevelt established the first U.S. bird reservation at Pelican Island in Florida.
1917 the U.S. Navy first succeeded in launching an aircraft.
1921 the Psychological Corporation was founded.
1939 the Republic of Czechoslovakia was dissolved as Nazi troops began their occupation.
1964 rioting broke out between Greeks and Turks on Cyprus. United Nations troops were sent to the island to keep peace.
1976 Ralph A. Mikkelson caught a thirty-three pound, ten ounce rainbow runner near Clarion Island in Mexico.

The following people were born on March 14:

Johann Strauss the elder in 1804.
Paul Ehrlich and Thomas R. Marshall in 1854.
Casey Jones in 1864.
Maxim Gorky in 1868.
Albert Einstein in 1879.
Les Brown in 1912.
Frank Borman in 1928.

Michael Caine and Quincy Jones in 1933.
Billy Crystal in 1950.

March 15	Buzzard Day (Hinckley, Ohio)
	DeSoto Celebration Day (Bradenton, Florida)
	Ides of March
	Andrew Jackson Day (Tennessee)
	Maine Admission Day
	J.J. Roberts Day (Liberia)
	National Poison Prevention Week (begins the third Sunday)
	National Wildlife Week (begins the third Sunday)

the buzzards return to Hinckley, Ohio.
  44 B.C., Julius Caesar was assassinated in the Roman Senate.
1812 a Russian settlement was established at Cazadero in what is now California.
1820 Maine was admitted to the Union.
1830 the American Institute of Instruction was formed.
1887 Michigan hired the first fish and game warden.
1887 Roxbury, Massachusetts authorized the first kindergarten for the blind.
1892 J.W. Reno obtained a patent for his escalator.
1897 the first indoor flycasting tournament was held.
1916 Austria declared war on Portugal.
1916 U.S. troops entered Mexico in pursuit of "Pancho" Villa.
1917 Czar Nicholas II abdicated.
1930 the U.S.S. Nautilus was launched at Mare Island, California.
1939 Germany occupied Bohemia-Moravia.
1939 Hungary occupied Carpatho-Ukraine.
1957 Paul E. Foust caught a five pound black crappie in South Carolina.
1966 riots broke out in the Watts section of Los Angeles for the second time in less than a year.

The following people were born on March 15:

Andrew Jackson in 1767.
Lightnin' (Sam) Hopkins in 1912.
Harry James in 1916.
Sly Stone in 1944.

March 16   Goodard Day

 597 B.C., Nebuchadnezzar's army captured Jerusalem.
  37 A.D., the Roman emperor Tiberius died at Misenum at the age
      of seventy-nine.
1521 Ferdinand Magellan sighted the Philippines.
1802 a military academy was established at West Point, New York.
1827 Freedom's Journal was first published in New York.
1882 the U.S. was accepted as a member of the International Red Cross.
1915 the Federal Trade Commission was organized.
1917 the Russian Duma, an elected representative body, established
      a provisional government to replace the Czar.
1926 Robert H. Goddard fired the first liquid fuel rocket.
1935 Germany formally denounced the clauses in the Treaty of Ver-
      sailles dealing with the disarmament of the German nation.
1939 the annihilation of the Czechoslovak state was completed. Ger-
      many either occupied or declared protectorates of the various
      regions. No resistance was offered.
1962 a Flying Tiger Super Constellation, with 111 aboard, vanished
      in the western Pacific.
1968 the Mylai massacre was perpetrated.
1978 the Amoco Cadiz oil spill occurred near Portsall, France.

The following people were born on March 16:

James Madison in 1751.
George Ohm in 1787.
Lloyd Waner in 1906.
Jerry Lewis in 1926.

March 17   Camp Fire Girls Founders Day
                                      Canberra Day (Australian Capital
                                          Territory)
                                      Evacuation Day (Massachusetts)
                                      St. Patrick's Day
                                      World Maritime Day

1824 the Dutch ceded Malacca to Great Britain in return for Bengkulen
      in Sumatra.
1845 Stephen Perry of London patented the rubber band.
1861 the independent kingdom of Italy was proclaimed. It was to
      be a constitutional monarchy with a parliament, and Victor
      Emmanuel as king.
1884 John J. Montgomery of Otay, California made the first glider
      flight.
1891 the British steamer Utopia sank off Gibraltar: 574 lives were
      lost.
1910 the Camp Fire Girls was founded in Casco, Maine.

1912 the Camp Fire Girls became a public organization.
1921 the Kronstadt Mutiny came to an end.
1921 the Soviet Union instituted the "New Economic Policy" in response
     to severe shortages caused by the Allied blockade, civil war,
     and sharp cutbacks in production in industry and agriculture.
1921 Poland adopted a constitution.
1934 Hungary, Italy, Austria and Germany formed an alliance.
1948 the Brussels Pact was signed.
1950 the discovery of californium was announced.
1958 the U.S. Navy launched "Vanguard I."

The following people were born on March 17:

James Bridger in 1804.
Gottlieb Daimler in 1834.
Kincsem in 1876.
Bobby Jones in 1902.
Sammy Baugh in 1914.
Nat "King" Cole in 1919.
Rudolf Nureyev in 1938.
John Sebastion in 1944.

March 18   Day of the Supreme Sacrifice
                                    (People's Republic of the Congo)

1813 David Melville patented his apparatus for making coal gas.
1834 the first American railroad tunnel was completed in Pennsylvania.
1848 the Five Days of Milan marked the beginning of the Italian
     War of Independence.
1865 the Congress of the Confederate States of America adjourned
     for the last time.
1890 the Massachusetts Naval Battalion was organized.
1895 the first petrol driven motor bus began operations.
1913 King George of Greece was assassinated.
1922 British magistrates in India sentenced Mahatma Gandhi to six
     years in prison for his acts of civil disobedience.
1931 Schick, Inc. manufactured and delivered the first electric shaver.
1938 Mexico seized $450,000,000 worth of U.S. and British oil proper-
     ties.
1949 the North Atlantic Treaty Organization was formed.
1963 Mount Agung on Bali erupted resulting in 1,584 recorded deaths.
1965 Lt. Col. A.A. Leonov made the first tethered "space walk."
1967 the Torrey Canyon oil spill occurred off Land's End, England.
1970 Cambodian Prince Norodom Sihanouk was deposed by the army.
1978 Philip Terry, Jr. caught an eight pound, fifteen ounce spotted
     bass in Alabama.
1981 the Pawtucket (Rhode Island) Times reported development of

a one-handed typewriter at the Technion-Israel Institute of Technology.

The following people were born on March 18:

John C. Calhoun in 1782.
Grover Cleveland in 1837.
Nikolai Rimsky-Korsakov in 1844.
Rudolf Diesel in 1858.
Ralph Waldo Tyler in 1860.
Edgar Cayce in 1877.
Edward Everett Horton in 1888.
Irving Wallace in 1916.
Peter Graves in 1926.
George Plimpton in 1927.
John Updike in 1932.
Charlie Pride in 1938.
Wilson Pickett in 1941.

March 19   St. Joseph's Day

the swallows return to San Juan Capistrano.
25,637 B.C., ancestors of the American Indians first arrived in Alaska.
1831 America's first bank robbery was pulled by Edward Smith at the City Bank in New York.
1918 New York City inaugurated Daylight Savings Time in the United States.
1920 the United States Senate refused to sanction the League of Nations.
1928 Charles Lindbergh received the Wilson Medal.
1949 the American Museum of Atomic Energy opened in Oak Ridge, Tennessee.
1951 Herman Wouk's The Caine Mutiny was first published.
1954 the Joe Giardello-Willie Troy prize fight became the first fight to be telecast (from Madison Square Garden) in color.
1954 a rocket sled on rails was tested at Alamogordo, New Mexico.
1956 M. Salazar caught a 283 pound tarpon in Venezuela.
1965 Rembrandt's portrait of his son, Titus, was purchased by Norton Simon for $2,234,000.

The following people were born on March 19:

Wilhelm von Biela in 1782.
David Livingstone in 1813.
Sir Richard Burton in 1821.
Wyatt Earp in 1848.
William Jennings Bryan in 1860.

Joe McGinnity in 1871.
Earl Warren in 1891.
Bill Wambsganss in 1894.
"Moms" Mabley (Loretta Aiken) in 1897.
Patrick McGoohan in 1928.
Phillip Roth in 1933.

March 20   Falgun Purnima (Nepal)
                                  Oil Day (Iran)
                                  Tunisia Independence Day
                                  Vernal Equinox

497 B.C., Pythagoras died at Metapontum at the age of eighty-five.
929 A.D., Albategnius, an Arabian astronomer, died in Damascus
    at the age of seventy-nine.
1815 "The Hundred Days" began, marking Napoleon's brief return
    to power.
1833 the U.S. and Siam concluded a Treaty of Amity and Commerce.
1890 the General Federation of Women's Clubs was organized in
    New York City.
1896 U.S. Marines landed in Nicaragua.
1909 the Navajo National Monument in Arizona was established.
1911 the National Squash Tennis Association was formed.
1934 the first test of a practical radar apparatus was made in Germany.
1948 NBC broadcast a symphonic performance simultaneously over
    AM and FM radio and television.
1956 France agreed to withdraw from Tunisia and grant it indepen-
    dence.
1963 Hope Cooke married Prince Palden Thondup Namgyal and became
    Maharajkumarani (Crown Princess) of the Kingdom of Sikkim.
1965 President Johnson ordered federal troops to protect Alabama
    Civil Rights marchers.
1980 the Council on Environmental Quality reported that environmental
    impact studies on Three Mile Island, and other nuclear reactors,
    ignored risks and potential effects of major accidents.

The following people were born on March 20:

Ovid in 43 B.C.
Henrik Ibsen in 1828.
B.F. Skinner in 1904.
Abe Beame in 1906.
Sir Michael Redgrave in 1908.
Carl Reiner in 1922.
Hal Linden in 1931.
Jerry Reed in 1937.
Bobby Orr in 1948.

March 21   Be Kind to Your Astrologer Day
                                           Bird Day
                                           Day of the Indian Child (Mexico)
                                           International Day for the Elimination
                                             of Racial Discrimination
                                           Juarez' Birthday (Mexico)
                                           No Ruz or New Year (Iran)
                                           Vernal Equinox Day (Japan)

the sun enters the house of Aries.
1790 Thomas Jefferson became the first United States Secretary of State.
1791 Captain Hopley Yeaton became the first commissioned U.S. Naval officer.
1859 the Philadelphia Zoological Garden was incorporated.
1868 Sorosis was founded.
1905 the Pennsylvania legislature passed legislation to provide for sterilization of undesirables, but it was vetoed by Governor Samuel Whitaker Pennypacker.
1918 Germany began the Great March Offensive.
1935 Persia was officially renamed Iran.
1939 Germany annexed Memel.
1939 some sixty people on Glencairn Beach at the tip of South Africa sighted the Flying Dutchman.
1946 the United Nations moved into temporary headquarters at Hunter College in New York City.

The following people were born on March 21:

Johann Sebastian Bach in 1685.
Florenz Ziegfeld in 1869.

March 22   Arab League Day (Jordan and Syria)
                                           Emancipation Day (Puerto Rico)

 843 A.D., Charles the Bald became emperor of the Western Franks.
1622 a battle took place between European settlers at Jamestown, Virginia and local Indians. The settlers suffered 1,240 casualties while Indian casualties numbered 347.
1630 Boston, Massachusetts made gambling illegal.
1765 the Stamp Act was imposed on Great Britain's American colonies.
1822 the New York Horticultural Society was incorporated.
1861 the School of Nursing of the Woman's Hospital of Philadelphia was chartered.
1871 North Carolina's Governor William W. Holden's impeachment hearings resulted in a guilty verdict. He was removed from office.

1872 Illinois passed a women's equal employment law.
1874 the Young Men's Hebrew Association was founded.
1882 federal legislation was passed prohibiting polygamy.
1888 Ms. Irene Adler cleverly eluded Sherlock Holmes' trap.
1965 United States authorities confirmed that its troops had used
chemical warfare against the Vietcong.
1967 Cassius Clay (Muhammad Ali) knocked out Zora Folley but was
stripped of the world heavyweight title by the World Boxing
Association because he had refused to serve in the military.
1979 about six UFO's buzzed St. Paul, Minnesota.

The following people were born on March 22:

Anthony Van Dyck in 1599.
Leonard "Chico" Marx in 1891.
Werner Klemperer in 1920.
Marcel Marceau in 1923.
William Shatner in 1931.
George Benson in 1943.

March 23   Liberty Day
National Tree Planting Day (Lesotho)
Otago Provincial Anniversary (New
Zealand)
Pakistan Day
Southland Provincial Anniversary
(New Zealand)
World Meteorological Day

1775 Patrick Henry gave his famous, "Give me liberty or give me
death!" speech in Virginia.
1794 Josiah Gilbert Pierson patented the rivet.
1802 the Magdalen Society Home for Girls was established with the
idea of providing, "more normal opportunities of development
and inculcating good habits."
1857 the five story E.V. Haughwout and Co. building introduced its
installation of an elevator by Elisha Graves Otis.
1858 Eleazer A. Gardner of Philadelphia patented the first plans
for a cable car system.
1880 John Stevens patented the flour rolling mill.
1910 a trial race was held on the new board track automobile raceway
at Playa de Rey, California.
1919 Benito Mussolini founded the Fascist Party in Milan, Italy.
1925 the State of Tennessee enacted legislation that made it unlawful
to teach children about the theory of evolution.
1933 the passage of the Enabling Act firmly established the Nazi
dictatorship in Germany.

1957 the U.S. Army sold the last of its homing pigeons at Fort Monmouth, New Jersey.

The following people were born on March 23:

Schuyler Colfax in 1823.
Erich Fromm in 1900.
Joan Crawford in 1908.
Wernher von Braun in 1912.

March 24   Feast of St. Gabriel the Archangel

1603 James VI, King of Scotland, son of Mary Stuart, was proclaimed James I, King of England.
1629 Virginia passed a game law that prohibited the exportation of hides or skins.
1765 the Quartering Act decreed that American civilians could be required to provide board for British soldiers.
1792 Benjamin West became president of the Royal Academy of London.
1794 there was an unsuccessful Polish uprising led by Thaddeus Kościuszko.
1920 the U.S. Coast Guard opened its first air station at Morehead City, North Carolina.
1932 WABC made the first radio broadcast from a moving train.
1935 "Major Bowes' Original Amateur Hour" made its initial coast to coast broadcast on NBC radio.
1949 father and son, Walter and John Huston, were awarded Oscars for their performances as actor and director in The Treasure of Sierra Madre.
1955 the first sea-going oil drill rig was put into service.

The following people were born on March 24:

Georgius Agricola in 1490.
Roscoe "Fatty" Arbuckle in 1887.
George Sisler in 1893.
Thomas E. Dewey in 1902.
Steve McQueen in 1930.
David Suzuki in 1936.
Jesus Alou in 1942.

March 25   Feast of the Annunciation to the
                                          Virgin Mary
                                          Greek Independence Day (Greece
                                          and Cyprus)
                                          Maryland Day

5,603,921 B.C., Homo habillus declared itself an independent species.
1639 the first American canal for the purpose of providing hydropower
    was ordered built at Dedham, Massachusetts to furnish mill
    power.
1776 Continental Congress awarded a medal to George Washington
    for his exploits against the British in Boston on the 17th.
1802 Dr. James Smith of Baltimore, Maryland opened a vaccine clinic
    offering free vaccinations to the poor.
1821 the Greek war of independence against Turkey began.
1894 "Coxey's Army" set out from Massillon, Ohio on their march
    to Washington, D.C.
1900 the Socialist Party was formed in Indianapolis, Indiana.
1911 fire at the Triangle Shirt Waist Co. in New York killed 147.
1915 twenty-one men were lost when the submarine F-4 sank just
    outside the harbor at Honolulu, Hawaii.
1937 Yugoslavia and Italy concluded a non-aggression pact.
1941 the Carolina Paprika Mills was incorporated in Dillon, South
    Carolina, thereby becoming America's first paprika mill.
1954 the German Democratic Republic (East Germany) was granted
    the rights of an independent sovreign nation.
1957 the European Common Market and Euratom were established.
1960 a guided missile was launched from a nuclear powered submarine
    for the first time.

The following people were born on March 25:

Arturo Toscanini in 1867.
Gloria Steinem in 1934.
Hoyt Axton in 1938.
Anita Bryant in 1940.
Aretha Franklin in 1942.
Elton John in 1947.

March 26   Bangladesh Independence Day
                                          Prince Jonah Kuhio Kalanianaole
                                          Day
                                          Seward's Day (Alaska)

2850 B.C., Menes, having united Egypt under a single rule, established
    Egypt's first dynasty.
1804 the United States government enacted a policy of removal for
    Indians east of the Mississippi River.

1845 Joseph Francis patented the corrugated life boat.
1848 Dr. John Parker Maynard announced his invention of the plaster cast for treating bone fractures.
1885 Louis Riel helped lead the Northwest Rebellion.
1937 the Popeye statue in Popeye Park in Crystal City, Texas was unveiled during the Second Annual Spinach Festival.
1943 Second Lieutenant Elsie S. Ott became the first woman to receive the Air Medal "for meritorious achievement while participating in an aerial flight."
1953 Dr. Jonas Salk announced the development of a polio vaccine.
1956 a gas turbine powered automobile left New York City on a demonstration transcontinental drive to Los Angeles.
1958 the U.S. Army launched "Explorer III."
1971 Bangladesh declared itself independent of Pakistan.
1979 Anwar Sadat and Menachem Begin signed the treaty that formally ended the state of war between Egypt and Israel.

The following people were born on March 26:

Ahmed Fuad I in 1868.
Robert Frost in 1875.
Thomas L. "Tennessee" Williams in 1911.
Leonard Nimoy in 1931.
Alan Arkin in 1934.
James Caan in 1939.
Diana Ross in 1944.

March 27   Resistance Day (Burma)
                                      Youth Day (Eastern Nigeria)

1513 Ponce de León first sighted Florida.
1802 the Treaty of Amiens brought peace to Europe.
1849 Joseph J. Couch patented the percussion rock drill.
1855 Dr. Abraham Gesner patented kerosene.
1860 M.L. Byrn was granted a patent for the corkscrew.
1871 Scotland beat England in the first international rugby match.
1884 the first long distance phone call was made from Boston to New York.
1897 200 people saw a large object fly over Topeka, Kansas, including the governor who said, "I don't know what the thing is, but I hope it may yet solve the railroad problem."
1958 Nikita Khrushchev replaced Marshal Nikolai Bulganin as premier of the Union of Soviet Socialist Republics.
1964 an earthquake near Anchorage, Alaska killed over 100 persons.
1974 Harm Steyn caught a 128 pound Atlantic sailfish off the coast of Angola.
1977 a KLM 747 collided with a PanAm 747 on a runway at Tenerife in the Canary Islands killing 581 people.

1977 Donald L. Stalker caught a two pound, four ounce yellow bass
     in Indiana.
1980 Mount St. Helens in Washington erupted after 123 years of dor-
     mancy.

The following people were born on March 27:

Nathaniel Currier in 1813.
Wilhelm Roentgen in 1845.
Miller Huggins in 1879.
Gloria Swanson in 1899.
Sarah Vaughn in 1924.
David Janssen in 1930.
Annemarie Proell in 1953.

March 28   Libya Evacuation Day (British
                                  Troops)
                                Teachers' Day (Czechoslovakia)

 193 A.D., the office of the Emperor of Rome was auctioned off
     to Didius Julianus for a bid of 300,000,000 sesterces.
1796 the Bethel African Methodist Episcopal Church of Philadelphia
     was incorporated. It was the first African church established
     in the United States.
1797 Nathaniel Briggs patented a washing machine.
1806 the first art organization in the United States, the Pennsylvania
     Academy of Fine Arts, was incorporated.
1848 Pennsylvania law decreed that no child under twelve could engage
     in commercial labor.
1854 France and Great Britain joined forces with the Ottoman Empire
     against Russia in the Crimean War.
1895 construction of the municipal subway in Boston was begun.
1939 the Spanish Civil War was formally ended.
1953 Jim Thorpe died.
1959 following two weeks of rebellion in Tibet, Chou En-lai dissolved
     the Tibetan government. The Dalai Lama fled to India and
     was supplanted by Panchen Lama.
1978 the Three Mile Island nuclear power plant first sustained a nuclear
     reaction.
1979 a major nuclear accident occurred at the Three Mile Island
     nuclear power plant after three months of commercial operation.

The following people were born on March 28:

Paul Whiteman in 1891.
Edmund Muskie in 1914.
Thad Jones in 1923.

March 29   Anniversary of President Boganda's
                                      Death (Central African Republic)
                                      Delaware Swedish Colony Day
                                      Martyrs' Day/Youth Day (Republic
                                      of China-Taiwan)
                                      Memorial Day (Madagascar)

1597 "Dafne," the first opera, was performed in Florence.
1626 Plymouth Colony enacted forestry legislation requiring approval
     for the exportation of lumber.
1638 Swedish settlers established what is now Wilmington, Delaware.
1728 the Edinburgh Music Society was founded.
1852 the state of Ohio made it illegal for "children under eighteen,
     and women" to work over ten hours a day.
1867 the British North America Act established the Dominion of
     Canada (to take effect on July 1) uniting Ontario, Quebec,
     Nova Scotia and New Brunswick.
1882 the Knights of Columbus were chartered in Connecticut.
1886 Dr. John Pemberton, the inventor of Coca-Cola, introduced
     the drink as an "esteemed brain tonic and intellectual bev-
     erage."
1927 Major Henry O. de Hane became the first person to drive a
     car at over 200 miles per hour.
1929 Michigan introduced a prohibition on the use of fireworks by
     the general public, but continued to allow displays by licensed
     operators.
1932 the Chinese Women's Association was organized in New York
     City.

The following people were born on March 29:

John Tyler in 1790.
Cy Young in 1867.
Eugene McCarthy in 1916.
Pearl Bailey in 1918.
Denny McLain in 1944.
Walt Frazier in 1945.

March 30   Feast of St. Zosimus

1822 the Pennsylvania College of Pharmacy was incorporated.
1842 an anaesthetic was first used for (minor) surgery.
1843 Napoleon E. Guerin patented the egg incubator.
1852 Dr. Albert Sonnenberg and Philip Rechten of Bremen, Germany
     patented an electric whale killing machine.
1856 the Treaty of Paris ended the Crimean War.
1858 Hyman Lipman of Philadelphia patented a pencil with an attached
     eraser.

1867 the United States bought Alaska from Russia for $7,200,000. The purchase became known as "Seward's Folly."
1870 Texas was readmitted to the Union.
1897 the New York State Society of Certified Public Accountants was formed.
1909 the Queensboro Bridge was opened to traffic.
1923 the Laconia returned to New York City from a round the world cruise.
1956 France announced plans to withdraw its 20,000 troops from South Vietnam. The United States pledged its continued support of the South Vietnamese government.

The following people were born on March 30:

Maimonides in 1135.
Francisco Goya in 1746.
Vincent Van Gogh in 1853.
Richard Helms and Frankie Laine in 1913.
Warren Beatty in 1938.
Eric Clapton in 1945.

March 31   Jum il-Helsien (Malta)
                                       Taranaki Provincial Anniversary
                                       (New Zealand)
                                       Virgin Islands Transfer Day

1282 the people of Sicily rose up against French rule in the rebellion known as the Sicilian Vespers.
1814 John Lineback patented a cottonseed hulling machine.
1848 the ghost of Charles Rosmer communicated with the Fox family at their home in Hydesville, New York.
1870 Thomas Peterson-Mundy of Perth Amboy, New Jersey became the first black man to vote under the authority of the fifteenth amendment.
1880 Wabash, Indiana became the first town to have a complete electric street lighting system.
1903 man's second powered flight was made by Richard Pearse in a monoplane that flew several hundred yards along a roadway near Temuka, New Zealand.
1917 the United States took formal possession of the Virgin Islands.
1932 Ford Motor Company introduced its V-8 engine.
1933 the Civilian Conservation Corps was authorized.
1946 transcontinental Pullman sleeping car service was inaugurated.
1949 Newfoundland became Canada's tenth province.
1951 North and South Korean positions were stabilized along the 38th parallel.
1953 L.C. Baumgardner caught an eighty-three pound, twelve ounce seabass off the coast of Mexico.

1958 the Soviet Union announced unilateral suspension of nuclear
     weapons tests, and urged the United States and Great Britain
     to do the same.
1959 the Dalai Lama requested political asylum in India.

The following people were born on March 31:

René Descartes in 1596.
Franz Josef Haydn in 1732.
Robert von Bunsen in 1811.
Jack Johnson in 1878.
Henry Morgan in 1915.
Cesar Chavez in 1927.
Gordie Howe in 1928.
Shirley Jones in 1934.
Herb Alpert and Richard Chamberlain in 1935.
Gabriel Kaplan in 1945.

April

The first day of April marks the following commemorations:

April Fool's Day (All Fools' Day)
Captain Regents Day (San Marino)
Intolerance Day
Iranian Islamic Republic Day
(St.) Lazarus' Day (Bulgaria)
Nafels Pilgrimage (first Thursday in Switzerland)
Student Government Day (first Friday in Massachusetts)
Youth Day (Benín)

National Drafting Week (begins the first Sunday)
National Laugh Week (the first through the ninth)
Publicity Stunt Week
Week of the Young Child (begins the first Sunday)

Cancer Control Month
National Home Improvement Month

April 1

1621 the Pilgrim colonists on Strawberry Hill at Plymouth, Massachu-
     setts, concluded an alliance with Massasoit, war chief of
     the Wampanoags. It was the first treaty between Indians
     and white European colonists.
1665 during the month of April, the great plague hit London.
1826 Samuel Morey patented the internal combustion engine.
1838 the College of Charleston (South Carolina) opened. It was the
     first community college to operate under municipal control.
1909 the federal law prohibiting the importation of opium went into
     effect.
1929 Louis Marx began marketing the yo-yo.
1933 Nazi Germany announced an official policy of boycotting Jewish
     businesses.
1935 General Electric announced the development of the first metal
     radio tube.

1945 U.S. troops invaded Okinawa.
1977 Curt Wiesenhutter caught a 388 pound, twelve ounce yellowfin tuna off the coast of Mexico.
1979 Iran was proclaimed an Islamic republic.

The following people were born on April 1:

Otto von Bismarck in 1815.
Sergei Rachmaninoff in 1873.
Lon Chaney in 1883.
Wallace Beery in 1886.
Hans Conried in 1915.
Toshiro Mifune in 1920.
Debbie Reynolds in 1932.
Ali McGraw in 1939.
Daniel J. "Rusty" Staub in 1944.

April 2   International Children's Book Day
                                     Iranian Revolution Day
                                     Pascua Florida Day

 200 A.D., Galen died in Sicily at the age of seventy.
1513 Ponce de León first landed in Florida.
1744 Leith, Scotland: John Rattray won the first golf tournament.
1792 Congress approved the establishment of a mint in Philadelphia.
1794 the National Armory was established at Springfield, Massachusetts.
1872 George B. Brayton patented a gas powered automobile.
1877 a human cannonball circus act was performed for the first time.
1889 Charles Martin Hall patented aluminum.
1947 the United Nations placed Japan's Pacific islands under United States trusteeship.
1956 "As the World Turns" debuted on CBS.
1956 "Edge of Night" debuted on CBS.
1982 an Argentine invasion force overran a British garrison and seized the Falkland Islands.

The following people were born on April 2:

Charlemagne in 742.
Giovanni Casanova in 1725.
Hans Christian Andersen in 1805.
Emile Zola in 1840.
Hughie Jennings in 1869.
Luke Appling in 1907.
Buddy Ebsen in 1908.
Alec Guiness in 1914.

Jack Webb in 1920.
Jack Brabham in 1926.
Engelbert Humperdinck in 1936.
Marvin Gaye in 1939.
Leon Russell in 1942.

April 3   Feast of St. Richard of Chichester

1451 Johann Gutenberg used movable type for the first time in Europe
     when he produced Donatus Latin Grammar.
1776 Harvard College conferred the honorary degree of "Doctor
     of Laws, the Law of Nature and Nations and the Civil Law"
     on George Washington.
1829 James Carrington patented the coffee mill.
1860 riders set out on the Pony Express' inaugural run.
1866 Rudolph Eickemeyer patented a hat blocking and shaping machine.
1882 Robert Ford shot and killed Jesse James at St. Joseph, Missouri.
1889 the savings "bank for Negroes operated by Negroes" of the Grand
     Fountain of the United Order of True Reformers began opera-
     tions.
1913 an eye conservation class for the education of children with
     serious vision defects was opened in Boston.
1954 Oxford defeated Cambridge in the 100th annual Thames River
     rowing race in England.
1974 Richard M. Nixon announced that he was going to pay $432,787.13
     that he owed in back taxes.

The following people were born on April 3:

Washington Irving in 1783.
George Jessel and Henry R. Luce in 1898.
Marlon Brando and Doris Day in 1924.
Wayne Newton in 1942.
Tony Orlando in 1944.
Don Schollander in 1946.
Lyle Alzado in 1949.

April 4   Anniversary of the Liberation of
                                         Hungary
                                         Senegal Independence Day
                                         Hate Week

1818 the steamboat Walk-in-the-Water was launched.
1841 President William Henry Harrison died of pneumonia.

1870 the New York Athletic Club was incorporated.
1887 a woman was elected to a mayor's office for the first time in the United States when Susanna Medora was elected mayor of Argonia, Kansas.
1891 the American Academy of Political and Social Science was incorporated.
1949 the North Atlantic Pact was signed in Washington, D.C., and the United States ratified the formation of N.A.T.O.
1958 a group of scientists sued the Atomic Energy Commission to put a stop to nuclear weapons testing.
1968 the Reverend Dr. Martin Luther King, Jr. was assassinated.
1974 Hank Aaron hit his 714th home run.
1975 a U.S. Air Force Galaxy C-58 crashed near Saigon after taking off with a load of orphans. One hundred and seventy-two died.

The following people were born on April 4:

Tris Speaker in 1888.
Arthur Murray in 1895.
Muddy Waters (McKinley Morganfield) in 1915.
Anthony Perkins in 1932.
Hugh Masekela in 1939.

April 5   Arbor Day (Korea)
                                     Ching Ming Festival (Macao)
                                     Rosa Parks Day (New York)

1609 Indian maize was first planted by Englishmen in America.
1653 the use of postage stamps was initiated in Paris.
1806 Isaac Quintard patented the cider mill.
1815 the Tamboro volcano on Sumbawa Island erupted setting off whirlwinds and tsunamis that killed 12,000.
1864 William Nicholson of the Nicholson File Company of Providence, Rhode Island patented a file cutting machine.
1881 the South African Republic was granted independence under British suzerainty.
1892 Walter H. Coe of Providence, Rhode Island obtained a patent for gold leaf in roll form.
1909 the Neurological Institute of New York was incorporated.
1923 Firestone produced the first balloon tires.
1951 Israel conducted retaliatory bombings of Syrian positions.
1951 Julius and Ethel Rosenberg were sentenced to death.

The following people were born on April 5:

Thomas Hobbes in 1588.

Elihu Yale in 1648.
Joseph Lister in 1827.
Booker T. Washington in 1856.
Bette Davis and Mary Hemingway in 1908.
Gregory Peck in 1916.
Gale Storm in 1922.
Nguyen Van Thieu in 1923.
Michael Moriarty in 1941.

April 6   Chakri Day (Thailand)
                                     Patriots' Victory Day (Ethiopia)
                                     Van Riebeeck Day (South Africa)

1712 six persons committed suicide and twenty-one were executed
     in the New York slave revolt.
1830 Joseph Smith established the Church of Jesus Christ of Latter
     Day Saints (Mormons) in Fayette, New York.
1857 the New York College of Veterinary Surgeons was incorporated.
1866 the Grand Army of the Republic was established.
1869 Nicholas H. Borgfeldt patented a snow melting apparatus.
1893 Andy Bowen and Jack Burke fought a 110 round lightweight
     boxing match that resulted in a draw.
1896 the first modern Olympiad opened in Athens.
1909 Robert E. Peary became the first to reach the North Pole and
     return to tell about it.
1917 the United States declared war on Germany.
1941 Germany invaded Yugoslavia and Greece.
1941 the British captured Addis Ababa.

The following people were born on April 6:

Butch Cassidy (Robert Parker) in 1866.
Harry Houdini (Ehrich Weiss) in 1874.
Lowell Thomas in 1892.
Mickey Cochrane in 1903.
Gerry Mulligan in 1927.
Andre Previn in 1929.
Merle Haggard in 1937.
Michelle Phillips in 1944.

April 7   Mozambican Women's Day
                                     World Health Day

1614 "El Greco" died in Toledo at the age of 73.

1652 Jan Van Riebeeck established the Dutch colony of Capetown.
1788 the first white settlement in Ohio was established at Marietta.
1864 America's first recorded camel race was held at Sacramento, California.
1906 the Society of American Artists merged with the National Academy of Design.
1917 Cuba and Panama declared war on Germany.
1939 Italian troops invaded and conquered Albania.
1948 the World Health Organization was established.
1953 Dag Hammarskjöld assumed the office of Secretary General of the United Nations.
1956 Spain recognized Morocco as an independent nation.
1959 a radar signal was bounced off the sun from Stanford University.
1966 the United States recovered an H-bomb it had lost three months earlier in the ocean off the coast of Spain.

The following people were born on April 7:

St. Francis Xavier in 1506.
William Wordsworth in 1770.
William R. King in 1786.
John McGraw in 1873.
Bronislaw Malinowski in 1884.
Walter Winchell in 1897.
Percy Faith in 1908.
Billie Holliday in 1915.
Ravi Shankar in 1920.
James Garner in 1928.
Jerry Brown, Jr. in 1938.
Francis Ford Coppola and David Frost in 1939.
John Havlicek in 1940.

April 8   Buddha Day (Hawaii)
                                Hana Matsuri or Flower Festival
                                (Japan)
                                National Library Week (begins
                                second or third Sunday)

222,619,801 B.C., the first birth of a true mammal occurred in Poland.
1730 the Shearith Israel (Spanish-Portuguese) Jewish congregation in New York City was consecrated.
1834 Cornelius V. Lawrence became the first mayor to win a popular election in the United States when he was elected mayor of the City of New York.
1848 the Homeopathic Medical College of Pennsylvania was incorporated.
1854 the United States introduced a registered letter system.

1873 Alfred Paraf patented a process for the manufacture of oleomar-
     garine.
1879 Echo Farms Dairy introduced the glass milk bottle.
1935 the Emergency Relief Appropriation Act was approved.
1956 six Marine Corps recruits drowned in a boot camp drill at Parris
     Island, North Carolina.
1974 Hank Aaron hit his 715th home run.
1977 Robyn Davidson set out on a 195 day trek across the Gibson
     Desert of Australia's outback.

The following people were born on April 8:

Mary Pickford in 1893.
Sonja Henie in 1912.
Betty Ford in 1918.
John Hiller in 1943.
James A. "Catfish" Hunter in 1946.

April 9   Appomattox Day
                                     Tunisia Martyrs' Day

1667 the world's first art exhibition was held at the Palais-Royale
     in Paris.
1847 a state reformatory for boys (later the Lyman School for Boys)
     was authorized by the state of Massachusetts.
1865 General Robert E. Lee surrendered to General Ulysses S. Grant
     at Appomattox.
1872 Samuel R. Percy patented dried milk.
1909 busses with an enclosed upper deck were first introduced.
1928 Turkey ended its official support of Islam.
1937 the state of Vermont enacted anti-sit-down strike legislation.
1940 Germany invaded Norway and occupied Denmark.
1942 U.S. forces surrendered as Bataan fell to Japan.
1950 T.S. Hudson caught a four pound, twelve ounce bluegill in Ala-
     bama.
1965 Houston's Astrodome opened.

The following people were born on April 9:

Efrem Zimbalist in 1889.
Paul Robeson in 1898.
Ward Bond and J. William Fulbright in 1909.
Hugh Hefner in 1926.
Jean-Paul Belmondo in 1933.

April 10
           Liberia's National Fast and Prayer Day
           Commodore Matthew C. Perry Day
           Salvation Army Founders' Day

1833 the Hahnemann Society was organized.
1845 Erastus Brigham Bigelow received a patent for his gingham manufacturing machinery.
1849 Walter Hunt patented the safety pin.
1866 the American Society for the Prevention of Cruelty to Animals was incorporated.
1877 Nathanael G. Herreshoff of Providence, Rhode Island patented his catamaran.
1892 the Pennsylvania Society for the Prevention of Tuberculosis was founded.
1933 Michigan became the first state to ratify the repeal of the eighteenth amendment.
1941 the United States occupied Greenland.
1944 researchers at Harvard University produced synthetic quinine for the first time.
1963 the atomic submarine Thresher was lost in the North Atlantic. One hundred and twenty-nine lives were lost.

The following people were born on April 10:

Lewis Wallace in 1827.
Joseph Pulitzer in 1847.
Clare Boothe Luce in 1903.
Howard "Howdie" Grosskloss in 1908.
Harry Morgan in 1915.
Kevin J. "Chuck" Connors in 1921.
Max von Sydow in 1929.
Omar Sharif in 1932.

April 11
           Barber Shop Quartet Day
           Cost Rica National Heroes Day
           (Anniversary of the Battle of Rivas)
           International Resistance Movement Day
           Uganda Liberation Day

1640 in defiance of the King's Court's order, Wethersfield, Connecticut held an election to select the town recorder.
1789 the Gazette of the United States began publishing.
1803 John Stevens patented the twin screw steamboat.
1814 Napoleon abdicated and was exiled to Elba.

1876 John C. Zachos patented the stenotype.
1921 Iowa imposed the first state cigarette tax.
1941 the Office of Price Administration and Civilian Supply was created to regulate prices in the United States.
1945 U.S. troops formally liberated the prisoners in the Nazi concentration camp at Buchenwald.
1947 Jackie Robinson became the first black man to play major league baseball.
1951 General Douglas MacArthur was relieved of command in the Far East.
1961 Adolph Eichmann went on trial in Jerusalem.
1982 Sir Ranulph Fiennes and Charles Burton reached the North pole.

The following people were born on April 11:

William Harvey in 1575.
Macedonio Melloni in 1798.
Ethel Kennedy in 1928.
Joel Grey in 1932.

April 12   Halifax Independence Day (North Carolina)
                               Ram Navami (Nepal)

418,927 B.C., the second interglacial period ended and the Riss or Illinoisan period of glaciation began.
1204 the forces of the Fourth Crusade stormed and mercilessly sacked Constantinople.
1606 England adopted the Union Jack as its flag.
1633 Galileo went on trial for heresy before the Inquisition in Rome.
1776 a North Carolina provincial congress meeting at Halifax voted in favor of declaring independence from Great Britain.
1859 the first billiard match of international prominence took place in Detroit, Michigan between Michael Phelan and John Seereiter.
1861 Confederate forces under General Pierre Gustave Toutant Beauregard fired the shore batteries of Fort Johnson on the detachment at Fort Sumter, forcing its surrender.
1864 the Fort Pillow massacre took place.
1918 the First Aero Squadron of the United States Army saw its first combat action.
1927 three hundred died in Shanghai, China in a purge of Communists and their sympathizers on the order of Chiang Kai-shek.
1945 President Franklin D. Roosevelt died and Harry S Truman became president.
1961 Yuri Gagarin made the first successful manned orbital space flight.

1981 the space shuttle <u>Columbia</u> was launched. It was piloted by John Young and Robert Crippen.

The following people were born on April 12:

Bill Bailey in 1889.
Tiny Tim (Herbert Khaury) in 1930.
Jack Gelber in 1932.
David Cassidy in 1950.

April 13   Chadian National Holiday
                                  Thomas Jefferson's Birthday (Ala-
                                      bama)
                                  Songkram Festival Day (Thailand)
                                  Spring Holiday (Scotland)

 922 B.C., King Solomon of Israel died after a thirty-nine year reign.
1759 the first military Masonic lodge was formed at Crown Point, New York.
1796 an elephant landed in New York City.
1808 the Union Temperate Society was organized in Saratoga Springs, New York.
1863 the Hospital for Ruptured and Crippled, America's first orthopedic hospital, was incorporated in New York City.
1896 the American Guild of Organists was organized.
1902 the first J.C. Penney store opened in Kemmerer, Wyoming.
1917 Bolivia severed relations with Germany.
1940 in Berkeley, California, Cornelius Warmerdam became the first pole vaulter to vault fifteen feet at an outdoor meet.
1962 Dennis Hall caught a nineteen and a half pound weakfish off Trinidad in the West Indies.
1964 Ian Smith succeeded Winston Field as Rhodesian Prime Minister.
1975 civil war broke out in Lebanon between Muslim and Christian factions.

The following people were born on April 13:

Thomas Jefferson in 1743.
F.W. Woolworth in 1852.
Harold Stassen in 1907.
Lyle Waggoner in 1935.
Al Green in 1946.

April 14   Bengali New Year's Day (Bangladesh)
                                      Día de las Américas (Guatemala
                                         and Honduras)
                                      Pan American Day

1775 the Society for the Relief of Free Negroes Unlawfully Held
     in Bondage was formed in Philadelphia.
1818 the United States Army medical corps was organized.
1865 Abraham Lincoln was assassinated.
1890 the International Bureau of American Republics was established.
1894 the Kinetoscope Parlor at 155 Broadway in New York City began
     showing Thomas Edison's "peep-shows."
1910 President William Howard Taft threw out the first ball to start
     the 1910 baseball season.
1912 the Titanic collided with an iceberg in the North Atlantic.
1914 the "non-skid" tire pattern was patented by Stacy G. Carkhuff
     in Akron, Ohio.
1931 the Spanish monarchy fell and a republic was proclaimed.
1956 the Ampex Corporation demonstrated their newly developed
     commercial video-tape recorder.
1981 after a two day, six hour, twenty minute and fifty-two second
     space flight, the Columbia landed at Edwards Air Force Base.

The following people were born on April 14:

Christiaan Huygens in 1629.
Arnold Toynbee in 1889.
Sir John Gielgud in 1904.
Rod Steiger in 1925.
Frank Serpico in 1936.
Julie Christie and Pete Rose in 1941.

April 15   Assumption of Power by CMS
                                         (Niger)
                                      National Hostility Day
                                      Railway Men's Day (Yugoslavia)
                                      Bike Safety Week (begins Sunday
                                         of the third full week)
                                      National Coin Week (begins Sunday
                                         of the third week)

71,229,499 B.C., the Cenozoic era began.
1598 Henry IV of France issued the Edict of Nantes.
1788 the first worsted mill operated entirely by water power was
     set up.
1794 the Courrier Français was established, thereby becoming the
     first daily French language newspaper in the United States.
1817 the first American school for the deaf opened.

1861 President Abraham Lincoln called out the Union troops.
1912 the Titanic sank with the loss of 1,517 lives.
1935 Laurens Hammond put the first pipeless organ on exhibit.
1956 General Motors announced the development of a free piston
      engined automobile.
1980 Jean-Paul Sartre died following a lengthy illness.
–––– United States income tax filings are due.

The following people were born on April 15:

Leonardo da Vinci in 1542.
Henry James in 1843.
Emile Durkheim in 1858.
Leonard "King" Cole in 1886.
Roy Clark and Elizabeth Montgomery in 1933.
Claudia Cardinale in 1939.

April 16   DeDiego's Birthday (Puerto Rico)
                                       Queen's Birthday (Denmark)

1746 the Battle of Culloden marked the end of Scottish resistance
      to British rule.
1851 the iron pile light house at Minot's Ledge, Massachusetts was
      swept away in a gale.
1900 postage stamps were first issued in books.
1912 Harriet Quimby flew across the English Channel.
1917 Lenin arrived in Moscow from Switzerland.
1917 the Second Battle of the Aisne and the Third Battle of Champagne
      began.
1922 the Treaty of Rapallo was concluded between Germany and
      the Soviet Union.
1926 the Book-of-the-Month Club distributed its first book of the
      month.
1935 "Fibber McGee and Molly" debuted on NBC radio.
1947 a zoom lens was demonstrated for the first time in New York
      City.
1956 the first solar powered radios went on sale in Chicago.
1964 Joshua Nkomo was summarily banished from Rhodesia.

The following people were born on April 16:

Anatole France in 1844.
Wilbur Wright in 1867.
Charlie Chaplin in 1889.
Paul Waner in 1903.
Lily Pons in 1904.
Peter Ustinov in 1921.

Henry Mancini in 1924.
Eydie Adams in 1929.
Herbie Mann in 1930.
Bobby Vinton in 1935.
Dusty Springfield in 1939.
Kareem Abdul Jabbar in 1947.

April 17   American Samoan Flag Day
                                  Kampuchea Independence Day
                                  Syrian Arab Republic Independence
                                      Day
                                  Verrazano Day

1524 Giovanni da Verrazano sailed into the harbor that later became
     known as New York.
1810 Lewis M. Norton patented a "vat for forming pineapple cheese."
1824 the United States gave Alaska to Russia.
1861 Virginia seceded from the Union.
1895 the Hennepin Canal opened for traffic.
1897 war broke out between Greece and Turkey.
1916 the American Academy of Arts and Letters was incorporated.
1935 "Lights Out" opened on the NBC Red network.
1942 U.S. flyers bombed Tokyo.
1954 Gamal Abdel Nasser became the Egyptian premier.
1957 Dr. Russel Lee caught a 435 pound Pacific bigeye tuna off the
     coast of Peru.
1961 the rebel invasion of the Bay of Pigs began.
1963 Alex Karras and Paul Hornung were suspended indefinitely for
     betting on NFL games.

The following people were born on April 17:

Adrian C. "Cap" Anson in 1851.
Nikita Khrushchev in 1894.
Thornton Wilder in 1897.
William Holden in 1918.

April 18   Paul Revere Day
                                  Zimbabwe Independence Day
                                  National Secretaries Week (the last
                                      full week: this Wednesday is
                                      Secretaries Day)
                                  National YWCA Week (begins Sun-
                                      day of the last full week)

489 A.D., the Indian mathematician Aryabhata began teaching about
the rotation of the earth and the value of pi as 3.1416.
1521 Martin Luther was called before the Diet of Worms.
1775 Paul Revere made his famous ride.
1846 Royal E. House patented a telegraph ticker that printed letters
of the alphabet.
1855 Siam opened trade and initiated consular relations with Great
Britain.
1885 Japan and China concluded the Convention of Tientsin and nar-
rowly averted open warfare in Korea.
1906 a tremendous earthquake shook San Francisco setting off fires
that devastated the city for three days.
1916 the Irish Easter Rebellion erupted.
1923 a baseball game was played for the first time in the newly finished
Yankee Stadium.
1925 the Chinese Hospital of San Francisco was opened.
1925 the Woman's World Fair opened in Chicago.
1934 America's first laundromat opened in Fort Worth, Texas.
1949 the Republic of Ireland was proclaimed in Dublin and was officially recognized by Great Britain.
1955 Albert Einstein died.
1956 Eddie A. Rommel became the first major league umpire to
wear glasses.
1980 Great Britain recognized Rhodesia, Africa's last European colony,
as the independent nation of Zimbabwe.

The following people were born on April 18:

Clarence Darrow in 1857.
Sam Crawford in 1880.
Max Weber in 1881.
Leopold Stokowski in 1882.

April 19   Landing of the 33 Orientales (Uru-
guay)
Patriots' Day (Maine, Massachusetts)
Sierra Leonean Republic Day
Venezuela Declaration of Indepen-
dence Day

1775 the Battles of Lexington and Concord were fought. The American
revolutionary Minutemen suffered eight casualties, the British
suffered 273.
1897 the American Marathon Race from Hopkinton to Boston was
first run.
1897 Alexander Hamilton, a Kansas farmer, reported seeing a 300
foot cigar shaped airship over his cow pasture. The beings
inside lassoed one of his cows and hauled it aboard.

1917 the U.S. Navy took its first shot in World War I.
1923 the Egyptian constitution was promulgated.
1931 King Prajadhipok of Siam arrived in Portal, North Dakota.
1943 a rebellion began in the Jewish ghetto in Warsaw. It was suppressed by Nazi forces who killed 50,000 Jews in the process.
1948 Burma joined the United Nations.
1951 Kiki Haakonson won the first "Miss World" title.
1955 a turbine powered 1955 Plymouth was first operated on the streets of Detroit.
1956 Grace Kelly was married to Prince Ranier of Monaco.
1968 Pierre E. Trudeau became the Prime Minister of Canada.
1971 Sierra Leone proclaimed itself a republic.
1971 Joseph Caboche, Jr. caught a forty pound skipjack tuna off the coast of Mauritius.
1981 a Pawtucket Red Sox-Rochester Red Wings baseball game was halted after thirty-two innings with the score tied at two to two.

The following people were born on April 19:

Don Adams in 1927.
Hugh O'Brian in 1930.
Dudley Moore in 1936.

April 20   Family Day (South Africa)

the sun enters the house of Taurus.
1769 Pontiac was assassinated in Cahokia.
1852 the Women's State Temperance Society was founded in Rochester, New York.
1859 the Dutch and Portuguese divided Timor between them.
1876 the American Chemical Society was organized.
1902 Marie and Pierre Curie isolated radium.
1908 according to his account, Dr. Frederick Albert Cook reached the North Pole.
1940 the electron microscope was first demonstrated for the public.
1948 Walter Reuther was shot and wounded in Detroit.
1961 the rebel invasion at the Bay of Pigs in Cuba ended in failure.
1972 Benny E. Hull caught a fifty-four and a half pound freshwater drum in Tennessee.
1976 William E. Allison caught a twenty-seven pound little tunny near Key Largo, Florida.
1978 Michael James caught a sixty-five pound longtail tuna near Port Stephens, Australia.

The following people were born on April 20:

James P. "Steamer" Flanagan in 1881.
Adolf Hitler in 1889.
Joan Miró in 1893.
Lionel Hampton in 1914.
Ryan O'Neal in 1941.

April 21   Kartini Day (Indonesia)
                                      San Jacinto Day (Texas)
                                      Tiradentes Day (Brazil)
                                      Canada-U.S. Goodwill Week (begins
                                        Sunday of the week with the
                                        twenty-seventh)

1,327,418 B.C., Rul-Tu of the Krul band discovered both a technique
        for putting an edge on a piece of flint and a new first aid
        method for stopping bleeding which he called the cold compress.
753 B.C., Romulus founded Rome on the banks of the Tiber River.
1500 Pedro Cabral claimed Brazil in the name of Portugal.
1856 the first railroad bridge over the Mississippi River was completed
        at Glasgow, Missouri.
1857 Alexander Douglas patented the bustle.
1869 for the first time in its thirty-seven years of operation, the
        appointee for the U.S. Indian Affairs Commissioner was an
        Indian: Do-Ne-Ho-Geh-Weh (E.S. Parker).
1881 the David Dows, a five masted schooner, was launched in Toledo,
        Ohio.
1899 the Juvenile Court of Cook County (Chicago Juvenile Court)
        was authorized.
1914 the U.S. Marines occupied the city of Veracruz in Mexico.
1918 Roy Brown of the Royal Canadian Air Force shot down the
        "Red Baron."
1945 Soviet troops fought their way into Berlin.
1959 Alfred Dean caught a 2,664 pound white shark off Australia.
1979 the first universal franchise election in Zimbabwe (Rhodesia)
        history took place.

The following people were born on April 21:

John Muir in 1838.
Edmund G. (Pat) Brown in 1905.
Choh Hao Li in 1913.
Anthony Quinn in 1915.
Queen Elizabeth II in 1926.

April 22
Arbor Day
Discovery of Brazil Day
Fast Day (fourth Monday in New
Hampshire)
Lenin's Birthday (U.S.S.R.)
Oklahoma Day

1370 construction was begun on the Bastille in Paris.
1793 George Washington went to the circus.
1794 Pennsylvania abolished the death penalty except for the crime of first degree murder.
1823 R.J. Tyers obtained a patent for roller skates.
1833 the first self-propelled (steam powered) omnibus service was inaugurated.
1884 Thomas Stevens left San Francisco on an around the world bicycle trip.
1889 the first Oklahoma land rush began.
1915 the Second Battle of Ypres began in which Germany introduced the use of poison gas.
1917 United States Day was celebrated in France.
1931 James G. Ray landed an autogiro on the White House lawn.
1952 KTLA-TV broadcast a test explosion of a nuclear device.
1954 Senator Joe McCarthy led the televised hearings on Communist influence in the U.S. Government.

The following people were born on April 22:

Queen Isabella of Spain in 1451.
Immanuel Kant in 1724.
Lenin (Vladimir Ilyich Ulyanov) in 1870.
J. Robert Oppenheimer in 1904.
Eddie Albert in 1908.
Yehudi Menuhin in 1916.
Glen Campbell in 1936.
Jack Nicholson in 1937.
Peter Frampton in 1950.

April 23
Children's Day (Turkey)
Commemoration of the Martyrdom
of Saint George (England)
First Day of Summer (Iceland)
Turkey's National Sovereignty Day

1750 Dr. Thomas Walker and party settled on the site for Barbourville, Kentucky; the first civilian settlement west of the Allegheny Mountains.
1867 William E. Lincoln patented the zoetrope.
1890 the General Federation of Women's Clubs held its first convention.

1895 the Far Eastern Crises began, involving Russia, Germany, France
       and Japan.
1897 the Gillette State Hospital for Crippled Children was authorized.
1904 the American Academy of Arts and Letters was founded.
1917 Turkey severed relations with the United States.
1918 Guatemala declared war on Germany.
1954 Hank Aaron hit his first home run.
1962 the Ranger IV moon rocket was launched from Cape Canaveral.

The following people were born on April 23:

William Shakespeare in 1564.
James Buchanan in 1791.
Stephen Douglas in 1813.
Max Planck in 1858.
Warren Spahn in 1921.
Shirley Temple in 1928.
Roy Orbison in 1936.
Lee Majors in 1940.
Sandra Dee in 1942.

April 24   Arbor Day (Utah)
                                    Armenian Martyrs' Day
                                    Victory Day (Togo)

1800 the Library of Congress in Washington, D.C. was established.
1833 Jacob Ebert and George Dulty patented their soda fountain
       equipment.
1851 the Boston Society of Civil Engineers was incorporated.
1873 the N.Y. Diet Kitchen Association began serving free lunches.
1877 Russia declared war on Turkey.
1884 the Medico-Chirurgical Society of the District of Columbia
       was organized.
1895 Joshua Slocum set out from Boston on a solo circumnavigation
       of the earth.
1898 Spain declared war on the United States.
1918 history's first tank battle took place at Villers-Bretonneaux.
1928 Herbert G. Dorsey patented the fathometer.
1950 the incorporation of Arab Palestine into Jordan was finalized.
1956 Willard Cravens caught a 360 pound white sturgeon in Idaho.
1962 technicians at the Massachusetts Institute of Technology accom-
       plished the first transcontinental telecast by satellite.

The following people were born on April 24:

Shirley MacLaine in 1934.
Barbra Streisand in 1942.

April 25   Anzac Day (Australia, New Zealand,
                                            Samoa and Tonga)
                                            Feast of Saint Mark, Patron Saint
                                            of Venice
                                            Italy Liberation Day
                                            Swazi National Flag Day
                                            Portugal's Day
                                            Remembrance Day (Papua New
                                            Guinea)

1792 Claude Joseph Rouget de Lisle composed "La Marseillaise."
1841 Paul Hodge completed the first self propelled fire engine.
1846 shots were fired at La Rosia, Mexico that eventually led to
     the declaration of the Mexican-American War.
1898 the United States declared war on Spain.
1901 New York began requiring automobile license plates.
1939 the Federal Security Agency was established.
1939 the Federal Works Agency was authorized.
1945 Soviet and U.S. troops converged at Torgau.
1957 an atomic sodium reactor in the Santa Susana Mountains went
     into operation.
1959 the St. Lawrence Seaway opened to traffic.
1962 Ranger IV landed on the moon.
1974 General Antonio de Spinola seized control of the government
     of Portugal.
---- Daylight Savings Time in the United States begins at 2:00 a.m.
     (the last Sunday in April).

The following people were born on April 25:

Oliver Cromwell in 1599.
Guglielmo Marconi in 1874.
Edward R. Murrow in 1908.
Ella Fitzgerald in 1918.
Al Pacino in 1940.

April 26   Cape Henry Day
                                            Confederate Memorial Day (Ala-
                                            bama, Georgia, Mississippi)
                                            Tanzanian Union Day
                                            Virgin Islands Carnival

1819 Odd Fellows Lodge Number One was established in Baltimore.
1826 Rensselaer School (Rensselaer Polytechnic Institute) graduated
     its first class consisting of ten students.
1848 the Boston Society of Civil Engineers was organized.
1925 Paul von Hindenburg was elected president of Germany.

1929 the Academy of Natural Sciences of Philadelphia opened a fluorescent mineral exhibit.
1937 German aircraft bombed the Basque city of Guernica.
1954 Michigan began immunizing 1,829,916 children in a mass polio vaccination program.
1957 Captain N.M. McCracken became the first woman to be assigned to duty at the U.S. Air Force Academy.
1964 Tanganyika and Zanzibar announced their merger into the United Republic of Tanzania.
1973 the Anderson quintuplets were born.

The following people were born on April 26:

David Hume in 1711.
John James Audubon in 1785.
Alfred Krupp in 1812.
Frederick Law Olmstead in 1822.
Syngman Rhee in 1875.
Sal Maglie in 1917.
Carol Burnett in 1936.
Duane Eddy in 1938.
Erica Jong and Bobby Rydell in 1942.

April 27   Osvobodilna Fronta Formation
                               (Yugoslavia)
                               Sawr Revolution Day (Afghanistan)
                               Sham El Nessim (Egypt)
                               Sierra Leone Independence Day
                               Togo Independence Day

1521 Ferdinand Magellan was killed in the Philippine Islands.
1805 Lt. Presley O'Bannon of the U.S. Marine Corps raised the flag of the United States over the Tripolitan fortress at Derne.
1828 Regent's Park Zoo opened.
1873 the Apache War in Arizona ended.
1880 Miller R. Hutchinson patented a bone conduction electrical hearing aid.
1931 Pahala, Hawaii registered a temperature of 100° F.
1938 a yellow baseball was used in the game between Columbia and Fordham.
1950 South Africa designated separate residential areas for different races.
1951 Iran nationalized the Iranian oil industry.
1960 Togo became an independent republic.
1961 Sierra Leone became an independent nation.
1967 Cassius Clay (Muhammad Ali) refused induction into the U.S. Army.

The following people were born on April 27:

Samuel Morse in 1791.
Herbert Spencer in 1820.
Ulysses S. Grant in 1822.
Rogers Hornsby in 1896.
Jack Klugman in 1922.
Coretta King in 1927.
Ace Frehley in 1951.

April 28   Maryland Ratification Day
                                      Washington State Apple Blossom
                                      Festival

1780 the London Morning Post carried an ad for an abortion clinic.
1788 Maryland ratified the constitution of the United States.
1789 Fletcher Christian led a mutiny on H.M.S. Bounty.
1855 the Boston Veterinary Institute was incorporated.
1866 the steam powered whaler Pioneer was launched.
1896 Joseph S. Duncan patented the addressograph.
1909 in enacting a child delinquency law, Colorado became the first
      state to adopt a code for juvenile delinquents.
1923 the Bolton Wanderers beat West Ham United, 2-0, in the Wembley
      Cup Final.
1932 a yellow fever vaccine for immunization of humans was an-
      nounced.
1945 Benito Mussolini was captured and executed.
1952 King Farouk inherited the throne of Egypt.
1952 national sovereignty was restored to Japan.
1955 Vietnamese rebels rose up against Ngo Dinh Diem's rule.
1958 the United States began a new series of tests of explosive nuclear
      devices at Eniwetok.
1965 fourteen thousand U.S. Marines were sent to the Dominican
      Republic.
1973 Edward P. Nelson caught a nine pound, two ounce shad in Connec-
      ticut.
1978 William M. Kenney caught a fifty-one pound, eight ounce permit
      in Florida.

The following people were born on April 28:

James Monroe in 1758.
Lionel Barrymore in 1878.
Ann-Margret (Olsson) in 1941.

April 29   Emperor's Birthday (Japan)
                                          Feast of Saint Catherine of Siena

1851 Cooper Union for the Advancement of Science and Art established
     a policy prohibiting discrimination in the acceptance of its
     students.
1854 Lincoln University, the first negro university, was chartered.
1859 Austria invaded Piedmont and the Italian struggle for indepen-
     dence was renewed.
1873 Eli H. Janney patented the railroad coupler.
1894 "Coxey's Army" reached Washington, D.C. protesting unemploy-
     ment.
1913 Gideon Sundback patented the zipper.
1916 the British suppressed the Easter Rebellion in Ireland.
1916 ten thousand British troops occupying Kut-El-Amara capitulated.
1932 "One Man's Family" was first broadcast.
1943 the Civil Air Patrol was transferred to the War Department.
1945 U.S. troops liberated the prisoners in the Nazi concentration
     camp at Dachau.
1945 German armies in Italy surrendered.
1957 the military nuclear power plant at Fort Belvoir was dedicated.

The following people were born on April 29:

William Randolph Hearst in 1863.
Frank G. "Noodles" Hahn in 1879.
Duke Ellington in 1899.
Hirohito in 1901.
Tom Ewell in 1909.
George Allen in 1922.
Lonnie Donegan in 1931.
Rod McKuen in 1933.
Luis Aparicio in 1934.
Johnny Miller and Jim Ryun in 1947.

April 30   Buddha Purnima (Bangladesh)
                                          Louisiana Admission Day
                                          Queen's Birthday (The Netherlands)
                                          Walpurgis Eve (Scandinavia)

1789 George Washington was inaugurated as the first president of
     the United States of America.
1798 the United States Navy Department was established.
1798 the United States Marine Corps was placed under the jurisdiction
     of the U.S. Navy.
1803 the United States purchased Louisiana from France.
1812 Louisiana was admitted to the Union.

1864 hunting license fees were instituted by the state of New York.
1889 the United States Congress declared the first national holiday: the centennial commemoration of George Washington's inauguration.
1900 Casey Jones was killed in a train wreck.
1942 the submarine Peto was launched at Manitowoc, Wisconsin.
1945 Adolf Hitler committed suicide in Berlin.
1945 "Arthur Godfrey Time" was first heard on CBS radio.
1948 the Organization of American States was formed.
1955 the discovery of element 101, mendelevium, was announced.
1970 President Nixon announced the U.S. invasion of Cambodia which was supposed to cut communist supply lines.
1973 H.R. "Bob" Haldeman, John Ehrlichman, John Dean and Richard Kleindienst resigned from President Richard Nixon's staff.
1975 twenty-nine years of civil war ended when the South Vietnamese government collapsed under Vietcong pressure.
1977 Tommy D. Cason, Jr. caught a one pound, eight and one-half ounce redbreast sunfish in Florida.

The following people were born on April 30:

Karl Friedrich Gauss in 1777.
Walter G. "Jumbo" Brown in 1907.
Eve Arden in 1912.

May

The first day of May marks the following commemorations:

Americanism Day (Pennsylvania)
Feast of SS. Philip and James (Protestant)
Festival of the Hare
International Labor Day
International Working Class Day (U.S.S.R. and Cuba)
Kentucky Derby Day (first Saturday)
Law Day
Lei Day (Hawaii)
Loyalty Day
May Day
May Fellowship Day (first Friday)
Spring Festival (Luxembourg)
(St.) Tamenend's Day
Walpurgis Day (Scandinavia)
Workers Day (Mozambique)
Working People's Day (Yugoslavia)

American Heritage Week (Rhode Island)
Be Kind to Animals Week (begins the first Sunday)
National Extension Homemakers Week (begins the first Sunday)
National Family Week (begins the first Sunday)
National Music Week (begins the first Sunday)
National Youth Hostel Week (begins the first Sunday)
Senior Comedians Week (the first through the eighth)

Bike Month
Car Care Month
National Radio Month
Senior Citizens Month

May 1

305 A.D., Diocletian and Maximian abdicated and were succeeded by Galerius and Constantius.

1857 Massachusetts passed the first literacy requirement for voting.
1872 the Liberal Republican Party held its first convention.
1898 Admiral George Dewey's fleet destroyed the Spanish fleet in Manila Bay.
1904 the Socialist Party held its convention in Indianapolis.
1915 the S.S. Nantucket Chief was torpedoed by a German submarine.
1916 Germany initiated daylight savings time.
1920 the Brooklyn Dodgers and the Boston Braves played a twenty-six inning baseball game that ended in a 1-1 tie.
1924 Greece was proclaimed a republic following the fall of King George II.
1931 the Empire State Building was dedicated.
1939 Batman first appeared in Detective Comics.
1945 a German radio announcement from Hamburg declared that Adolf Hitler had died defending the Reichschancellery.
1948 the Democratic People's Republic of Korea was proclaimed.
1948 Eddie Arcaro won the Kentucky Derby for the fourth time.
1960 American pilot Gary Powers' U-2 spy plane was shot down in the Soviet Union.
1961 Tanganyika became self governing.
1979 Greenland received approval to institute home rule.

The following people were born on May 1:

Henry W. "Heinie" Meine in 1896.
Kate Smith in 1909.
Jack Paar in 1918.
Joseph Heller in 1923.
Judy Collins in 1939.
Rita Coolidge in 1945.

May 2   Birthday of His Late Majesty
                                 Jigme Dorji Wangchuck (Bhutan)

1003 Thorfinn Karlsefni became the first European colonist to set foot in America on the northern tip of Newfoundland where he and his expedition landed.
1670 England granted a charter to the Hudson's Bay Company.
1863 General Thomas J. "Stonewall" Jackson was mistakenly shot by his own sentry. He died eight days later.
1885 the Congo Free State was founded by Leopold II of Belgium.
1887 the Perkins Institute of Roxbury, Massachusetts opened the first kindergarten for the blind.
1887 Hannibal W. Goodwin applied for a patent for celluloid photographic film.
1900 the United Christian Party held its first convention.
1917 Jim Vaughn of the Cubs and Fred Toney of the Reds both pitched nine innings of no-hit baseball in the same game.

1923 Lt. Oakley G. Kelly and Lt. John A. Macready took off on the first transamerican flight.
1926 the United States Marines were sent to Nicaragua.
1932 "The Jack Benny Program" premiered on the NBC Blue network.
1939 after 2,130 consecutive games, Lou Gehrig did not start at first base for the New York Yankees.
1945 Berlin fell to Soviet troops.

The following people were born on May 2:

Catherine the Great of Russia in 1729.
John Galt in 1779.
Eddie Collins in 1887.
Dr. Benjamin Spock in 1903.
Harry L. "Bing" Crosby in 1904.
Theodore Bikel in 1924.
King Hussein in 1935.
Lesley Gore in 1946.

May 3   Day of the Holy Cross (Mexico)
                                       Feast of SS. Philip and James
                                         (Roman Catholic)
                                       Japanese Constitution Memorial
                                         Day
                                       Santa Cruz Feast Day (Taos Pueblo,
                                         New Mexico)
                                       Swieto Trzeciego Majo or Polish
                                         Constitution Day

435,420,481 B.C., the first land plant took root on the coast of present day Madras, India.
1481 Mohammed the Conqueror died on the verge of an Anatolian campaign.
1654 America's first toll bridge was erected at Rowley, Massachusetts over the Newbury River.
1765 the College of Philadelphia Department of Medicine (now the University of Pennsylvania School of Medicine) was established.
1791 Poland adopted a constitutional form of government.
1861 considerable controversy was generated when President Abraham Lincoln ordered the suspension of habeas corpus.
1881 Leonidas G. Woolley patented the electric locomotive headlight.
1913 the state of Ohio approved provisions for a motion picture censorship board.
1921 West Virginia approved the adoption of a sales tax.
1934 Dell became the first publisher to offer comic books for sale to the public.
1945 British troops captured Rangoon.

1945 official Portuguese government flags were flown at half mast
     in memory of Adolf Hitler.
1945 Queen Wilhelmina returned to The Netherlands.

The following people were born on May 3:

Niccolo Machiavelli in 1469.
Eppa Rixey in 1891.
Charles H. "Red" Ruffing in 1904.
Pete Seeger in 1919.
"Sugar" Ray Robinson in 1921.
Frankie Valli in 1937.

May 4   Rhode Island Independence Day
                                   Students Memorial Day

1776 Rhode Island declared itself independent of English rule.
1780 the American Academy of Arts and Sciences was incorporated.
1886 the Haymarket Square Riot broke out in Chicago.
1891 Provident Hospital in Chicago opened to become the United
     States' first interracial hospital.
1891 Sherlock Holmes disappeared at Reichenbach Falls and was
     presumed to have met a deadly fate at the hands of Professor
     Moriarty.
1942 the Battle of the Coral Sea began.
1943 William V.S. Tubman was elected president of Liberia.
1945 German armies in Holland and Denmark surrendered.
1956 the United States began a new series of nuclear bomb tests.
1970 four Kent State University students were shot and killed by
     National Guardsmen.
1974 Carlton Robbins caught a two pound warmouth in Georgia.
2040 the first fully operational, self-sustaining, earth orbiting space
     colony received its initial shipload of non-engineering support
     personnel (colonists).

The following people were born on May 4:

Horace Mann in 1796.
Thomas Huxley in 1825.
Audrey Hepburn in 1929.

May 5   Children's Day (Japan)
                                   Cinco de Mayo or Puebla Battle
                                   Day (Mexico)

Coronation Day Anniversary (Thailand)
Denmark Liberation Day
Netherlands Liberation Day

212 B.C., Archimedes died in Syracuse at the age of seventy-five.

1821 the vermilion phantom appeared to Napoleon Bonaparte for the fourth and last time. Napoleon died on this day.

1847 the American Medical Association was organized.

1860 Garibaldi and the Thousand Redshirts sailed for Sicily.

1862 Mexico won a significant victory over the French at Puebla.

1864 General William Tecumseh Sherman began his "March to the Sea" through Georgia.

1891 Carnegie Hall opened. Peter I. Tchaikovsky served as the guest conductor.

1908 Rhode Island passed an "Army Exclusion Law."

1913 the American College of Surgeons was organized.

1920 Nicola Sacco and Bartolomeo Vanzetti were arrested and accused of an April 15th robbery/homicide in South Braintree, Massachusetts.

1936 Edward A. Ravenscroft patented the screw cap bottle with a pour lip.

1941 Ethiopia's Haile Selassie re-entered Addis Ababa and his nation's independence was formally re-established.

1955 West Germany became a fully independent nation.

1961 Alan Shepard rocketed $116\frac{1}{2}$ miles into space in the "Freedom 7."

1977 Don Raley caught a twenty pound whiterock bass in Georgia.

1978 Barry Wrightson caught an eighty-five pound, six ounce Tanguigue off Western Australia.

The following people were born on May 5:

Søren Kierkegaard in 1813.
Karl Marx in 1818.
John B. Stetson in 1830.
Nellie Bly (Elizabeth Cochrane Seaman) in 1867.
Charles A. "Chief" Bender in 1883.
Freeman Gosden in 1899.
Spencer Tracy in 1900.
Tammy Wynette in 1942.

May 6   Kagitingan Day (Philippines)
                                   Syria Martyrs' Day
                                   National Hospital Week (begins
                                      the Sunday of the week with
                                      the twelfth)

1527 Rome was sacked by troops of Emperor Charles V.
1626 Peter Minuit bought the island of Manhattan from the Man-a-hat-a Indians.
1794 Haiti revolted against French rule.
1840 Great Britain issued the first postage stamp.
1861 Tennessee seceded from the Union.
1877 Crazy Horse surrendered to General George Crook at Camp Robinson.
1882 the Chinese Exclusion Act was passed by the United States Congress. It remained in force until December 17, 1943.
1891 the Amateur Fencers League of America was organized.
1896 a sustained flight by an unmanned "heavier-than-air" aircraft was first achieved by Samuel Langley.
1915 Babe Ruth hit his first home run.
1937 the German zeppelin Hindenburg burst into flames at its mooring in Lakehurst, New Jersey.
1945 the German army in Austria surrendered.
1954 Roger Bannister ran the first sub-four minute mile.

The following people were born on May 6:

Maximilien Robespierre in 1758.
Sigmund Freud and Robert Peary in 1856.
Barron William Ironside in 1880.
Rudolph Valentino in 1913.
Orson Welles in 1915.
Willie Mays in 1931.
Bob Seger in 1945.

May 7   Ploughing Ceremony (Thailand)

1784 the Society of the Cincinnati held its first general meeting in Philadelphia.
1789 President George Washington's inaugural ball was held in New York City.
1861 Arkansas seceded from the Union.
1907 Charles Collier won the first Isle of Man TT Races on a Matchless.
1915 the Lusitania was torpedoed and sunk. There was a loss of 1,198 lives.
1918 the Treaty of Bucharest was concluded.
1943 the Allies captured Tunis and Bizerte.
1945 Germany submitted its unconditional surrender.
1953 L. Marron caught a 1,182 pound swordfish off the Chilean coast.
1954 French troops suffered a major defeat at Dienbienphu.

The following people were born on May 7:

Johannes Brahms in 1833.
Peter I. Tchaikovsky in 1840.
Gary Cooper in 1901.
Edwin H. Land in 1909.
Anne Baxter in 1923.
Teresa Brewer in 1931.
Johnny Unitas in 1933.
Jimmy Ruffin in 1939.
Janis Ian in 1951.

May 8   American Indian Day (the second
                                            Saturday)
                                        Armistice Day (France)
                                        Cat Festival (the first Sunday in
                                            Belgium)
                                        German Democratic Republic
                                            Liberation Day
                                        Mother's Day (the second Sunday)
                                        Harry Truman's Birthday (Missouri)
                                        V-E Day
                                        World Red Cross Day
                                        Salvation Army Week (begins the
                                            second Monday

1429 Joan of Arc raised the siege of Orleans.
1541 Hernando DeSoto located the Mississippi River.
1660 Charles II was proclaimed King of England.
1783 the British ship Ceres fired a seventeen gun salute to George
     Washington in New York Harbor.
1787 the Philadelphia Society for Alleviating the Miseries of Public
     Prisons was formed.
1792 the United States instituted its first military draft.
1847 Robert W. Thomson patented the rubber tire.
1878 Paul Hines of the Providence Greys made the first major league
     triple play on record.
1902 Mont Pelee erupted on the island of Martinique, destroying
     the city of St. Pierre and killing over 30,000 people.
1915 the filly Regret won the Kentucky Derby.
1918 Nicaragua declared war on Germany and Austria.
1945 World War II came to an end in Europe.
1951 dacron men's suits were first introduced.
1954 Parry O'Brien became the first to put a shot over sixty feet.
1970 "hard hat" workers attacked a group of peace demonstrators
     in New York City.
———— the storks return to Ribe, Denmark.

The following people were born on May 8:

Jean Henry Dunant in 1828.
Dan Brouthers in 1858.
Harry S Truman in 1884.
Edd Roush in 1893.
Fulton J. Sheen in 1895.
Peter Benchley and Rick Nelson in 1940.
Angel Cordero, Jr. in 1942.
Toni Tennille in 1943.

May 9   Cotton Carnival (Memphis, Tennes-
                                     see)
                                   Czechoslovakia Liberation Day
                                   Feast of St. Christopher
                                   Romania Independence Day
                                   Victory Day (U.S.S.R., Yugoslavia)

1386 England and Portugal concluded the Treaty of Windsor.
1662 the first "Punch and Judy" show on record was presented by
       Pietro Gimonde at Covent Garden
1775 Ethan Allen crossed Lake Ticonderoga at night.
1860 the Constitutional Union Party was organized.
1915 the Second Battle of Artois began.
1926 Commander Richard Byrd flew over the North Pole.
1936 Italy annexed Ethiopia.
1937 "The Charlie McCarthy Show" was broadcast for the first time.
1944 an eye bank was opened in New York City.
1945 Soviet forces occupied Prague and began a purge of Nazi collabor-
       ators.
1957 Ezio Pinza died.
1963 Nyasaland achieved self government.
1974 the House Judiciary Committee opened impeachment hearings
       on Richard Nixon.

The following people were born on May 9:

John Brown in 1800.
Hank Snow in 1914.
Pancho Gonzales in 1928.
Albert Finney and Glenda Jackson in 1936.
Candice Bergen in 1946.
Billy Joel in 1949.

May 10   Confederate Memorial Day (North
                                         Carolina, South Carolina)
                                         Golden Spike Day (Utah)

 105 A.D., Tsai Lun invented paper in China.
1775 Ethan Allen captured Fort Ticonderoga.
1775 the Second Continental Congress opened in Philadelphia.
1869 the golden spike was driven at Promontory, Utah.
1872 the National Radical Reformers party nominated Victoria C.
     Woodhull for president of the United States and Frederick
     Douglass for vice-president.
1879 the Archaeological Institute of America was founded.
1892 the American School of Osteopathy in Kirksville, Missouri was
     chartered.
1923 J. Edgar Hoover became head of the Federal Bureau of Investiga-
     tion.
1930 the Adler Planetarium was opened.
1933 Nazi party members began conducting mass book burnings
     throughout Germany.
1940 Germany invaded Belgium, Luxembourg and The Netherlands.
1940 Neville Chamberlain resigned and Winston Churchill became
     the British Prime Minister.

The following people were born on May 10:

William "Klondike" Douglas in 1872.
Fred Astaire in 1899.
David O. Selznick in 1902.
Donovan (Leitch) in 1946.

May 11   Laotian Constitution Day
                                         Minnesota Day

 330 A.D., Constantine dedicated his new capitol at Constantinople.
 868 A.D., the <u>Diamond Sutra</u> became the first book to be produced
     on a printing press. It was printed from wood blocks.
1502 Columbus left Portugal on his fourth voyage.
1816 the American Bible Society was formed.
1825 the American Tract Society was organized.
1858 Minnesota was admitted to the Union.
1860 Garibaldi landed in Sicily.
1875 George "Charmer" Zettlein pitched the first major league nine
     inning shutout.
1929 codeball (a combination of golf and soccer) was played for the
     first time in Chicago.
1931 the Creditanstalt, Austria's largest bank, folded.
1939 fighting broke out between Soviet and Japanese troops in Mon-
     golia.

1947 B.F. Goodrich announced the manufacture of tubeless automobile tires.
1949 Siam changed its name to Thailand.
1949 Israel joined the United Nations.
1960 the submarine Triton completed the first submerged circumnavigation of the earth.

The following people were born on May 11:

Charles W. Fairbanks in 1852.
Irving Berlin in 1888.
Ellsworth Bunker in 1894.
Charlie Gehringer in 1903.
Salvador Dali in 1904.
Phil Silvers in 1912.
Mort Sahl in 1927.
Eric Burden in 1941.

May 12   Fatima Annual Pilgrimage (Portugal)

1841 the Liberty Party held its national convention in New York.
1894 the 120 ton torpedo boat Ericsson was launched in Dubuque, Iowa.
1896 the city of New York passed an ordinance making it unlawful to spit on the sidewalk.
1926 Marshal Joseph Pilsudski led a military coup in Poland.
1933 the Federal Emergency Relief Administration was created.
1938 Sandoz Labs synthesized LSD (lysergic acid diethylamide).
1943 the Axis forces in North Africa, consisting of 252,415 Germans and Italians, surrender to the Allies.
1945 Falangist officials in Generalissimo Franco's Spain attended a requiem mass for Adolf Hitler.
1949 the Berlin blockade was lifted.
1953 the first noncommercial educational television station, KUHT, began broadcasting its first test patterns.
1980 father and son Maxie and Kris Anderson successfully completed the first non-stop transamerica balloon flight.

The following people were born on May 12:

Florence Nightingale in 1820.
William "Chicken" Wolf in 1862.
Eugene "Rubber" Krapp in 1888.
Howard K. Smith in 1914.
Lawrence "Yogi" Berra in 1925.
Burt Bacharach in 1929.
Felipe Alou in 1935.
Tom Snyder in 1936.

May 13   Jamestown Day

1607 John Smith founded Jamestown on the Virginia coast.
1610 the vermilion phantom appeared to Henry IV and foretold his
     death on the fourteenth.
1821 Samuel Rust patented a printing press.
1829 the American Peace Society held its first annual meeting.
1830 the Republic of Ecuador was created.
1846 the United States declared war on Mexico.
1873 Ludwig M.N. Wolf patented the sewing machine lamp holder.
1917 three children reported seeing a vision of the Virgin Mary at
     Fatima in Portugal.
1918 the United States began issuing airmail stamps.
1951 H.R. Rider caught an eight pound black sea bass in Nantucket
     Sound.
1968 peace talks between the United States and North Vietnam began
     in Paris.

The following people were born on May 13:

Joe Louis in 1914.
James L. "Dusty" Rhodes in 1927.
Robert W. "Riverboat" Smith in 1928.
Richie Valens in 1941.
Stevie Wonder (Steveland Hardaway) in 1950.

May 14   Feast of St. Matthias (Roman
                                      Catholic)
                                    Guinean Democratic Party Anni-
                                      versary
                                    Israel Independence Day
                                    Kamuzu Day or the President's
                                      Birthday (Malawi)
                                    Liberia's National Unification Day
                                    Paraguay Independence Day

1610 Francois Ravaillac assassinated Henry IV of France.
1634 Massachusetts passed a property tax law.
1796 Edward Jenner discovered a vaccine for smallpox.
1804 the Lewis and Clark expedition left St. Louis.
1847 H.M.S. Driver became the first steamship to circumnavigate
     the earth.
1853 Gail Borden applied for a patent on condensed milk.
1884 the Anti-Monopoly Party was formed in Chicago.
1940 the German army began a blitzkrieg against France.
1942 the United States Congress authorized the Women's Army Corps.
1945 the Democratic Republic of Austria was re-established.

1948 the state of Israel was proclaimed in Tel Aviv.
1955 the Warsaw Pact was signed.
1963 Kuwait joined the United Nations.
1965 the People's Republic of China exploded its second atomic bomb.

The following people were born on May 14:

Gabriel Daniel Fahrenheit in 1686.
Thomas Gainsborough in 1727.
Ed Walsh in 1881.
Bobby Darin in 1936.

May 15   Aoi Matsuri or Hollyhock Festival
                                    (Japan)
                                   Prayer's Day (Denmark)
                                   San Isidro Day (Mexico)
                                   International Pickle Week (the
                                      week with the next to the last
                                      Thursday)

 409 B.C., Lao-tzu completed his book The Canon of the Way and
     of Virtue.
1796 Napoleon occupied Milan.
1851 the Adelphean Society was organized.
1854 the U.S. Inebriate Asylum was founded in Binghamton, New York.
1888 the Union Labor Party held a convention in Cincinnati.
1902 Lyman Gilmore flew his twenty horsepower steam-engined
     aircraft to become the first person to achieve powered flight.
1911 the U.S. Supreme Court invoked the Sherman Anti-Trust Act
     and dissolved Standard Oil.
1918 the first airmail flight was made from Washington to New York.
1922 the Arbitration Society of America was formed.
1937 the first Keedoozle Store was opened in Memphis.
1939 DDT was used for the first time in combatting the Colorado
     beetle in Switzerland.
1940 nylon stockings were introduced to the public.
1957 the British tested an H-bomb over Christmas Island.
1958 the U.S.S.R. launched Sputnik III.
1970 two Jackson State College students were killed by the National
     Guard in Mississippi.

The following people were born on May 15:

Richard Daley in 1902.
Eddy Arnold in 1918.
Anna Maria Alberghetti in 1936.
Trini Lopez in 1937.

May 16   Feast of St. Simon Stock

79 A.D., Pliny the Elder died near Mount Vesuvius at the age of
    56.
1862 Jean Joseph Etienne Lenoir built the first motor car.
1866 Charles Elmer Hires first produced root beer.
1871 U.S. Marines landed in Korea in an unsuccessful attempt to
    open the country to foreign trade.
1882 Henry Van Hoevenbergh patented the flicker.
1888 the United Labor Party was formalized in Cincinnati.
1893 Herman L. Wagner patented the "visible" typewriter.
1914 the Grand League of the Horse Shoe Pitchers Association was
    organized in Kansas City.
1919 L.Cdr. Albert C. Read and a crew of five set out on the first
    transatlantic flight.
1929 the first "Oscars" were awarded by the Academy of Motion
    Picture Arts and Sciences.

The following people were born May 16:

Levi P. Morton in 1824.
Henry Fonda in 1905.
(Wlad Ziu Valentino) Liberace in 1919.
Alfred Manuel "Billy" Martin in 1928.
Lainie Kazan in 1940.

May 17   Nauruan Constitution Day
                                              Norwegian Constitution Day
                                              World Telecommunication Day

4,127,496,231 B.C., life originated on the planet earth just outside
    of present day Mexico City.
1620 the first merry-go-round was introduced in Turkey.
1792 the New York Stock Exchange was established.
1803 Richard French and John Hawkins patented a reaper.
1809 Napoleon annexed the Papal States.
1875 the first Kentucky Derby was run.
1876 the Greenback Party held its convention in Indianapolis.
1919 a civilian government was re-established in Libya.
1939 Pitney-Bowes installed a coin operated mailbox (the "Mailomat")
    in New York City.
1954 the U.S. Supreme Court ruled on Brown vs. the Board of Education
    of Topeka, holding racial segregation in public schools to
    be unconstitutional.

The following people were born on May 17:

Edward Jenner in 1749.
J. Pierpont Morgan in 1837.
Maureen O'Sullivan in 1911.
Dennis Hopper in 1936.

May 18   Discovery Day (Cayman Islands)
                                        Haitian Flag Day
                                        Las Piedras Battle (Uruguay)
                                        Vesak Day (Singapore)
                                        Victoria Day (first Monday before
                                           the twenty-fifth)
                                        Visakha Bucha Day (Thailand)

1631 John Winthrop was elected governor of Massachusetts in the
     first accredited election in colonial America.
1652 the Rhode Island General Court of Election, meeting in Warwick,
     passed ordinances strictly regulating slavery and bondage
     within the state.
1804 less than twelve years after the abolition of the French monarchy,
     Napoleon Bonaparte was crowned emperor for life over France.
1852 Massachusetts enacted a compulsory school attendance law.
1893 the Cherokee Strip was added to Oklahoma.
1917 the first U.S. troop contingent landed in England.
1926 Aimee Semple McPherson was reported to have been kidnapped
     in California.
1933 the Tennessee Valley Authority was created.
1944 Allied forces took the German stronghold at Cassino.
1953 Jacqueline Cochrane became the first woman to pilot an airplane
     in excess of the speed of sound.

The following people were born on May 18:

Bertrand Russell in 1872.
Perry Como in 1912.
Margot Fonteyn in 1919.
Robert Morse in 1931.
Brooks Robinson in 1937.
Reggie Jackson in 1946.

May 19   Cup Day (South Australia)
                                        May Ray Day
                                        Youth and Sports Day (Turkey)

1536 Anne Boleyn was beheaded.

---- now every year the ghost of Anne Boleyn returns to Blickling Hall in Norfolk, which was the place of her birth.
1571 Miguel Lopez de Legazpi founded Manila in the Philippines.
1774 Ann Lee and eight Shakers sailed from Liverpool for New York. They eventually became the first conscientious objectors on religious grounds and were jailed during the American War of Independence in 1776.
1848 the United States and Mexico signed a peace treaty.
1857 William Francis Channing and Moses G. Farmer patented an electric fire alarm system.
1876 Sarah Bernhardt became the first woman to wear trousers as an intentional article of feminine apparel.
1891 the People's Party was organized in Cincinnati.
1911 Caesar Cella was convicted of burglary through the use of a new identification technique known as fingerprinting.
1921 an immigration quota act was enacted by the United States.
1928 the first annual Frog Jumping Jubilee was held in Calaveras County, California.
1980 after smouldering since March 27, Mount St. Helens in Washington blew its top and killed sixty-three people.

The following people were born on May 19:

Ho Chi Minh in 1890.
Malcolm X (Malcolm Little) in 1925.
David Hartman in 1935.

May 20   Cameroonian Republic Day
                                    Cuba Independence Day
                                    Eliza Doolittle Day
                                    Ferrary Day
                                    Lafayette Day (Massachusetts)
                                    Mecklenburg Day (North Carolina)
                                    M.P.R. Anniversary (Zaire)
                                    Weights and Measures Day

 526 A.D., an earthquake in Antioch, Syria caused 250,000 deaths.
1536 Henry VIII married his third wife, Jane Seymour.
1639 schools in Dorchester, Massachusetts became the first American public schools to be supported by direct taxation.
1749 a fire engine was used in America for the first time in Salem, Massachusetts.
1775 at Charlotte, Mecklenburg County, North Carolina, a group of citizens formally declared independence from Great Britain.
1785 Thomas Hutchins was appointed as the first Geographer of the United States.
1830 D. Hyde patented the fountain pen.

1861 North Carolina seceded from the Union.
1862 the U.S. Homestead Act was enacted.
1882 Germany, Austria and Italy formed the Triple Alliance.
1895 the Latham Panoptikon had its first commercial showing.
1927 Charles Lindbergh took off from New York bound solo for Paris.
1932 Amelia Earhart took off on the first transatlantic solo flight by a woman.
1961 Lynn Joyner caught a 680 pound jewfish off the Florida coast.

The following people on May 20:

Honoré de Balzac in 1799.
James Stewart in 1908.
Moshe Dayan in 1915.
George Gobel in 1919.
Joe Cocker in 1944.
Cher LaPierre (Bono) in 1946.

May 21   Naval Battle of Iquique (Chile)
                                    Yugoslav Air Force Day

the sun enters the house of Gemini.
1819 bicycle velocipedes were introduced in New York.
1840 Governor William Hobson proclaimed British sovereignty over New Zealand.
1853 Regent's Park Zoo opened its "Aquatic Vivarium."
1881 Clara Barton organized the American Red Cross.
1906 Louis H. Perlman applied for a patent for a demountable tire carrying rim for automobiles.
1908 the first horror film, Dr. Jekyll and Mr. Hyde, was released in Chicago.
1916 Great Britain initiated daylight savings time.
1941 the U.S.S. Robin Moor became the first U.S. warship to be sunk by a German U-boat in World War II.
1956 the U.S. conducted an atmospheric test of a hydrogen bomb over Bikini Atoll.
1968 the U.S. atomic submarine Scorpion was lost at sea.

The following people were born on May 21:

Albrecht Dürer in 1471.
Alexander Pope in 1688.
Thomas "Fats" Waller in 1904.
Harold Robbins in 1912.
Raymond Burr and Dennis Day in 1917.
Leo Sayer in 1948.
Jane Olivor in 1952.

May 22   National Maritime Day
                                              Sri Lanka Republic Day

1498 Vasco da Gama reached Calicut on the Malabar coast.
1649 lawmakers in Warwick, Rhode Island, enacted a fraudulent elec-
      tion law.
1819 the first sea-going U.S. built steamboat, the U.S.S. Savannah,
      set out on its first transatlantic voyage from Georgia to Liver-
      pool.
1849 Abraham Lincoln received a patent for a device designed for
      "buoying vessels over shoals."
1892 Dr. Washington Sheffield invented the toothpaste tube.
1900 Allen De Vilbiss patented an automatic computing pendulum-type
      scale.
1900 Edwin S. Votey patented the pneumatic piano player.
1906 the Wright brothers received a patent on their airplane.
1927 an earthquake in Nan-Shan, China killed 200,000.
1931 canned rattlesnake meat went on sale in Arcadia, Florida.
1939 Adolf Hitler and Benito Mussolini signed a ten year alliance.
1942 Mexico declared war on Germany, Italy and Japan.
1960 Patrice Lumumba and his party won a plurality in elections
      in the Republic of the Congo (Leopoldville).
1972 the Republic of Sri Lanka was proclaimed.
1972 Richard Nixon set out on a presidential visit to Moscow.

The following people were born on May 22:

Wilhelm Wagner in 1813.
Sir Arthur Conan Doyle in 1859.
Al Simmons in 1902.
Laurence Olivier in 1907.
Peter Nero in 1934.
Richard Benjamin in 1938.

May 23   Linnaeus Day
                                              South Carolina Ratification Day

1498 Girolamo Savonarola was burned at the stake.
1785 Benjamin Franklin wrote out a description of bifocal glasses.
1788 South Carolina ratified the Constitution of the United States.
1827 the Infant School Society of New York established the first
      American kindergarten.
1879 the Iowa State College at Ames established a veterinary school.
1915 Italy declared war on Austria-Hungary.
1918 Costa Rica declared war on Germany.
1926 the French proclaimed Lebanon to be a republic under French
      administration.

1945 Heinrich Himmler committed suicide.
1949 the German Federal Republic (West Germany) officially came
        into existence as a republic.
1953 two yetis on a foraging excursion sighted a party of humans
        making their way up Mount Everest.
1960 Israel announced the capture of Adolf Eichmann.

The following people were born on May 23:

Carolus Linnaeus in 1707.
Franz Anton Mesmer in 1734.
Deacon Phillippe in 1872.
Douglas Fairbanks in 1883.
Zachariah "Buck" Wheat in 1888.
Rosemary Clooney in 1928.
Joan Collins in 1933.
John Newcombe in 1944.

May 24   Day of Slavonic Letters (Bulgaria)
                                    Empire Day (Belize, Malawi)
                                    Independence Battle (Ecuador)
                                    Kirtland's Warbler Day

1004 Thorfinn Karlsefni reached Cape Cod.
1430 Joan of Arc was captured and tried for heresy.
1865 the first Bessemer steel railroad rails were rolled in Wyandotte,
        Michigan.
1869 Major John Wesley Powell left Green River City on an expedition
        to explore the Grand Canyon.
1883 the Brooklyn Bridge opened.
1893 the Ohio Anti-Saloon League was formed in Oberlin.
1918 the Croix de Guerre was awarded to Henry Johnson.
1935 the first major league night baseball game was played in Cincin-
        nati.
1962 Malcolm Scott Carpenter orbited the earth three times.
1977 Lorraine Carlton caught a fourteen and a half pound black skip-
        jack in Mexico.

The following people were born on May 24:

Queen Victoria in 1819.
Lilli Palmer in 1914.
Peggy Cass in 1924.
Bob Dylan (Robert Zimmerman) in 1941.

May 25   African Freedom Day
                                                Argentine National Holiday
                                                Bermuda Day
                                                Jordan Independence Day
                                                Spring Holiday (United Kingdom)
                                                Sudanese Revolution Day
                                                Youth Day (Yugoslavia)

1602 Florian Mathis performed the first successful abdominal surgery
      when he removed a dagger from the stomach of a sword swal-
      lower.
1844 Samuel F.B. Morse sent a telegram from Washington, D.C. to
      Baltimore, Maryland using Morse code.
1850 the first hippopotamus landed in Great Britain.
1880 the American Jersey Cattle Club was incorporated.
1898 an American expeditionary force sailed for Manila to take posses-
      sion of the Philippines.
1915 British troops were issued gas masks.
1917 the first U.S. troop contingent arrived in Rouen, France.
1935 Babe Ruth hit home runs number 713 and 714 in Pittsburgh.
1935 Jesse Owens broke or tied six world records in track in one
      afternoon in Ann Arbor, Michigan.
1935 the U.S. Narcotic Farm in Lexington, Kentucky was dedicated.
1946 the independent Kingdom of Transjordan was proclaimed.
1963 the Organization of African States was formed.
1980 Oral Roberts saw and talked with a 900 foot tall Jesus Christ
      in Tulsa, Oklahoma.

The following people were born on May 25:

Ralph Waldo Emerson in 1803.
Lip Pike in 1845.
Tip O'Neill in 1858.
Igor Sikorsky in 1889.
Tito (Josip Broz) in 1892.
Bennett Cerf and Gene Tunney in 1897.
Miles Davis in 1926.
Beverly Sills in 1929.
Tom T. Hall in 1936.
Leslie Uggams in 1943.

May 26   Feast of St. Augustine of Canterbury
                                                Guyana Independence Day
                                                Al Jolson Day
                                                Lady Mary Wortley Montagu Day

735 A.D., the Venerable Bede, historian, scientist, ecclesiastic,

and one of the earliest of English scholars, died at the age
of sixty-two.

1721 a smallpox epidemic broke out in Boston.

1781 the Bank of North America was incorporated in Philadelphia.

1906 the Archaeological Institute of America was incorporated.

1923 Emir Abdullah ibn Hussein organized Transjordania into an autonomous state.

1923 the first twenty-four hour race at Le Mans began.

1924 President Calvin Coolidge signed a bill setting immigration
quotas.

1926 the Riffian War ended when Abd-El-Krim surrendered.

1928 Andrew Payne won a Los Angeles to New York foot race with
a running time of 573:4:34.

1959 after pitching twelve no-run, no-hit, no-walk innings, Harvey
Maddix of the Pittsburgh Pirates lost 2-0 to the Milwaukee
Braves in the thirteenth inning.

1962 Brian W. Batchelor caught a nineteen pound bonefish off South
Africa.

1966 Guyana became an independent nation.

1975 John T. Holton caught a forty-six pound, seven ounce pollock
in New Jersey.

The following people were born on May 26:

Al Jolson in 1886.
John Wayne in 1907.
Robert Morley in 1908.
Peggy Lee (Norma Delores Egstrom) in 1920.
James Arness in 1923.
Brent Musburger in 1939.

May 27   Afghanistan Independence Day
                                    Feast of St. Bede the Venerable
                                    Nicaraguan Armed Forces Day
                                    Turkish Constitution Day

1607 a group of about 200 Indians attacked, and were repulsed by,
an English settlement in Virginia.

1647 Achsah Young was hanged in Massachusetts for witchcraft.

1796 James S. McLean patented the piano.

1860 Garibaldi took Palermo.

1905 the Battle of Tsushima was fought.

1918 the Third Battle of the Aisne began.

1923 the first twenty-four race at Le Mans was completed.

1935 the U.S. Supreme Court declared the National Industrial Recovery
Act to be unconstitutional.

1937 San Francisco's Golden Gate Bridge opened.

1941 the Bismarck was sunk by British naval forces.
1943 Edwin Barclay of Liberia addressed the United States Senate
     and became the first head of state from black Africa to do
     so.
1951 the People's Republic of China announced the liberation of
     Tibet.
1978 Greenville, Georgia registered a temperature of 113° F.
1980 Ms. Kathleen Tooker-O'Shaughnessy moved to Boston.
1981 Willie Shoemaker won his 8,000th career victory.

The following people were born on May 27:

Amelia Bloomer in 1818.
"Wild Bill" Hickok in 1837.
Isadora Duncan in 1878.
Hubert Humphrey and Vincent Price in 1911.
Sam Snead in 1912.
Caryl Chessman in 1921.
Henry Kissinger in 1923.
Ramsey Lewis in 1935.

May 28   Feast of St. Bernard of Montjoux
                               Feast of the London Martyrs of
                               1582

1539 Hernando de Soto landed in Florida.
1602 Bartholomew Gosnold's crew began construction of the first
     verifiable English settlement in America on Cuttyhunk Island.
1879 the state of Illinois passed a law prohibiting the employment
     of women in mines.
1881 New York City enacted its pure food and drug legislation.
1929 On with the Show, the first talking picture entirely in color,
     was shown in New York City.
1934 the Dionne quintuplets were born.
1937 Neville Chamberlain became prime minister of Great Britain.
1953 Edmund Hillary and Tenzing Norkay planted the flags of Great
     Britain, India, Nepal and the United Nations on the peak of
     Mount Everest.
1959 monkeys Able and Baker survived a U.S. space shot.
1967 Sir Francis Chichester completed his solo circumnavigation
     of the world.
1977 William Katko caught a sixteen pound spotted seatrout in Virginia.

The following people were born on May 28:

Patrick Henry in 1736.
Jean Louis Agassiz in 1807.

Jim Thorpe in 1888.
Jerry West in 1938.
Gladys Knight in 1944.

May 29   Day of Buddha's Parinirvana (Bhutan)
                                    Rhode Island Ratification Day
                                    Wisconsin Admission Day

1453 Constantinople fell to the Turks.
1765 Patrick Henry expressed his opposition to the British government
     in the Virginia House of Burgesses.
1790 Rhode Island ratified the constitution of the United States.
1827 Admiral Sir Isaac Coffin's Lancasterian (nautical) School was
     established at Nantucket in Massachusetts.
1844 James K. Polk became the first "dark horse" candidate to be
     nominated for the presidency of the United States.
1848 Wisconsin was admitted to the Union.
1884 the U.S. Bureau of Animal Industry was established.
1909 the state of New York gave its approval to the City Court of
     Buffalo to become the first U.S. court to be empowered to
     hear domestic relations cases.
1916 the United States President's flag was adopted.
1935 the U.S. Narcotic Farm in Lexington, Kentucky received its
     first patients.

The following people were born on May 29:

Bob Hope in 1903.
John F. Kennedy in 1917.
Johnny Lee "Blue Moon" Odom in 1945.

May 30   Feast of St. Joan of Arc
                                    Memorial Day

10,041 B.C., Kiruk of the Tur tribe planted the world's first garden
     marking the beginning of agriculture in present-day Lebanon
1431 Joan of Arc was burned at the stake in Rouen.
1635 the Treaty of Prague was concluded.
1806 Andrew Jackson was involved in a duel in Red River, Kentucky.
1821 James Boyd patented a rubber-lined cotton web fire hose.
1848 William G. Young patented the ice cream freezer.
1896 the first automobile accident happened in New York City.
1909 the National Conference on the Negro led to the founding of
     the National Association for the Advancement of Colored
     People.

1911 an automobile race took place on a race track for the first
     time. This yearly event has now become known as the Indian-
     apolis 500.
1922 the Lincoln Memorial was dedicated.
1959 the first full size hovercraft was launched.

The following people were born on May 30:

Benny Goodman in 1909.
Gayle Sayers in 1943.

May 31   South African Republic Day

1594 Tintoretto died in Venice.
1790 the United States enacted a copyright law.
1853 the first American arctic expedition set out under Elisha Kane.
1865 Dr. C.C. Abbott's catch of a four pound, three and a half ounce
     yellow perch in New Jersey went in the record books.
1870 Professor Edward J. De Smedt patented sheet asphalt pavement.
1880 the League of American Wheelmen was formed in Newport,
     Rhode Island.
1902 the Peace of Vereeniging ended the Boer War.
1910 the Union of South Africa became an independent nation.
1916 the Battle of Jutland began.
1929 a jet black reindeer calf was born at the Lodgepole Ranch at
     North Beverly, Massachusetts.
1930 Bobby Jones won the British Amateur golf championship at
     St. Andrew's in Scotland.
1961 South Africa severed its ties with the British Commonwealth.
1962 Adolf Eichmann was hanged in Israel.
1967 the Ibos of Nigeria declared their territory to be the independent
     state of Biafra.
1974 hostilities between Egyptian and Syrian forces and the forces
     of Israel came to an end.

The following people were born on May 31:

Peter the Great in 1672.
Walt Whitman in 1819.
Fred Allen in 1894.
Norman Vincent Peale in 1898.
Ray "Peaches" Davis in 1905.
Clint Eastwood in 1930.
Peter Yarrow in 1938.
Joe Namath in 1943.

June

The first day of June marks the following commemorations:

Anniversary of the Royal Brunei Malay Regiment
Children's Day (Cape Verde)
International Child's Day (Poland)
Kentucky Admission Day
Madaraka Day (Kenya)
Nathaniel Ulysses Turtle Day
Samoa Independence Day
South African Public Holiday
Summer Holiday (Ireland)
Teachers' Day (first Sunday in Massachusetts)
Tennessee Admission Day
Victory Day (Tunisia)

    National Humor Week (begins first Sunday)
    National Safe Boating Week (the first through the seventh)
    National Soaring Week (begins first Sunday)

    Dairy Month
    Fight the Filthy Fly Month
    National Ragweek Control Month
    National Rose Month
    Philatelic Writers Month

June 1

1638 at 2:00 p.m., an earthquake shook the town of Plymouth, Massachusetts.
1792 Kentucky was admitted to the Union.
1796 Tennessee was admitted to the Union.
1847 the Communist League covened in London.
1869 Thomas Alva Edison patented an electric voting machine.
1880 the first pay telephone was installed in the Yale Bank Building in New Haven, Connecticut.
1888 the first seismograph was installed at the Lick Observatory at Mount Hamilton, California.

1938 Superman first appeared in Action Comics.
1947 "The Jack Paar Show" began on NBC radio.
1947 the development of photosensitive glass was announced in Corn-
        ing, New York.
1954 Senator Joseph McCarthy was at the height of his career during
        thirty-five days of televised hearings of his Senate internal
        security commission "investigations" of government operations.
1960 Abe Sackheim caught a 114 pound roosterfish in Mexico.

The following people were born on June 1:

Jacques Marquette in 1637.
Brigham Young in 1801.
Nelson Riddle in 1921.
Andy Griffith in 1926.
Marilyn Monroe in 1928.
Pat Boone in 1934.

June 2   Coronation Day of the Fourth Here-
                                    ditary King (Bhutan)
                                    Foundation Day (Western Australia)
                                    Hristo Botev Day (Bulgaria)
                                    Italian Republic Day

1835 Phineas Taylor Barnum's circus started on its first tour of Ameri-
        can cities.
1857 James E.A. Gibbs patented the first practical chain-stitch single-
        thread sewing machine.
1883 the first trial trip was run over Chicago's electric elevated
        railroad at the Chicago Railway Exposition. It remained in
        operation for the following three weeks.
1883 the first baseball (non-league) night game was played in Fort
        Wayne, Indiana.
1886 President Grover Cleveland was married to Frances Folsom
        in a ceremony at the White House.
1896 Guglielmo Marconi patented the radio in Great Britain.
1924 American Indians were granted citizenship in the United States
        of America by the Snyder Act.
1925 Lou Gehrig played his first major league baseball game.
1930 the Mariner's Museum in Newport News, Virginia was established.
1932 George W. Perry caught a twenty-two and a quarter pound large-
        mouth bass in Georgia.
1941 Lou Gehrig died of amyotrophic lateral sclerosis.
1946 a referendum in Italy rejected the monarchy and made Italy
        a republic.
1949 Transjordan was renamed the Hashemite Kingdom of Jordan.
1953 the coronation of Elizabeth II of England was held.

1978 Alan J. Card caught a 42 pound blackfin tuna in Bermuda.

The following people were born on June 2:

Martha Washington in 1731.
Marquis de Sade in 1740.
Thomas Hardy in 1840.
Wilbert Robinson in 1863.
Hedda Hopper in 1890.
Hollis "Sloppy" Thurston in 1899.
Johnny Weissmuller in 1904.
Chuck Barris in 1929.
Charlie Watts in 1941.

June 3   Confederate Memorial Day (Ken-
                                  tucky, Louisiana, Tennessee)
                                  Jefferson Davis' Birthday (Alabama,
                                      Florida, Georgia, Mississippi,
                                      South Carolina)
                                  Yang di-Pertuan Agong's Birthday
                                      (Malaysia)

1509 Henry VIII married his first wife, Catherine of Aragon.
1856 Cullen Whipple of Providence patented a screw machine.
1878 the American Laryngological Association was founded.
1899 the Chapel of the Transfiguration on Conanicut Island was conse-
     crated. It was the first mobile church in the United States.
1915 San Marino declared war on Austria.
1921 the United States imposed immigration quotas for the first
     time.
1932 Lou Gehrig hit four consecutive home runs for the New York
     Yankees against the Philadelphia Athletics.
1942 the Battle of Midway began.
1946 the trial of Japanese war criminals began in Tokyo.
1948 Daniel F. Malan, who had campaigned on a platform of apartheid,
     became the new prime minister of the Union of South Africa.
1949 Wesley Anthony Brown became the first black midshipman to
     graduate from the United States Naval Academy.
1959 the United States Air Force Academy graduated its first class.
1959 Singapore became self governing under British supervision.
1963 Orville Welch caught a five pound mountain whitefish in Alberta.
1979 the Ixtoc I oil well blowout in the Gulf of Mexico led to the
     spilling of 130,200,000 gallons of crude oil.

The following people were born on June 3:

James Hutton in 1726.

Jefferson Davis in 1808.
Henry James in 1811.
Garret A. Hobart in 1844.
Roland Hayes in 1887.
Tony Curtis in 1925.
Allen Ginsberg in 1926.
Curtis Mayfield in 1942.

June 4   Emancipation Day (Tonga)
                                             Old Maids' Day

1070 roquefort cheese was discovered in a cave near Roquefort,
     France,
1674 Massachusetts passed a law prohibiting horse racing on public
     streets or commons.
1816 the double decked steamboat Washington was launched in Wheel-
     ing, West Virginia.
1912 Massachusetts enacted a minimum wage law.
1916 the Brusilov Offensive was initiated.
1940 200,000 British and 140,000 French troops retreated from Dunkirk.
1940 Winston Churchill said, "We shall fight on the beaches, we shall
     fight on the landing-grounds, we shall fight in the fields and
     in the streets, we shall fight in the hills; we shall never surren-
     der."
1944 the German submarine U-505 was captured and boarded by
     the U.S. Navy.
1944 the United States' 5th Army took Rome.
1949 Mrs. E. Small caught a four and three quarter pound white perch
     in Maine.
1970 Tonga became an independent member of the British Common-
     wealth.
1974 ABC newsman Robert Le Donne reported seeing a flying object
     he could not identify in Woodcliffe Lake, New Jersey.

The following people were born on June 4:

Gene Barry in 1922.
Dennis Weaver in 1925.
John Barrymore, Jr. in 1932.
Bruce Dern in 1936.
Freddy Fender in 1937.

June 5   Danish Constitution Day
                                             Iranian Revolution Day

The Seychelles Liberation Day
World Environment Day

66,010 B.C., the glacial interstadial ended and the Main Würm period of glaciation began.
1411 Musa and his supporters attacked and killed Suleiman at Edirne.
1846 the first telegraph line was opened between Philadelphia and Baltimore.
1849 Denmark adopted its basic constitution.
1855 the first national convention of the "Know-Nothing Party" was held.
1862 the Treaty of Saigon permitted the French to occupy the three eastern provinces of Cochin China.
1939 the Dard Hunter Paper Museum of the Massachusetts Institute of Technology was opened.
1942 the United States declared war on Bulgaria, Hungary and Romania.
1947 George C. Marshall proposed the Marshall Plan.
1967 the Six Day War began: Israel vs. Egypt, Syria and Jordan.
1968 Robert F. Kennedy was shot by assassin Sirhan B. Sirhan.
1978 Jerry Reid caught a fifty pound California yellowtail in Mexico.

The following people were born on June 5:

Adam Smith in 1723.
Johan Gadolin in 1760.
Jack Chesbro in 1874.
John Keynes in 1883.
Bill Moyers in 1924.

June 6
D-Day
Memorial Day (Korea)
Philatelic Writers Day
Swedish Flag Day
Tuen Ng Festival (Hong Kong)

659 B.C., Zarathustra, founder of zoroastrianism, was born in Media.
1727 James Figg defeated Ned Sutton for the boxing championship cf England.
1816 ten inches of snow fell in New England.
1844 the Young Men's Christian Association was founded in London, England.
1846 the English corn laws were repealed.
1850 Levi Strauss made his first blue jeans.
1882 Henry W. Seely patented the electric flatiron.
1890 the United States Polo Association was formed.
1918 the Battle of Belleau Wood began.

1925 the Chrysler Corporation was formed.
1928 Xavier University in New Orleans conferred its first degrees.
1932 the federal government of the United States instituted a gasoline
        tax.
1933 the first drive-in movie theater opened in Camden, New Jersey.
1934 the U.S. Securities and Exchange Commission was created.
1944 Allied forces landed on the beaches of Normandy.

The following people were born on June 6:

Nathan Hale in 1755.
Alexander Pushkin in 1799.
Karl Braun in 1850.
Thomas Mann in 1875.
Bill Dickey in 1907.
Dalai Lama in 1935.
Gary "U.S." Bonds in 1939.
Janice M. Mooradian in 1944.
Bjorn Borg in 1956.

June 7   Feast of St. Vulflagius

 632 A.D., Mohammed, founder of Islam, died in Medina.
1099 Christian Crusaders reached Jerusalem.
1123 'Omar Khayyám died at the age of seventy-three.
1494 Spain and Portugal divided up South America according to the
        provisions of the Treaty of Tordesillas.
1692 the buccaneer city of Port Royal, Jamaica was dumped into
        the Caribbean Sea by an earthquake.
1801 the American Company of Booksellers was organized in New
        York.
1854 the Young Men's Christian Association held its first international
        convention in Boston.
1870 Thomas S. Hall patented the automatic electric block railroad
        signal system.
1887 Tolbert Lanston patented the monotype typesetting machine.
1892 John F. Palmer patented the cord construction bicycle tire.
1892 John J. Doyle became baseball's first "pinch-hitter."
1898 the Social Democracy of America Party was formed.
1905 the Norwegian Storting declared their union with Sweden dis-
        solved.
1913 Gustaf W. Elmen developed permalloy.
1929 the Italian government ratified an agreement making the Vatican
        City an independent state.
1939 King George VI arrived at Niagara Falls.
1945 "Topper" debuted on NBC radio.
1971 Manuel Elizalde, Jr. became the first representative of modern
        civilization to contact the stone age Tasaday tribe of Mindanao.

The following people were born on June 7:

Beau Brummell in 1778.
Paul Gaugin in 1848.
George Washington in 1907.
Rocky Graziano in 1922.
Tom Jones in 1940.
Thurman Munson in 1947.

June 8   Children's Day (the second Sunday)
                                    Race Unity Day (the second Sunday)
                                    National Fraternal Week (the eighth
                                        through the fourteenth)

1723 the Honourable Society of Improvers of the Knowledge of Agricul-
     ture in Scotland was founded.
1783 Mount Skaptar erupted and killed one fifth of the population
     of Iceland.
1815 German confederation was achieved.
1869 Ives W. McGaffey patented the suction type vacuum cleaner.
1911 Connecticut began the licensing and registration of aircraft.
1921 the U.S. Public Health Service, having purchased the facility
     from the state of Louisiana in January, reopened the Leper
     Hospital in Carville, Louisiana.
1940 Edwin M. McMillan and Philip H. Abelson announced the discovery
     of neptunium.
1948 John E. Rudder became the first black commissioned officer
     in the U.S. Marine Corps.
1953 the Union Pacific Railroad put a gas turbine, propane fueled
     locomotive into service.
1959 United States mail was sent from the submarine U.S.S. Barbero
     to Jacksonville, Florida via a Regulus 1 missile.
1966 the National and American Football Leagues announced a merger
     to be fully implemented in 1970.
1969 Alphonse Bielevich caught a ninety-eight and three quarter
     pound cod in New Hampshire.

The following people were born on June 8:

Frank Lloyd Wright in 1869.
Francis H.C. Crick in 1916.
Byron R. "Whizzer" White in 1917.
Nancy Sinatra in 1940.
Mark Belanger and William R. "Boz" Scaggs in 1944.

June 9   Feast of St. Columba
                                            Senior Citizens Day (Oklahoma)

1628 Thomas Morton was deported from Plymouth Colony for living
     with a licentious group and trading guns to the Indians.
1790 The Philadelphia Spelling Book was registered for copyright.
1846 John P. Hale was elected to represent New Hampshire in the
     United States Senate on the basis of an anti-slavery campaign.
     He was the first senator to publicly take this position.
1880 the Greenback Labor Party held its national convention in Chi-
     cago.
1902 the first vending machine-type Automat Restaurant opened
     in Philadelphia.
1923 Brink's, Inc. introduced armored security vans.
1949 Ms. Georgia Neese Clark was confirmed as the first woman
     Treasurer of the United States.
1959 the first submarine equipped to fire ballistic missiles, the U.S.S.
     George Washington, was launched.
1973 Secretariat won the Belmont Stakes to become the first American
     triple crown winner in twenty-five years.
1975 Jerry Verge caught a six pound, nine and three quarter ounce
     kokanee in Idaho.

The following people were born on June 9:

Roger Bresnahan in 1879.
William "Wheezer" Dell in 1887.
Cole Porter in 1893.
Robert Cummings in 1910.
Robert McNamara and Les Paul in 1916.
Jackie Wilson in 1934.

June 10   Camoes Memorial Day
                                            Camoen and Portuguese Communi-
                                                ties Day (Macao)
                                            Portugal Day (Madeira)

1329 the Turks defeated a Byzantine force at Pelakanon.
1682 a tornado hit New Haven, Connecticut. It was the first to be
     recorded by white settlers in North America.
1772 the Gaspee Affair occurred in Narragansett Bay.
1793 the Jardin des Plantes Zoo was established.
1808 Pope Pius VII excommunicated Napoleon Bonaparte.
1842 the Wilkes expedition returned to New York City from its explora-
     tion and survey of the Pacific Ocean.
1892 Wilbert Robinson got seven hits in seven times at bat for Balti-
     more.

June   126

1898 U.S. Marines occupied Guantánamo Bay in Cuba.
1902 the window envelope was patented by Americus F. Callahan.
1903 King Alexander I of Serbia, his wife and a number of the members
      of their court were assassinated.
1915 the Girl Scouts were incorporated.
1919 six days after passing through Congress, the woman suffrage
      (19th) amendment was ratified by Michigan, Illinois and Wiscon-
      sin.
1935 William G. Wilson and Dr. Robert Smith established Alcoholics
      Anonymous in Akron, Ohio.
1940 Italy declared war on Great Britain and France.
1942 Nazi troops obliterated Lidice, Czechoslovakia as retribution
      for the death of Gestapo leader Reinhard Heydrich in that
      country.
1963 War broke out between Iraqi and Kurdish troops.
1978 Stanley Gibbon caught a 220 pound, 7 ounce south bluefin tuna
      off the coast of Tasmania.

The following people were born on June 10:

Saul Bellow in 1915.
Judy Garland in 1922.
Maurice Sendak in 1928.
F. Lee Bailey in 1933.

June 11   Al-Esra (Oman)
                                   Kamehameha Day (Hawaii)
                                   Libya Evacuation Day (U.S. Troops)
                                   Time Memorial Day (Japan)

2720 B.C., the Minoan civilization on Crete entered the bronze age.
 671 A.D., the water clock was invented in Japan.
1793 the first American stove patent was granted to Robert Haeterick.
1901 the American Society of Orthodontists held its first annual
      meeting in St. Louis.
1912 Silas Christoferson took off in an airplane from the roof of
      the Multnomah Hotel in Portland, Oregon.
1919 Sir Barton completed his sweep of the triple crown by winning
      the Belmont Stakes, becoming the first horse to do so.
1927 the distinguished flying cross was presented to Charles Lindbergh.
1938 Johnny Vander Meer pitched his second consecutive no-hit,
      no-run baseball game.
1961 A.F. Plim caught a 111 pound southern yellowtail off New Zea-
      land.
1963 a South Vietnamese Buddhist monk immolated himself.
1977 Robert A. Jahnke caught a twenty-seven pound, three ounce
      chum salmon in Alaska.

The following people were born on June 11:

Richard Strauss in 1864.
Alfred Kroeber in 1876.
Jeannette Rankin in 1880.
Vince Lombardi in 1913.
Gene Wilder in 1935.

June 12   Peace with Bolivia Day (Paraguay)
                                         Philippines Independence Day
                                         The Twelfth (Northern Ireland)

32,217 B.C., the first individual was born into the sub-species <u>Homo</u>
        <u>sapiens sapiens</u>. His parents named him Bob.
1206 Temujin was proclaimed Genghis Khan ("Emperor within the
        Seas") at Karakorum.
1665 New York City was incorporated.
1701 the Act of Settlement was passed which declared that no Roman
        Catholic may become the King of England.
1800 the United States purchased a navy yard in Portsmouth, New
        Hampshire.
1849 Lewis Haslett patented the first gas mask.
1898 the Philippines proclaimed freedom from Spanish rule under
        Emilio Aguinaldo.
1901 the Platt Amendment was passed by the United States Congress
        empowering the U.S. to intervene in Cuban affairs.
1913 the animated cartoon "The Dachshund" was released.
1920 the Farmer Labor Party was organized.
1933 Dr. Russell P. Schwartz exhibited the electrobasograph in Milwau-
        kee.
1935 the Chaco War between Bolivia and Paraguay ended.
1939 the museum housing the Baseball Hall of Fame in Cooperstown
        was dedicated.
1940 Norway surrendered to Germany.
1954 R.N. Sheafer caught a twenty-one pound, six ounce tautog in
        New Jersey.
1957 weightlifter Paul Anderson lifted three tons of weights.
1963 Medgar Evers was assassinated in Jackson, Mississippi.

The following people were born on June 12:

Fritz Lipmann in 1899.
Vic Damone in 1928.
Jim Nabors in 1933.

June 13   Feast of St. Anthony of Padua
                                               Queen's Birthday (Montserrat)
                                               Reform Movement's Anniversary
                                               (Yemen Arab Republic)

323 B.C., Alexander the Great died of a fever in Babylonia.
1633 the Maryland charter was issued to Lord Cecil Baltimore.
1774 Newport, Rhode Island outlawed the importation of slaves and
     provided that if they were brought into the colony, they would
     be declared free.
1878 the Congress of Berlin convened.
1890 the Supreme Council of the Mystic Order of Veiled Prophets
     of the Enchanted Realm (Freemasons) was instituted.
1893 a 1000 mile horse race (from Chadron, Nebraska to Chicago)
     was started at 5:30 p.m.
1893 Lady Margaret Scott won the first British Ladies Golf Champion-
     ship at Royal Lytham, England.
1900 the Boxer Rebellion began.
1917 a meeting of the International Congress of Soil Science opened
     in Washington, D.C.
1933 the Federal Savings and Loan Association was authorized.
1944 Marvin Camras patented the wire recorder.
1944 Germany began launching V-1 attacks against England.
1955 seventy-seven people were killed in a crash at the start of the
     Le Mans twenty-four hour endurance race.
1967 Thurgood Marshall was nominated to the U.S. Supreme Court.
1968 the hull of the S.S. World Glory failed leading to a massive
     oil spill off the coast of South Africa.
1971 publication of the "Pentagon Papers" was begun by the New
     York Times.
1972 Clyde McPhatter died of a heart attack at forty-one years of
     age.

The following people were born on June 13:

Thomas Young in 1773.
Sir Charles A. Parsons in 1854.
William Butler Yeats in 1865.
Wallace C. Sabine in 1868.
Jules Bordet in 1870.
Carlos Chavez in 1899.
Harold "Red" Grange in 1903.
Erwin Mueller in 1911.
Josiah Stinkney Carberry in 1913.
Paul Lynde in 1926.
Bobby Freeman in 1940.

June 14   Rice Planting Festival (Japan)
                                         United States Army Birthday
                                         United States Flag Day

1642 Massachusetts passed a compulsory education law.
1645 the Battle of Naseby led to the surrender of Charles I to the
     Scots.
1777 the flag of the United States of America was formally adopted.
1816 William Allen founded the Peace Society in Great Britain.
1834 the first practical underwater diving suit was patented by Leonard
     Norcross.
1834 Isaac Fischer, Jr. patented sandpaper.
1846 the Republic of California was established.
1870 the Cincinnati Red Stockings lost 8-7 to the Brooklyn Atlantics
     and their 92 game undefeated streak came to an end.
1919 Captain John Alcock and Lieutenant Arthur Whitten Brown
     set out on the first non-stop transatlantic flight.
1938 Benjamin Grushkin patented chlorophyll.
1940 the German army occupied Paris. Marshal Petain sued for peace.
1955 the United States and Great Britain concluded an agreement
     regarding the peaceful use of nuclear power.
1956 British forces left Suez.
1964 Walter Maxwell caught a 1,780 pound tiger shark off South
     Carolina.

The following people were born on June 14:

Charles Coulomb in 1736.
Harriet Beecher Stowe in 1811.
Major Edward Bowes in 1874.
Burl Ives in 1909.
Dorothy McGuire in 1919.

June 15   Arkansas Admission Day
                                         Father's Day (the third Sunday)
                                         Magna Carta Day
                                         Valdemar's Day (Denmark)

1215 the Magna Carta was adopted in England.
1752 Benjamin Franklin first showed the relationship between lightning
     and electricity (and damn near killed himself).
1775 George Washington was made commander-in-chief of the Conti-
     nental Army.
1836 Arkansas was admitted to the Union.
1844 Charles Goodyear patented vulcanized rubber.
1846 the Oregon Treaty between the United States and Great Britain
     was concluded.

1858 Eli W. Blake patented a stone crusher.
1859 Joseph C. Hutchison performed the first mastoid operation.
1867 John Stough Bobbs performed the first gallstone operation.
1869 John W. and Isaiah S. Hyatt patented celluloid.
1904 the General Slocum, an excursion steamer, burned in the East
      River, resulting in the loss of 1,030 lives.
1909 Benjamin F. Shibe patented the cork center baseball.
1944 U.S. troops landed on Saipan.
1962 John Pirovano caught a 149 pound wahoo in the Bahamas.

The following people were born on June 15:

William "Peek-A-Boo" Veach in 1863.
Erik H. Erikson in 1902.
Everett "Pid" Purdy in 1904.
Morris K. Udall in 1922.
Waylon Jennings in 1937.
Harry Nilsson in 1941.

June 16   Bloomsday (Dublin, Ireland)
                                    Soweto Day

1686 B.C., Hammurabi the Great, emperor of Babylon, died after
      a prosperous forty-two year reign.
1871 the Ancient Arabic Order of Nobles of the Mystic Shrine was
      established in New York City.
1922 Henry A. Berliner demonstrated a helicopter for a gathering
      of representatives of the U.S. Bureau of Aeronautics.
1932 the Lausanne Conference opened.
1933 the United States' Consumers' Counsel was authorized.
1933 the Federal Deposit Insurance Corporation was created.
1933 the Industrial Recovery Act was enacted.
1955 armed revolt broke out in Argentina against the regime of Presi-
      dent Juan Peron.
1961 the United States agreed to increase its military manpower
      in South Vietnam.
1963 Valentina Tereshkova became the first woman in space.

The following people were born on June 16:

Geronimo in 1829.
Stan Laurel in 1890.
Jack Albertson in 1910.

June 17   Bunker Hill Day (Massachusetts)
                                         Federal Republic of Germany's
                                           National Day
                                         German Unity Day (Federal Re-
                                           public of Germany)
                                         Icelandic Republic Day

1775 the Battle of Bunker Hill was fought.
1789 the French National Assembly met for the first time.
1836 the North American Academy of the Homeopathic Healing
     Art was chartered in Allentown, Pennsylvania.
1856 the Republican Party held its first national convention in Phila-
     delphia.
1863 the first U.S. accident insurance company was chartered.
1867 in Glasgow, Scotland, Joseph Lister became the first surgeon
     to perform surgery under antiseptic conditions.
1876 Crazy Horse and General George Crook engaged in a battle
     on the banks of the Rosebud River.
1894 a poliomyelitis epidemic broke out in Rutland, Vermont.
1928 Wilmer Stultz, Louis Gordon and Amelia Earhart took off from
     Trepassy, Newfoundland bound for Burry Port, Wales.
1930 Herbert Hoover signed the Smoot-Hawley Tariff which helped
     to worsen the world depression.
1942 an American expeditionary force landed in Africa.
1942 "Suspense" premiered on CBS radio.
1950 Dr. Richard H. Lawler performed the first kidney transplant.
1963 the U.S. Supreme Court ruled that school prayer is unconstitu-
     tional.
1972 five men were arrested for burglarizing the Watergate office
     complex.

The following people were born on June 17:

Elbridge Gerry in 1744.
Sir William Crookes in 1832.
Igor Stravinsky in 1882.
Ralph Bellamy in 1904.
John Hersey in 1914.
Dean Martin in 1917.
James Brown in 1928.
Barry Manilow in 1946.

June 18   Egypt Evacuation Day

6195 B.C., the neolithic period began in Anatolia.
1778 the British evacuated Philadelphia.
1812 the War of 1812 started when the United States declared war
     on Great Britain.

1815 the Battle of Waterloo ended Napoleon's power in France.
1861 the first fly casting tournament was held in Utica, New York.
1885 the New York Library Club was formed.
1898 a half mile long amusement pier was opened to the public in Atlantic City.
1922 a Kurdish insurrection began in Iraq which was not suppressed until four years later.
1936 the Union Party was organized.
1950 Mayo, Yukon Territories, registered a temperature of 35° C.
1971 Paul M. Dilley caught a two pound, two ounce green sunfish in Missouri.

The following people were born on June 18:

E.G. Marshall in 1910.
Lou Brock in 1939.
Paul McCartney in 1942.

June 19   Artigas Day (Uruguay)
                               Emancipation Day (Texas)
                               Juneteenth
                               Midsummer Eve (Finland, Sweden)
                               Righting Day (Algeria)
                               Rizal's Birthday (Philippines)

1846 the first official baseball game was played. The New York Nine defeated the New York Knickerbockers twenty-three to one.
1849 C. Austin patented the melodeon.
1885 the United States received the Statue of Liberty from France.
1893 Lizzie Borden was acquitted of the brutal murder of her father and stepmother.
1912 the Progressive Party of the United States was organized.
1934 the Federal Communications Commission was created.
1939 Atlanta, Georgia banned pinball machines.
1953 Julius and Ethel Rosenberg were executed for treason.
1961 Kuwait gained its independence.
1963 Valentina Tereshkova, the first woman in space, returned to earth after three days in orbit.
1964 the United States Senate passed the Civil Rights Bill.
1970 Maurice E. Ball caught a four and a half pound redear sunfish in Virginia.

The following people were born on June 19:

James I in 1566.
Blaise Pascal in 1623.
Guy Lombardo in 1902.
Lou Gehrig in 1903.

June 20   Argentine Flag's Day
                               Midsummer Day (Finland, Sweden)
                               West Virginia Day

1726 the Beverly, Yorkshire municipal fire brigade was founded.
1756 Nawab of Bengal captured Calcutta and imprisoned the Britons
     who were there.
1782 "E Pluribus Unum" was adopted by the United States as its motto.
1789 the French National Assembly took the "Oath of the Tennis
     Court."
1793 Eli Whitney applied for a patent on his cotton gin.
1837 William IV died and Victoria became queen of England.
1863 West Virginia was admitted to the Union.
1898 the Spanish on the island of Guam surrendered to the U.S. Navy.
1907 the Army War College opened in Washington, D.C.
1930 Bobby Jones won the British Open at Hoylake, England.
1933 the U.S. Labor Advisory Board was organized.
1948 Ed Sullivan's "Toast of the Town" was first telecast.
1960 Senegal and the Sudanese Republic formed the Mali Federation.
1960 Floyd Patterson knocked out Ingemar Johansson and became
     the first boxer to regain the heavyweight title.
1978 Stephen Schwenk caught a fifty-one pound crevalle jack in Flor-
     ida.

The following people were born on June 20:

Lloyd A. Hall in 1894.
Lillian Hellman in 1905.
Errol Flynn in 1909.
Chet Atkins and Audie Murphy in 1924.
Anne Murray in 1947.

June 21   New Hampshire Ratification Day
                               Pya Martyrs' Day (Togo)
                               Summer Solstice

the sun enters the house of Cancer.
2310 B.C., the last marker in the Ring of Brogar in the Orkney Islands
     was erected at the completion of the first annual observational
     cycle at that site.
2183 B.C., the first large scale Druid ceremonies were held at Stone-
     henge.
1788 New Hampshire ratified the constitution of the United States.
1834 Cyrus H. McCormick patented a practical reaper.
1869 the Massachusetts Health Board was organized.
1876 a gorilla landed in Liverpool.
1933 the barge steamer Vicksburg arrived in Chicago with the first
     cargo barges from New Orleans.

1934 the United States National Mediation Board was approved.
1943 a race riot in Detroit left thirty-four people dead and 700 injured.
1948 Chakravarti Rajagopalachari became governor-general of India.
1948 Columbia Records introduced the LP record album.
1964 Peter Simons caught a 149 pound amberjack in Bermuda.

The following people were born on June 21:

Daniel D. Tompkins in 1774.
Arnold Gesell in 1880.
Jean Paul Sartre in 1905.
"Steady" Eddie Lopat in 1918.
Maureen Stapleton in 1925.

June 22   Corrective Move (People's Demo-
                                         cratic Republic of Yemen)
                                     Morat Battle Commemoration
                                         (Switzerland)
                                     Teachers' Day (El Salvador)

1476 the Battle at Murten took place.
1535 John Fisher was beheaded at the order of King Henry VIII.
1815 Napoleon abdicated again and was banished to St. Helena.
1832 John I. Howe patented a pin making machine.
1841 Adrien Delacambre and J.H. Young patented a typesetting machine.
1868 Arkansas was readmitted to the Union.
1894 the world's first recorded auto race was held from Paris to Rouen.
1914 Alice Gertrude Bryant and Florence W. Duckering became the
     first women members of the American College of Surgeons.
1940 France surrendered to Germany.
1941 Finland attacked the U.S.S.R. in collaboration with Germany.
1943 Allied forces landed in New Guinea.
1959 Eddie Lubanski rolled two 300 games in a row.
1966 U.S. planes began bombing N. Vietnam on orders from Washington.
1970 David R. White caught a forty-two pound, two ounce rainbow
     trout in Alaska.
1970 the voting age in the United States was lowered to eighteen.

The following people were born on June 22:

Julian Huxley in 1887.
Carl Hubbell in 1903.
Karl Malden in 1913.
Kris Kristofferson in 1936.
Todd Rundgren in 1948.

June 23   Discovery Day (Newfoundland)
Guru Padma Sambhava's Birthday
(Bhutan)
Luxembourg's National Holiday
(The Grand Duke's Birthday)

1501 Pedro Cabral arrived in Lisbon with a fleet of ships loaded with
spices from India.
1771 Jose Candido Exposito became the first matador in history
to be killed in a bullfight.
1784 the first American balloon flight was made.
1868 Christopher L. Sholes patented a practical typewriter.
1887 the Babies Hospital of the City of New York was chartered.
1888 Frederick Douglass' name was put in for the nomination for
president at the Republican convention.
1938 Marineland, in St. Augustine, Florida, was formally opened.
1947 the United States Congress over-rode President Truman's veto
and the Taft-Hartley Bill became law.
1954 Overton, Nevada registered a temperature of 122° F.
1956 Gamal Abdel Nasser was elected president of Egypt.
1976 Lewis W. Lomerson caught a ten pound, five ounce white catfish
in New Jersey.
1981 the Pawtucket-Rochester baseball game that began on April
18th, and had to be suspended on the 19th, was completed
after 33 innings, Pawtucket 3, Rochester 2.

The following people were born on June 23:

Alfred Kinsey in 1894.
June Carter in 1929.
Wilma Rudolph in 1940.

June 24   Battle of Carabobo (Venezuela)
Countryman's Day (Peru)
Day of the Fish (Zaire)
Feast of St. John the Baptist
Feriado Municipal Angra (Azores)
St. Jean Day (Quebec)
Thailand's National Day

2946 B.C., the bronze age began in Armenia.
1314 the Battle of Bannockburn secured Scotland's independence.
1340 the English defeated the French in the naval battle of Sluys
on the North Sea.
1497 John Cabot's expedition reached Cape Breton Island.
1647 Margaret Brent, "America's first feminist," demanded a voice
and vote in the Maryland colonial assembly.

1650 Charles II landed in Scotland and was proclaimed king.
1675 King Philip's War began at Swansea, Massachusetts.
1898 the first battle of the Spanish-American War was fought at Las Guasimas, Cuba.
1940 German armies reached their furthest advance line in France.
1947 flying saucers were reported in the area of Mount Ranier in Washington.
1952 Eddie Arcaro won his 3,000th horse race.
1963 Zanzibar became self governing.
1977 Howard C. Rider caught a ninety-three pound chinook salmon in Alaska.

The following people were born on June 24:

Ambrose Bierce in 1842.
Jack Dempsey in 1895.
Phil Harris in 1906.

June 25   Mozambique Independence Day
                                     Virginia Ratification Day

511,210 B.C., the first true Homo sapiens were born near Lake Tanganyika.
1530 the Augsburg Confession was presented at the Diet of Augsburg.
1788 Virginia ratified the constitution of the United States.
1798 the United States passed an immigration act requiring the recording of pertinent information upon arrival of all immigrants.
1844 President John Tyler married Julia Gardiner in New York City and became the first president to get married while in office.
1868 Alabama, Florida, Louisiana, North Carolina and South Carolina were readmitted to the Union.
1876 the Battle of the Little Big Horn was fought.
1946 a Northrop XB35 "flying wing" type bomber made its initial flight.
1950 North Korean troops invaded South Korea.
1951 CBS broadcast the first commercial color TV program.
1961 Frank Budd set the new world record for the 100 yard dash at nine and two tenths seconds.
1975 Mozambique became an independent nation.

The following people were born on June 25:

Lord Louis Mountbatten in 1900.
George Orwell in 1903.
Peter Lind Hayes in 1915.
Carly Simon in 1945.

June 26   Madagascar Independence Day
                                   Somali Republic Independence of
                                   the Northern Region

1498 the toothbrush was invented in China.
1721 Dr. Zabdiel Boylston began administering smallpox vaccinations
      in Boston.
1797 Charles Newbold patented the cast iron plow.
1847 James Nasmyth patented the steam pile driver.
1870 the Atlantic City Boardwalk was completed.
1911 John J. McDermott won the U.S. Open golf tournament.
1917 U.S. troops landed at St. Nazaire, France.
1919 the New York Daily News published its first issue.
1933 the Consumer's Advisory Board was organized.
1945 fifty nations signed the United Nations Charter in San Francisco.
1959 ceremonies marked the formal opening of the St. Lawrence
      Seaway.
1960 the Malagasy Republic achieved independence.
1964 Joseph Kasavubu dismissed Cyrille Adoula and recalled Moise
      Tshombe from exile.

The following people were born on June 26:

Abner Doubleday in 1819.
William Kelvin in 1824.
Pearl Buck in 1892.
Peter Lorre in 1904.
Mildred "Babe" Didrickson in 1914.
Billy Davis, Jr. in 1940.

June 27   Djibouti Independence Feast Day

1652 New Amsterdam imposed a speed limit specifying that it would
      be illegal for traffic within the city to proceed at a gallop.
1776 Thomas Hickey was executed after being found guilty of treason-
      ous plotting against George Washington.
1884 Larry Corcoran pitched his third no-hitter.
1915 Fort Yukon, Alaska registered a temperature of 100° F.
1916 Hussein ibn-Ali proclaimed the establishment of an Arab state
      in the Hejaz.
1917 Greece declared war on Austria, Bulgaria, Germany and Turkey.
1934 the Federal Savings and Loan Insurance Corporation was created.
1950 Truman ordered U.S. troops to Korea and the Korean War got
      into full swing.
1950 the United States sent thirty-five military advisors to South
      Vietnam.
1954 the first atomic power station began producing electricity in
      Obninsk, U.S.S.R.

1960 chlorophyll "a" was synthesized by Robert B. Woodward.
1973 Richard Nixon's memo, proposing the use of "available federal machinery to screw our political enemies," was made public by John Dean.
1977 the Republic of Djibouti became an independent nation.

The following people were born on June 27:

Paul Lawrence Dunbar in 1872.
Helen Keller in 1880.
Bob Keeshan in 1927.
Anna Moffo in 1934.

June 28   Shab-e-Barat (Bangladesh)

1832 the first case of cholera in the New York City epidemic was reported. By the end of the epidemic, 2,251 had died.
1884 the American Derby horse race in Chicago was won by Modesty with Isaac Murphy up.
1892 St. George, Utah registered a temperature of 116° F.
1894 congress declared Labor Day to be a national holiday.
1914 the event that led to the first World War took place when Gavrilo Princip of Serbia assassinated Archduke Ferdinand of Austria-Hungary.
1919 the Treaty of Versailles was signed finalizing the end of World War I.
1919 under the Treaty of Versailles, Poland became recognized as an independent nation.
1929 Irene McFarland became the first woman member of the Caterpillar Club.
1948 Yugoslavia was expelled from Cominform.
1954 Camden, South Carolina registered a temperature of 111° F.
1956 Polish workers began rioting in Poznan.
1956 the nuclear reactor at the Illinois Institute of Technology began operating.

The following people were born on June 28:

King Henry VIII in 1491.
Peter Paul Rubens in 1577.
John Wesley in 1703.
Jean-Jacques Rousseau in 1712.
John Dillinger in 1902.
Ashley Montagu in 1905.

June 29   Feast of SS. Peter and Paul
                                        The Seychelles Independence Day

1317 movable type was first used in the printing of The Family Sayings
      of Confucius.
1456 Pope Calixtus III issued a papal bull against Haley's Comet.
1810 the first U.S. missionary society, the American Board of Commis-
      sioners for Foreign Missions, was organized at Bradford, Massa-
      chusetts.
1858 the Treaties of Tientsin opened eleven more Chinese ports to
      foreigners, and legalized the trafficking of opium.
1929 the first high speed jet wind tunnel in the United States was
      completed at Langley Field.
1931 Monticello, Florida registered a temperature of 109° F.
1934 Zaro Agha died in Istanbul at the age of 164.
1952 the Oriskany became the first aircraft carrier to round Cape
      Horn.
1956 the United States' war orphans education law was enacted.
1956 Charles Dumas became the first person to high jump over seven
      feet.
1976 The Seychelles became an independent nation.

The following people were born on June 29:

Sir Henry M. Stanley in 1841.
William J. Mayo in 1861.
Nelson Eddy in 1901.
Paul H. "Dizzy" Trout in 1915.
Harmon Killebrew in 1936.

June 30   Guatemalan Army Day (Anniversary
                                        of the Revolution of 1871)
                                        Mongolian Constitution Day
                                        Zaire Independence Day

220,945,663 B.C., the mesozoic era began.
1520 the Aztecs rebelled against Spanish domination and drove Cortés
      from Tenochtitlan who suffered heavy losses in the process.
1831 Thaddeus Fairbanks patented the platform scale.
1838 Philos Blake, Eli W. Blake and John A. Blake patented the caster.
1859 Emile Blondin crossed over Niagara Falls on a tight rope.
1870 Ada H. Kepley became the first American woman to graduate
      from law school.
1886 the United States Forest Service was organized.
1898 U.S. troops arrived in the Philippines.
1899 Charles C. Murphy rode a bicycle at over sixty miles per hour.

1906 the Pure Food and Drug Act was passed.
1908 an unexplained explosion (which may have resulted from an Apollo object or asteroid colliding with the earth), as powerful as a hydrogen bomb, shook Siberia. Some witnesses reported seeing a mushroom cloud.
1921 President Warren G. Harding signed a peace resolution with Germany.
1934 at the direction of Adolf Hitler, "the Great Blood Purge" was conducted in the German Reichstag.
1936 Margaret Mitchell's Gone with the Wind was published.
1936 the U.S. government approved a forty hour work week.
1956 a TWA Super-Constellation and a United DC-7 collided over the Grand Canyon and 128 people died.
1960 the Belgian Congo became the Republic of the Congo (Leopold-ville), which country later became the nation of Zaire.

The following people were born on June 30:

William Wheeler in 1819.
Davy Jones in 1880.
Lena Horne and Bernard "Buddy" Rich in 1917.
Pompeyo Antonio "Yo-Yo" Davalillo in 1931.
Harry Blackstone, Jr. in 1934.

July

The first day of July marks the following commemorations:

Burundi Independence Day
Caribbean Day (first Monday in Guyana)
Day of Freedom (Suriname)
Dominion Day (Canada)
First Republic Day (Ghana)
Half-year Holiday (Hong Kong)
Rwanda Independence Day
Somali Republic Day
Take Over Day (Nauru)
Territory Day (British Virgin Islands)
Zambia Heroes Day (first Monday)
Zambia Unity Day (first Thursday)

Let's Play Tennis Week (begins the first Saturday)

Hitch Hiking Month
Hot Dog Month
National July Belongs to Blueberries Month

July 1

1690 England crushed Irish resistance in the Battle of Boyne.
1823 the United Provinces of Central America declared their sovereignty.
1847 the first adhesive U.S. postage stamps went on sale.
1863 the Battle of Gettysburg began.
1867 Canadian confederation went into effect.
1871 British Columbia joined the Dominion of Canada.
1873 Prince Edward Island joined the Dominion of Canada.
1896 the British assumed control of Pelak, Selangor, Negri, Sembilan and Pahang.
1898 Teddy Roosevelt's Rough Riders charged up San Juan Hill.
1910 a completely automatic bread bakery opened in Chicago.
1913 the Massachusetts minimum wage law took effect.

1916 the Battle of the Somme began. It lasted until November 18, and was the first battle in which the British used tanks.
1934 Arthur W. Fuchs took the first entire-body X-ray photograph.
1946 technicians and scientists from the United States tested an atomic bomb at Bikini Atoll.
1952 Riverside Hospital, a narcotic sanatorium for minors, received its first patients.
1952 "The Guiding Light" debuted on CBS television.
1960 British Somaliland and Somalia were united and proclaimed to be an independent republic.
1962 Burundi and Rwanda became independent nations.

The following people were born on July 1:

Gottfried Wilhelm Leibniz in 1646.
John Clarkson in 1861.
Cletus "Boots" Poffenberger in 1915.
Olivia de Havilland in 1916.
Leslie Caron in 1931.
Karen Black in 1942.

July 2   Feast of the Visitation of the
                              Blessed Virgin Mary
                              Yar Nyidhok or Summer Solstice
                              (Bhutan)

 622 A.D., according to historical information, Mohammed's Hegira took place.
1644 Oliver Cromwell defeated English Royalist troops at the Battle of Marston Moor.
1776 New Jersey granted women suffrage.
1777 Vermont formally abolished slavery.
1798 Napoleon captured Alexandria.
1849 Garibaldi retreated from Rome.
1850 Benjamin J. Lane patented a gas mask with a self contained breathing apparatus.
1860 the National Rifle Association held its first long-range rifle shooting tournament at Wimbledon.
1881 President James A. Garfield was shot. The wound led to his death on September 19.
1890 the Sherman Anti-Trust Law was enacted.
1931 the first outdoor night polo game was played.
1937 Amelia Earhart and Fred Noonan were lost in the Pacific.
1941 "The Adventures of the Thin Man" debuted on NBC radio.
1955 ABC television broadcast the first "Lawrence Welk Show."
1961 Ernest Hemingway committed suicide.
1964 President Lyndon B. Johnson signed the Civil Rights Act.

The following people were born on July 2:

Hermann Hesse in 1877.
Olav V of Denmark in 1903.
Thurgood Marshall in 1908.
Dan Rowan in 1922.
Medgar Evers and Patrice Lumumba in 1925.
Cheryl Ladd in 1951.

July 3   Idaho Admission Day

1608 Samuel de Champlain founded the settlement of Quebec.
1754 the first battle of the French and Indian War was fought at Fort Necessity, Pennsylvania.
1890 Idaho was admitted to the Union.
1898 Joshua Slocum sailed into the harbor at Fairhaven, Massachusetts and became the first person to complete a solo circumnavigation of the earth.
1912 "Rube" Marquard set a major league pitching record with nineteen consecutive pitching victories.
1929 foam rubber was developed at the Dunlop Latex Development Laboratories.
1939 "Blondie" was broadcast for the first time by CBS.
1952 Dr. Forest Dodrill performed a surgical procedure in which he substituted a "Michigan Heart" in place of a patient's lower left ventricle.
1954 "Babe" Didrickson, although suffering from cancer, came out of the hospital to win the U.S. Women's Open golf tournament by twelve strokes.
1956 the hurricane research vessel Crawford went into service.
1962 independence was proclaimed for the nation of Algeria.

The following people were born on July 3:

Samuel de Champlain in 1567.
George M. Cohan in 1878.
Franz Kafka in 1883.
Anthony "Bunny" Brief in 1892.
Jose "Coco" Laboy in 1939.

July 4   Combatant's Day (Yugoslavia)
                                        Philippine-American Friendship
                                           Day
                                        Trades Holiday (Scotland)

United States Independence Day

1054 Earth observers first sighted the supernova, the remnants of which we now know as the Crab Nebula.
1631 the first employment agency was established: the Bureau d'Adresse in Paris.
1776 the United States Declaration of Independence was adopted.
1817 construction was started on the Erie Canal.
1828 Miguel, who had staged a coup d'etat in May and abolished the constitution, proclaimed himself King of Portugal.
1848 the cornerstone for the George Washington Monument in Washington, D.C. was laid.
1874 the Socialist Labor Party of North America was formed.
1883 "Buffalo Bill" Cody introduced his "Wild West Show."
1894 the Republic of Hawaii was established.
1898 the French steamer La Bourgogne collided with the British sailing ship Cromartyshire off Nova Scotia, causing 560 lives to be lost.
1911 Nashua, New Hampshire registered a temperature of 106° F.
1911 Vernon, Vermont registered a temperature of 105° F.
1928 Jean Lussier went over Niagara Falls in a rubber ball.
1946 the Philippine Islands were formally granted independence by the United States.
1976 Charlie Smith celebrated his 134th birthday.

The following people were born on July 4:

Nathaniel Hawthorne in 1804.
Giuseppe Garibaldi in 1807.
Stephen Foster in 1826.
Calvin Coolidge in 1872.
Louis Armstrong in 1900.
Meyer Lansky in 1902.
Mitch Miller in 1911.
Ann Landers in 1918.
Neil Simon in 1927.
Gina Lollabrigida in 1928.
Bill Withers in 1938.
Emerson Boozer in 1943.

July 5   Algeria Independence Day
                                  Cape Verde Independence Day
                                  Sempach Battle Commemoration
                                      (first Monday after July 4 in
                                      Switzerland)
                                  Venezuela Independence Anniversary

1811 Venezuela was proclaimed independent from Spain as part of the nation of Colombia under Simón Bolívar.
1884 the United States Navigation Bureau was authorized.
1908 "Young Turks" in Macedonia rebelled against the Ottoman Empire.
1916 Adelina and Augusta Van Buren left New York City bound for San Diego, California on a motorcycle.
1932 Antonio de Salazar became the Portuguese prime minister and assumed powers making him a virtual dictator.
1935 the National Labor Relations Act was approved.
1936 Gannvalley, South Dakota registered a temperature of 120° F.
1937 Medicine Lake, Montana registered a temperature of 117° F.
1937 Midale and Yellow Grass, Saskatchewan registered temperatures of 45° C.
1946 the bikini swimsuit was introduced in Paris.
1948 the British National Health Services Acts took effect.
1950 Kenneth Shadrick became the first U.S. soldier to be killed in the Korean War.
1951 Dr. William Shockley announced the invention of the junction transistor.
1975 the Cape Verde Islands became independent.
1975 H.B. Reasor caught a 703 pound hammerhead shark in Florida.

The following people were born on July 5:

Admiral David G. Farragut in 1801.
Phineas Taylor Barnum in 1810.
Georges Pompidou in 1911.

July 6   Caricom Day (St. Vincent)
                                     Cayman Islands' Constitution Day
                                     Commemoration Day of the Burning
                                        of the John Hus (Czechoslovakia)
                                     Family Day (Lesotho)
                                     Kadooment Day (Barbados)
                                     Malawian Republic Day

1415 John Hus was burned at the stake for heresy.
1798 the Alien Discriminatory Law was enacted.
1858 Lyman R. Blake patented a shoe manufacturing machine.
1903 George Wyman arrived in New York City having travelled from San Francisco on a motorcycle.
1917 Lawrence of Arabia and Arab forces captured Aqaba.
1919 the Mongolian People's Revolutionary Government was formed under Soviet auspices.
1928 Lights of New York premiered as the first "all-talking" feature motion picture film.

1933 "Babe" Ruth hit a home run in the first baseball all-star game
     which ended American League 5; National League 2.
1936 Moorhead, Minnesota registered a temperature of 114° F.
1936 Steele, North Dakota registered a temperature of 121° F.
1964 Nyasaland became the independent state of Malawi.
1967 civil war erupted between Biafra and Nigeria.
1971 Louis Armstrong died peacefully in New York.
1975 the Comoros became independent.

The following people were born on July 6:

John Paul Jones in 1747.
Andrei Gromyko in 1909.
Merv Griffin in 1925.
Della Reese in 1932.
Sylvester Stallone in 1946.

July 7   People of Serbia Uprising Day
                                      (Yugoslavia)
                                    Saba Saba Day (Tanzania)
                                    Solomon Islands Independence Day
                                    Tanabata or Star Festival (Japan)

1535 Thomas More was beheaded at the order of King Henry VIII.
1863 the first wartime U.S. draft call was made.
1891 King Jaja of Opodo died in exile at Santa Cruz de Tenerife.
1898 the United States annexed Hawaii.
1905 Parker, Arizona registered a temperature of 127° F.
1937 various Chinese political factions that had been engaged in
     civil war, joined forces to resist the invasion that signaled
     the beginning of the Japanese-Chinese War.
1941 the United States occupied Iceland.
1947 "You Are There" originated under the title "CBS Is There."
1948 the first regular commissioned U.S. Navy women officers were
     sworn in.
1949 "Dragnet" debuted on NBC radio with Jack Webb.
1953 J. Robert Oppenheimer, former Los Alamos Labs director, was
     barred from access to classified material as a result of having
     been an object of the investigations of Senator Joseph McCar-
     thy.
1964 W.B. Whaley caught a fifty-eight pound channel catfish in South
     Carolina.
1978 the Solomon Islands became an independent nation.
1981 Stephen Ptacek piloted a solar powered aircraft across the
     English Channel.

The following people were born on July 7:

Gustav Mahler in 1860.
Marc Chagall in 1887.
Leroy Robert "Satchel" Paige in 1906.
Ringo Starr (Richard Starkey) in 1940.

July 8   Feast of St. Grimbald

72,446,218 B.C., the first extended family grouping of hominids developed on the plains of Africa.
1497 Vasco da Gama sailed from Portugal for India via the Cape cf Good Hope.
1524 Giovanni da Verazzano reported to the King of France that his crew had succeeded in kidnapping an Indian child from America.
1709 Peter the Great won a decisive victory in the Battle of Poltava.
1835 the Liberty Bell in Philadelphia cracked.
1853 Commodore Matthew C. Perry's first attempt to open Japan to foreign commerce turned out to be counter-productive.
1856 Charles E. Barnes patented a machine gun.
1862 Theodore R. Timby patented the revolving gun turret.
1889 John L. Sullivan defeated Jake Kilrain in seventy-five rounds in the last bare knuckles championship prize fight.
1892 the American Psychological Association was organized.
1896 William Jennings Bryan delivered his "Cross of Gold" speech.
1907 the first "Ziegfeld Follies" opened.
1909 the first night-time, regularly scheduled (minor) league baseball game was played at Grand Rapids, Michigan.
1911 Nan Jane Aspinwall completed her solo transcontinental horseback ride.

The following people were born on July 8:

Count Ferdinand von Zeppelin in 1838.
John D. Rockefeller in 1839.
Alfred Binet in 1857.
Clyde Barfoot in 1891.
George Romney in 1907.
Nelson Rockefeller in 1908.
Billy Eckstine in 1914.
Roone Arledge in 1931.
Jerry Vale in 1932.
Steve Lawrence in 1935.

July 9   Argentina Declaration of Indepen-
                                              dence
                                              Aviation Day (U.S.S.R.)
                                              Feast of the Martyrs of China II
                                              Feast of the Martyrs of Orange

1386 the Swiss defeated Leopold III of Swabia in the Battle of Sempach.
1778 the Articles of Confederation were formally engrossed.
1808 Samuel Parker patented a leather splitting machine.
1816 the United Provinces (Argentina) proclaimed independence.
1847 New Hampshire passed a ten-hour working day law.
1872 John F. Blondel patented the doughnut cutter.
1878 Henry Tibbe patented a corn cob pipe for commercial manufac-
      ture.
1893 Daniel H. Williams made the first successful surgical suture
      of the heart.
1910 Walter R. Brookins flew a Wright biplane to an altitude of 6,234
      feet.
1916 the Deutschland, the first cargo submarine to cross the Atlantic,
      arrived in Baltimore.
1924 Rotha Lintorn-Orman founded the Fascist Party in Britain.
1943 U.S. and British forces invaded Sicily.
1955 David L. Hayes caught an eleven pound, fifteen ounce small
      mouth bass in Kentucky.
1957 the discovery of nobelium was announced.

The following people were born on July 9:

Elias Howe in 1819.
Daniel Guggenheim in 1856.
Franz Boas in 1858.
Paul Brown in 1908.
Ed Ames in 1927.
Richard Roundtree in 1942.
O.J. Simpson in 1947.

July 10   Bahamas Independence Day
                                              Día del Bibliotecario (Chile)
                                              Wyoming Admission Day

1543 Henry VIII married his sixth wife, Catherine Parr.
1866 Edson P. Clark patented the pencil.
1877 David Kahnweiler patented the cork life preserver.
1890 Wyoming was admitted to the Union.
1890 the government of the State of Wyoming continued its policy
      of suffrage for women which had originally been granted
      while under territory status.
1911 North Bridgton, Maine registered a temperature of 105° F.

1913 Greenland Ranch, California registered a temperature of 134° F.
1918 the Russian Socialist Federated Soviet Republics adopted a written constitution.
1936 Cumberland and Frederick, Maryland registered a temperature of 109° F.
1936 Runyon, New Jersey registered a temperature of 110° F.
1936 Phoenixville, Pennsylvania registered a temperature of 111° F.
1936 Martinsburg, West Virginia registered a temperature of 112° F.
1940 German aircraft attacked targets in England and the Battle of Britain began.
1951 negotiations for a cease fire in Korea began.
1952 Frank J. Ledwein caught a fifty-five pound, five ounce carp in Minnesota.
1960 Belgian troops returned to the Republic of the Congo (Leopold-ville) with orders to restore order.
1962 Telstar went into orbit.
1973 the Bahamas attained independence within the British Common-wealth.

The following people were born on July 10:

John Calvin in 1509.
George M. Dallas in 1792.
James Abbott McNeill Whistler in 1834.
Mary McLeod Bethune in 1875.
Jack Spratt in 1888.
David Brinkley in 1920.
Arthur Ashe in 1943.
Arlo Guthrie in 1947.

July 11   Mongolian People's Revolution Day
                                             National Cheer up the Sad and
                                                   Lonely Day
                                             Uganda's National Holiday

1302 Flemish forces defeated a contingent of French knights in the Battle of the Golden Spurs.
1613 Michael Romanov was crowned the Czar, thereby founding the Romanov dynasty which ruled Russia till 1917.
1798 Congress created that branch of the military which is now known as the United States Marine Corps.
1804 Vice-President of the United States Aaron Burr killed Alexander Hamilton, former United States Secretary of the Treasury, in a duel at Weehawken, New Jersey.
1888 Bennett, Colorado registered a temperature of 118° F.
1916 the Federal Aid Road Act was passed providing grant-in-aid to states for road construction.
1921 Mongolia became an independent nation.

1923 a railroad signal system of continuous cab signals was installed
      at Sunbury, Pennsylvania.
1934 Franklin D. Roosevelt sailed through the Panama Canal.
1955 the United States Air Force Academy established temporary
      headquarters in Denver, Colorado.
1960 Moise Tshombe announced the secession of Katanga from the
      Republic of the Congo (Leopoldville).

The following people were born on July 11:

Robert the Bruce in 1274.
John Quincy Adams in 1767.
Yul Brynner in 1920.
Leon Spinks in 1953.

July 12   São Tomé and Príncipe Independence
                                    Day

1536 Erasmus died of dysentery in Basel.
1613 Giovan-francesco Sagredo of Venice began recording daily tem-
      perature readings.
1774 the American Declaration of Independence was read in the
      First Presbyterian Church in Carlisle, Pennsylvania.
1844 Captain J.N. Taylor first demonstrated the fog horn.
1859 William Goodale patented a paper bag manufacturing machine.
1882 the Atlantic City, New Jersey ocean pier was completed.
1886 Medicine Hat, Alberta registered a temperature of 42° C.
1900 Basin, Wyoming registered a temperature of 114° F.
1909 the income tax (sixteenth) amendment to the Constitution was
      proposed to the states.
1918 Haiti declared war on Germany.
1930 Bobby Jones won the U.S. Open golf tournament at Minneapolis,
      Minnesota.
1933 the United States established minimum wage legislation requiring
      a pay rate of forty cents per hour.
1936 Emerson, Manitoba registered a temperature of 44° C.
1946 "The Adventures of Sam Spade" was first heard on CBS radio.
1974 John Ehrlichman was found guilty of conspiring to violate the
      civil rights of Dr. Lewis Fielding.
1975 São Tomé and Príncipe became an independent nation.
1979 Kiribati became an independent nation.
1984 Walter Mondale announced that Geraldine Ferraro was his choice
      for the Democratic Party's Vice-Presidential candidate.

The following people were born on July 12:

Gaius Julius Caesar in 100 B.C.
Josiah Wedgwood in 1730.

Henry David Thoreau in 1817.
George Eastman in 1854.
Amedeo Modigliani in 1884.
Buckminster Fuller and Oscar Hammerstein II in 1895.
Milton Berle in 1908.
Andrew Wyeth in 1917.
Van Cliburn in 1934.
Bill Cosby in 1937.

July 13   Bon Festival or Feast of Lanterns
                                               (Japan)
                                               Nathan Bedford Forrest's Birthday
                                               (Tennessee)
                                               People of Montenegro Uprising
                                               Day (Yugoslavia)
                                               La Retraite aux Flambeau or The
                                               Night Watch (France)

1793 Jean-Paul Marat was assassinated in his bath.
1812 New York City enacted a pawnbroking ordinance.
1836 the United States adopted a numbering system for its patents.
     Patent number one was granted to John Ruggles for locomotive
     traction wheels.
1863 the New York City draft riots began.
1875 David Brown patented a cash carrier system.
1878 the Treaty of Berlin gave Serbia, Montenegro and Romania
     their independence.
1880 Stephen D. Field patented an electric street car.
1908 women competed in modern Olympic events for the first time.
1931 the Danatbank failed and all the rest of the banks in Germany
     followed.
1936 Mio, Michigan registered a temperature of 112° F.
1936 Fort Frances, Ontario registered a temperature of 42° C.
1936 Wisconsin Dells, Wisconsin registered a temperature of 114°
     F.
1938 Howard Hughes and four assistants completed a round-the-world
     airplane flight.

The following people were born on July 13:

Stanislao Cannizzaro in 1826.
Stan Coveleski in 1889.
Clarence "Footsie" Blair in 1903.
Dave Garroway in 1913.

July 14   Bastille Day or Fête National
                                          (France and French Guiana)
                                          Community Day (Madagascar)
                                          Founders' Day or Cecil Rhodes
                                              Day (Rhodesia)
                                          Iraqi 14th of July Revolution
                                          Monaco's National Holiday
                                          Tahiti's National Holiday

1789 the French Revolution began with the storming of the Bastille.
1820 Dr. Frank James climbed Pikes Peak.
1832 Opium was exempted from U.S. narcotic import tariffs.
1868 Alvin J. Fellows patented the tape measure.
1881 Sheriff Pat Garrett shot and killed Billy "The Kid" Bonner.
1891 John T. Smith patented corkboard.
1911 Harry N. Atwood landed an airplane on the White House lawn.
1914 Robert Goddard patented the liquid fuel rocket.
1921 Sacco and Vanzetti were convicted of robbery and murder.
1933 all political parties in Germany other than the Nazi Party were
       declared illegal.
1934 Orogrande, New Mexico registered a temperature of 116° F.
1936 Collegeville, Indiana registered a temperature of 116° F.
1937 Mikhail Gromov and two companions flew from Moscow to River-
       side, California non-stop via the North Pole.
1951 Citation became the first race horse to win over $1,000,000.
1954 Warsaw and Union, Missouri registered temperatures of 118°
       F.
1954 East St. Louis, Missouri registered a temperature of 117° F.
1958 a coup in Iraq overthrew the monarchy and eventually led to
       the establishment of a republic.
1965 "Mariner IV" flew by Mars, sending photographs back to Earth.
1974 Robert L. Stintsman caught a thirteen pound lake whitefish
       in the Northwest Territories.

The following people were born on July 14:

Isaac Bashevis Singer in 1904.
Terry Thomas in 1911.
Woody Guthrie in 1912.
Gerald R. Ford in 1913.
Ingmar Bergman in 1918.
Lawrence "Crash" Davis in 1919.
Dale Robertson in 1923.
Polly Bergen in 1930.
Robert Bourassa in 1933.

July 15   Sultan's Birthday (Brunei)
                               St. Swithin's Day

 622 A.D., according to tradition, Mohammed's Hegira took place.
1099 the first Crusade ended when Godfrey of Bouillon and Raymond
     took Jerusalem from the Egyptians.
1410 a Polish/Lithuanian army defeated the Teutonic Knights in
     the Battle of Tannenberg.
1783 the steamboat Pyroscaphe made its trial run.
1869 Hippolyte Mege-Mouries patented margarine in France.
1870 Manitoba joined the Canadian Dominion.
1870 Georgia was readmitted to the Union.
1876 G.W. Bradley pitched the first major league baseball no-hitter
     for the St. Louis Reds.
1904 a Shinsu Sect Buddhist temple was established in Los Angeles.
1918 the Second Battle of Marne began.
1922 Gene Sarazen won the U.S. Open golf tournament.
1922 the first public exhibit of a duck-billed platypus was opened.
1940 the University of Illinois Betatron first went into operation.
1954 Balcony Falls, Virginia registered a temperature of 110° F.
1958 U.S. Marines landed in Lebanon.

The following people were born on July 15:

Rembrandt van Rijn in 1606.
Eugene "Bubbles" Hargrave in 1892.
Linda Ronstadt in 1946.

July 16   Asalaha Bucha Day (Thailand)
                               First Sermon of Lord Buddha
                                 (Bhutan)
                               La Paz Day (Bolivia)
                               National Blueberry Festival
                               Yugoslav People's Army Tank
                                 Units Day

1212 the Battle of Las Navas de Tolosa established the rule of Christian
     kings on the throne of Spain.
'1810 Chileans deposed the Spanish governor and proclaimed their
     independence.
1867 Joseph Monier of Paris obtained a patent for reinforced concrete.
1867 D.R. Averill patented ready-mixed paint.
1912 Bradley A. Fiske patented the airborne torpedo.
1918 Czar Nicholas II, Czarina Alexandra, and their family were
     executed by the Bolsheviks.
1935 Oklahoma City installed the first parking meters.
1941 Joe DiMaggio hit safely in his 56th consecutive game to set
     the major league record.

1945 the first atomic bomb in history was detonated in the New Mexico
     desert. The light from its one-mile diameter fireball was
     visible 400 miles away. It created a mushroom cloud that
     rose to an altitude of 40,000 feet and left a crater a quarter
     of a mile in diameter. The surface of the desert was fused
     into glass for a distance of 800 yards around the blast site.
1949 the Nationalist Chinese began to withdraw to Formosa.
1973 the United States Senate began investigating "allegations" of
     "secret" bombings of Cambodia by the U.S. in 1969 and 1970.

The following people were born on July 16:

Roald Amundsen in 1872.
Barbara Stanwyck in 1906.
Ginger Rogers and Sonny Tufts in 1911.
Margaret Court in 1942.

July 17   Iraqi 17th of July Revolution
                                     Korean Constitution Day
                                     Muñoz-Rivera's Birthday (Puerto
                                     Rico)

1429 Joan of Arc restored the French crown to Charles VII.
1734 the Ursulines opened an infirmary which served the people of
     New Orleans without restrictions of any kind.
1775 American forces lay siege to Boston.
1790 Thomas Saint patented a sewing machine.
1821 Spain formally ceded Florida to the United States.
1839 Isaac Babbitt patented Britannia Ware.
1841 Punch published its first issue.
1850 the first astrophotograph was taken at Harvard College Observa-
     tory.
1862 federal law authorized the acceptance of "persons of African
     descent, for the purpose of constructing intrenchments or
     performing camp competent," into the armed forces of the
     Union.
1867 Harvard established its School of Dental Medicine.
1938 Douglas Corrigan took off from New York bound for California.
     The next day, he landed in Dublin, Ireland.
1941 Chinock Cove, Lillooet and Lytton, British Columbia registered
     temperatures of 44° C.
1944 Iceland was established as an independent republic.
1945 the Allies opened their conference at Potsdam.
1955 residents of Arco, Idaho became the first Americans to profit
     from nuclear power generation in a successful Atomic Energy
     Commission experiment.
1955 Disneyland opened.

The following people were born on July 17:

John Clapp in 1851.
Erle Stanley Gardner in 1889.
James Cagney in 1899.
Art Linkletter in 1912.
Lou Boudreau and Phyllis Diller in 1917.
Donald Sutherland in 1934.
Diahann Carroll in 1935.
Phoebe Snow in 1952.

July 18   Antibigot Day
                                   National Uprising Day (Spain)
                                   Uruguayan Constitution Day

1627 two French missionaries reported finding an oil spring near
     Cuba, New York.
1846 the Salina and Central Square Plank Road Company completed
     a plank road between Syracuse and Central Square.
1853 trains began running over the first North American international
     railroad between Portland, Maine and Montreal, Quebec.
1908 the City of Cleveland banned fireworks.
1914 the United States Army Air Corps was created.
1927 Ty Cobb got his 4,000th base hit.
1936 civil war broke out in Spain.
1940 the Vought-Sikorsky VS-300 helicopter successfully made a
     fifteen minute flight.
1941 Fort Smith, Northwest Territories registered a temperature
     cf 39° C.
1944 Japanese prime minister Tojo resigned.
1969 Mary Jo Kopechne died at Chappaquiddick Island, Massachusetts.

The following people were born on July 18:

Robert Hooke in 1635.
Samuel Colt in 1814.
S.I. Hayakawa in 1906.
Richard "Red" Skelton in 1913.
Dion (Di Mucci) in 1939.

July 19   Burma Martyrs' Day
                                   Feast of St. Vincent de Paul
                                   Laos Independence Day
                                   Sandanista Revolution Anniversary
                                      (Nicaragua)

1784 Manasseh Cutler set out from Ipswich, Massachusetts on a botanic scientific expedition. He subsequently classified 350 species of plants.
1848 Lucretia Mott and Elizabeth Cady Stanton assembled the first women's rights convention at Seneca Falls, New York.
1848 Amelia Jenks Bloomer introduced bloomers at the women's rights convention in Seneca Falls, New York.
1881 Sitting Bull surrendered at Fort Buford in North Dakota.
1909 Neal Ball completed an unassisted triple play for the Cleveland Naps in a game against the Boston Red Sox, and when he came up to bat in that same inning, hit a home run.
1915 the Washington Senators stole eight bases in the first inning.
1918 Honduras declared war on Germany.
1928 King Fuad took control of Egypt and assumed dictatorial powers.
1939 Fiberglass sutures were first used by Dr. Roy P. Scholz.
1944 the Battle of the Philippine Sea began.
1949 the Kingdom of Laos became a constitutional monarchy.
1950 William H. Hastie became the first black Circuit Court of Appeals judge.
1957 an air-to-air missile with an atomic warhead was test fired at Yucca Flat, Nevada.

The following people were born on July 19:

Edgar Degas in 1834.
Lizzie Borden in 1860.
Charles H. Mayo in 1865.
George McGovern in 1922.
George Hamilton IV in 1937.
Vikki Carr in 1942.

July 20   Colombia Independence Day
                                   Moon Day

1808 Napoleon's forces occupied Madrid.
1859 spectators were charged admission (fifty cents) to see a baseball game for the first time.
1917 the Pact of Corfu established the nation of Yugoslavia.
1923 General Francisco "Pancho" Villa was assassinated.
1930 Washington, D.C. registered a temperature of 106° F.
1934 Keokuk, Iowa registered a temperature of 118° F.
1935 "Gang Busters" was first heard on NBC radio.
1944 U.S. troops landed on Guam and the Marianas Islands.
1944 a plot to assassinate Adolf Hitler was foiled.
1950 a Senate subcommittee dismissed Senator Joseph McCarthy's claims that the State Department was "infested" with Communists.

1954 Cambodian independence was confirmed by the Geneva Conference.
1960 the George Washington became the first submerged submarine
to fire a Polaris missile.
1969 Neil Armstrong and Edwin Aldrin became the first men to land
on the moon.
1976 "Viking I" landed successfully on Mars.

The following people were born on July 20:

Petrarch in 1304.
Theda Bara in 1890.
Heinie Manush in 1901.
Sir Edmund Hillary in 1919.
Diana Rigg and Natalie Wood in 1938.
Mickey Stanley in 1942.
Carlos Santana in 1947.

July 21   Belgium's National Day
                                     Bolivia Martyrs' Day
                                     Death Anniversary of His Late
                                       Majesty Jigme Dorji Wangchuck
                                       (Bhutan)
                                     Guam Liberation Day
                                     Shoelcher Day (French West
                                       Indies)

1774 the Treaty of Kuchuk Kainarji ended the first Russo-Turkish
War.
1798 Napoleon occupied Cairo following the Battle of the Pyramids.
1861 the First Battle of Bull Run was fought.
1866 Mahlon Loomis transmitted and received the first man made
radio signals.
1880 an accidental explosion of compressed air during construction
of the Hudson River tunnel caused the deaths of twenty work-
men.
1917 Alexander Kerensky became the Soviet Prime Minister.
1918 the German submarine U-156, fired on a tugboat towing four
barges of stone off Nauset Bluffs, Orleans, Massachusetts.
Some of the shots landed in Meeting House Pond.
1919 John Boettner became the first member of the Caterpillar Club.
1930 Millsboro, Delaware registered a temperature of 110° F.
1930 the Veterans Administration was created.
1934 Gallipolis, Ohio registered a temperature of 113° F.
1946 the carrier U.S.S. Franklin D. Roosevelt made the first recovery
of a jet aircraft.
1954 the Geneva Accords divided Vietnam at the seventeenth parallel.

The following people were born on July 21:

Johnny Evers in 1881.
Ernest Hemingway in 1899.
Marshall McLuhan in 1911.
Isaac Stern in 1920.
Don Knotts in 1924.
Cat Stevens (Steven D. Georgiou) in 1948.

July 22   Dornach Battle Commemoration
                                (Switzerland)
                                Feast of St. Mary Magdalene
                                Hurricane Supplication Day (fourth
                                    Monday in the Virgin Islands)
                                King's Birthday (Swaziland)
                                People of Slovenia Uprising Day
                                    (Yugoslavia)
                                Poland Liberation Day

1796 General Moses Cleaveland founded Cleveland, Ohio.
1896 the Silverites held their first national convention in St. Louis.
1917 Siam declared war on Germany and Austria.
1926 Waterbury, Connecticut registered a temperature of 105° F.
1926 Troy, New York registered a temperature of 108° F.
1932 the Federal Home Loan Bank Act was approved.
1933 Caterina Jarboro became the first black operatic prima donna
      when she performed in Aida with the Chicago Opera Company.
1933 Wiley Post landed in New York after his round-the-world flight
      via the Arctic Circle.
1934 John Dillinger was supposedly killed by F.B.I. agents although
      Jay Robert Nash makes a case for the theory that it was
      another hood who was killed and that Dillinger remained
      alive and free.
1939 Jane Bolin became the first black woman judge when she was
      appointed to the New York City Court of Domestic Relations.
1952 Puerto Rico became the first independent commonwealth nation
      of the United States.

The following people were born on July 22:

Friedrich Bessel in 1784.
Gregor Mendel in 1822.
Jesse Haines and Karl Menninger in 1893.
Stephen Vincent Benét and Alexander Calder in 1898.
Jason Robards, Jr. in 1922.
Orson Bean in 1928.
Bobby Sherman in 1945.

July 23   Egyptian Revolution Anniversary
Feast of St. Apollinaris
Soma No Umaoi or Wild Horse
Chasing (Japan)

the sun enters the house of Leo.

8897 B.C., Khali-Ar of Syria successfully fired a new clay compound and became the first person to intentionally produce pottery.

1715 the Little Brewster Island (Massachusetts) lighthouse was authorized. It subsequently became the first lighthouse in North America.

1829 William Austin Burt patented his typewriter.

1841 the Bunker Hill Monument was completed.

1886 Steve Brodie claimed to have jumped off the Brooklyn Bridge and lived.

1904 the ice cream cone was introduced in St. Louis, Missouri.

1920 British East Africa was renamed Kenya.

1937 Drs. Abraham White, Hubert R. Catchpole and Cyril N.H. Long announced the isolation of the pituitary hormone.

1952 King Farouk of Egypt was forced to abdicate by Egypt's Society of Free Officers.

1955 Donald Campbell piloted his speedboat, Bluebird, to an unprecedented speed of over 200 m.p.h.

1970 Sultan Said bin Taimur of Muscat and Oman was overthrown by his son who changed the nation's name to the Sultanate of Oman.

1976 Jorge Potier caught a 465 pound porbeagle shark in England.

The following people were born on July 23:

Haile Selassie I in 1891.
Harold "Pee Wee" Reese in 1918.
Don Drysdale in 1936.

July 24   Simón Bolívar's Birthday (Latin America)
Pioneer Day (Utah)

1701 Antoine de la Mothe Cadillac founded Detroit.

1824 the first public opinion poll was conducted in regard to the U.S. presidential election in Wilmington, Delaware.

1844 Henry R. Worthington patented the independent single direct-acting steam power pump.

1847 Richard M. Hoe patented the rotary type printing press.

1847 having fled persecution in Illinois, Mormons (the Church of the Latter Day Saints) first reached the Great Salt Lake.

1866 Tennessee was readmitted to the Union.

1925 John T. Scopes was found guilty of teaching evolution in Tennes-
    see.
1936 Alton, Kansas registered a temperature of 121° F.
1936 Minden, Nebraska registered a temperature of 118° F.
1948 Soviet occupation troops imposed the Berlin Blockade.
1967 Charles de Gaulle made his "Vive Quebec Libre" speech in Mon-
    treal which led to his being asked to leave Canada earlier
    than he had planned.
1974 the United States Supreme Court told President Richard Nixon
    to surrender his "Watergate" tape recordings to special prosecu-
    tor Leon Jaworski.

The following people were born on July 24:

Simón Bolívar in 1783.
Tommy McCarthy in 1864.
Amelia Earhart in 1898.
Bella Abzug in 1920.
Ruth Buzzi in 1936.

July 25   Annexation of Guanacaste (Costa
                                        Rica)
                                     Feast of St. James the Greater
                                     Puerto Rican Constitution Day
                                     Tunisian Republic Day

116,920 B.C., the third interglacial period ended and the Early Würm
    period of glaciation began.
1261 a Greek army under Alexius Stragopulos reconquered Constantin-
    ople.
1603 James VI of Scotland was crowned James I of England.
1854 Walter Hunt patented the paper collar.
1871 Wilhelm Schneider patented the carrousel.
1871 Seth Wheeler patented perforated wrapping paper.
1907 Japan seized control of the Korean government, which led at
    once to an unsuccessful war of independence.
1918 Annette A. Adams began serving as the first woman U.S. district
    attorney.
1919 New York to Chicago airplane service began.
1934 a Nazi coup took place in Vienna.
1938 Prince Francis Joseph II assumed the role of monarch of the
    sovereign state of Liechtenstein.
1943 Benito Mussolini was forced to resign and his Fascist Party
    was dissolved.
1943 the U.S.S. Leonard Roy Harmon was launched.
1946 the United States conducted an underwater atomic bomb test
    at Bikini Atoll.

1957 Tunisia became a republic.
1959 a hovercraft crossed the English Channel for the first time.
1975 Caesar Paul, an Algonquin Indian, believed to be Canada's oldest
     person, died at Pembroke, Ontario at the age of 112.

The following people were born on July 25:

Thomas Eakins in 1844.
Walter Brennan in 1894.
Eric Hoffer in 1902.
Carroll "Whitey" Lockman in 1926.

July 26   Celebration of the 26th of July
                                   Movement or National Rebellion
                                   Day (Cuba)
                                   Liberia Independence Day
                                   Maldives Independence Day
                                   New York Ratification Day

1775 United States postal service began.
1788 New York ratified the constitution of the United States.
1845 Sir John Franklin, who was looking for the Northwest Passage,
     was last seen entering Lancaster Sound.
1847 the Republic of Liberia was established.
1880 the New York Steam Corporation was formed.
1943 Tishmoningo, Oklahoma registered a temperature of 120° F.
1947 the United States National Security Council was established.
1947 "The Abe Burrows Show" premiered on the radio.
1956 the Andrea Doria and the Stockholm collided off Nantucket
     Island resulting in fifty-one deaths.
1956 Gamal Abdel Nasser announced Egypt's nationalization of the
     Suez Canal.
1965 the Maldives became an independent nation.

The following people were born on July 26:

George Clinton in 1739.
George Catlin in 1796.
George Bernard Shaw in 1856.
Carl Jung in 1875.
Aldous Huxley in 1894.
Gracie Allen in 1905.
Vivian Vance in 1912.
Stanley Kubrick in 1928.
Mick Jagger in 1944.
Vitas Gerulaitis in 1954.

July 27   Jose Barbosa's Birthday (Puerto
                                         Rico)
                                         People of Croatia, Bosnia, Herzego-
                                         vina Uprising Day (Yugoslavia)

587 B.C., the Babylonians captured Jerusalem and razed its temple.
1784 the Courrier de l'Amérique began publishing in Philadelphia,
     Pennsylvania.
1789 the U.S. State Department created the Department of Foreign
     Affairs.
1794 Maximilien Robespierre was executed and the Reign of Terror
     ended.
1869 the American Philological Association held its first convention.
1918 the Socony 200 was launched: the first barge to be made of
     concrete.
1933 the U.S. Central Statistical Board was created.
1933 Walter H. McGee was sentenced to death for kidnapping the
     daughter of the city manager of Kansas City.
1953 the Korean Armistice was signed at Panmunjom.
1963 Bobby Bare's recording of "Detroit City" hit the top twenty
     chart.

The following people were born on July 27:

Alexandre Dumas in 1824.
Joe Tinker in 1880.
Leo Durocher in 1906.
Keenan Wynn in 1916.
Norman Lear in 1922.
Bobby Gentry in 1944.
Peggy Fleming in 1948.
Maureen McGovern in 1949.

July 28   Peru Independence Day

1586 Sir Thomas Harriot introduced potatoes to Europe.
1777 Vermont did away with property and wealth prerequisites for
     voting eligibility.
1821 Peru proclaimed its independence.
1868 the civil rights (fourteenth) amendment was ratified.
1875 Joseph E. Borden pitched the first nine-inning no-hitter for
     the Philadelphia Athletics of the National Association of
     Professional Baseball Players.
1914 World War I began when Austria declared war on Serbia.
1915 U.S. troops landed in Haiti.
1930 Greensburg, Kentucky registered a temperature of 114° F.
1934 Orofino, Idaho registered a temperature of 118° F.

1942 Linden A. Thatcher patented a coin operated mailbox.
1945 an Army B-25 crashed into the Empire State Building killing fourteen.
1965 Namu arrived in Seattle.
1976 an earthquake that registered 8.2 on the Richter Scale killed 655,235 in Tangshan, China.

The following people were born on July 28:

Joe E. Brown in 1892.
Rudy Vallee in 1901.
Jacqueline Kennedy Onassis in 1929.
Peter Duchin in 1937.
Sally Struthers in 1948.
Vida Blue in 1949.

July 29   Feast of St. Olav
                                     Olsok Eve (Norway)
                                     Umutomboko Ceremony (Zambia)

981 A.D., Eric the Red reached Greenland.
1773 the Schoenbrunn, Ohio schoolhouse was completed. It was the first European school to be built west of the Allegheny Mts.
1794 the Bethel African Methodist-Episcopal Church opened in Philadelphia.
1868 the fourteenth amendment went into effect.
1870 America's first asphalt pavement was laid in Newark, New Jersey.
1899 America's first motocycle race was held at Manhattan Beach, New York.
1914 the Cape Cod Canal opened to traffic.
1930 Holly Springs, Mississippi registered a temperature of 115° F.
1933 the cornerstone was laid for the federal narcotic sanitorium in Lexington, Kentucky.
1935 the F.B.I. police training school was initiated in Washington, D.C.
1958 the National Aeronautics and Space Administration was authorized.

The following people were born on July 29:

Alexis de Tocqueville in 1805.
Benito Mussolini in 1883.
Dag Hammarskjöld in 1905.
R.B. "Ted" Lindsay in 1925.

July 30   Vanuata Independence Day

1619 the House of Burgesses first met in Jamestown, Virginia.
1844 the New York Yacht Club was organized.
1850 Gail Borden patented a meat biscuit: add hot water and you had instant soup.
1898 Kellogg's invented corn flakes.
1898 the Scientific American carried the first advertisement for an automobile, advertising the product of the Winton Motor Car Company.
1933 the U.S. National Planning Board was organized.
1946 a captured German V-2 rocket was fired from the White Sands Proving Ground. It attained an altitude of 104 miles.
1954 Townsend Miller caught a fifty pound, five ounce longnose gar in Texas.
1956 "In God We Trust" was established as an official motto for the United States.
1975 Jimmy Hoffa disappeared.

The following people were born on July 30:

Henry Ford in 1863.
Charles "Casey" Stengel in 1891.
Henry Moore in 1898.
Harold Ballard in 1903.
Peter Bogdanovich in 1939.
Paul Anka in 1941.
Arnold Schwarzenegger in 1947.

July 31   Congolese Revolution Day
                                         Feast of St. Ignatius Loyola

1498 Columbus sighted the island of Trinidad on his third voyage to the new world.
1588 English naval forces engaged the Spanish Armada in the English Channel.
1849 Benjamin Chambers patented the breech loading cannon.
1876 the Coast Guard officers' training school was established at New Bedford, Massachusetts.
1897 Frank Samuelson and George Harvo arrived at St. Mary's in the Scilly Islands after having rowed across the Atlantic Ocean.
1916 Dr. W.J. Cook's catch of a fourteen and one half pound brook trout in Ontario went into the record books.
1917 the Third Battle of Ypres began.
1919 Bela Kun's Hungarian Soviet Republic ended when Romanian troops invaded Hungary.
1919 Germany adopted the Weimar constitution.

1957 Fred L. Bright caught a five pound, three ounce white crappie
     in Mississippi.

The following people were born on July 31:

William C. Quantrill in 1837.
Art Nehf in 1892.
Whitney M. Young, Jr. in 1921.
Kenny Burrell in 1931.
Evonne Goolagong in 1951.

August

The first day of August marks the following commemorations:

Anniversary of the Angola People's Armed Forces
Benín Independence Day
Civic Holiday (Canada)
Colorado Day
Commemoration of the Pact of 1291 (Switzerland)
Emancipation Day (Bahamas, Grenada)
Hari Raya Puasa (Singapore)
National Non-Parenthood Day
Parents' Day (Zaire)
Ramazan Bayram (Cyprus)
Switzerland's National Day

> International Humor Exchange Week (the first through the seventh)
> National Clown Week
> National Smile Week (begins the first Monday)
> Turtles International Awareness Week (begins the first Sunday)
>
> Good Nutrition Month
> Sandwich Month

August 1

1007 Snorro Karlsefni was born, the first European child to be born in America.
1498 on his third voyage to the new world, Columbus found his way to South America, coming upon it near the mouth of the Orinoco.
1774 Joseph Priestly first isolated the element oxygen which he called dephlogisticated air.
1798 the Battle of the Nile took place and Napoleon became cut off from France.

1874 Othmar Zeidler announced in Strasbourg his discovery of Dichloro-Diphenyl-Trichloro-ethane (DDT).
1876 Colorado was admitted to the Union.
1893 Henry D. Perky and William H. Ford patented a machine for making shredded wheat biscuits for a breakfast cereal.
1894 war broke out between China and Japan over the control of Korea.
1907 Edward Blakely caught a twenty-two and a half pound landlocked salmon in Maine.
1909 on a voyage from Sydney to London, the British steamer Waratah vanished with 300 lives presumed lost.
1914 Germany declared war on Russia.
1939 Louis F. Fieser first synthesized vitamin K.
1946 the United States established the Atomic Energy Commission.
1951 Kani Evans caught an eight pound black bullhead in New York.
1954 Ernest Theoharis caught an eleven and a half pound sunapee trout in New Hampshire.
1960 the republic of Dahomey became the independent nation of Benin.
1960 Mabry Harper caught a twenty-five pound walleye in Texas.
1974 Peter Gulgin caught a three pound rock bass in Ontario.

The following people were born on August 1:

Jean Baptiste Lamarck in 1744.
William Clark in 1770.
Francis Scott Key in 1780.
Herman Melville in 1819.
Charles C. Spaulding in 1874.
Elmer "Slim" Love in 1893.
Jack Kramer in 1921.
Dom DeLuise in 1933.

August 2   St. Elias Day or Ilinden (Macedonia)
                                       Friendship Day
                                       Id Alfeter (Ethiopia)

1776 delegates at the Continental Congress signed the official Declaration of Independence of the United States of America.
1819 Charles Guille became the first person to make a parachute jump from a balloon.
1869 Gustav Simon performed the first surgical removal of a kidney.
1876 "Wild Bill" Hickok was shot and killed by Jack McCall.
1934 Adolf Hitler became the German Reichsführer.
1939 Albert Einstein informed President Franklin Roosevelt that the manufacture of an atomic bomb was feasible.

1943 the PT-109, under the command of Lt. John F. Kennedy was
     rammed and sunk by the Japanese destroyer Amigiri.
1964 the U.S.S. Maddox was fired on by North Vietnamese PT boats
     in retaliation for six months of clandestine U.S. attacks on
     North Vietnam. The event became known as "the Tonkin Gulf
     Incident."
1975 New Bedford and Chester, Massachusetts registered temperatures
     of 107° F.
1975 Providence, Rhode Island registered a temperature of 104°
     F.
1977 Edward Rudnicki caught a seventeen pound tiger trout in Lake
     Michigan.

The following people were born on August 2:

"Still" Bill Hill in 1874.
James Baldwin and Carroll O'Connor in 1924.

August 3   Autumn Holiday (Ireland)
                                    Habib Bourguiba's Birthday (Tunisia)
                                    Caricom Day (Barbados)
                                    Discovery Day (Trinidad and Tobago)
                                    Equatorial Guinea Army Forces Day
                                    Farmer's Day (Zambia)
                                    Feast of Our Savior (El Salvador)
                                    Niger Independence Day
                                    Summer Holiday (Scotland)

315,827,619 B.C., at the site of what is now Charleston, South Carolina,
     the first successful flight by an animal was made when a
     winged insect flew a total of 43.2 centimeters.
1571 the Turks finally succeeded in taking Famagusta.
1861 John LaMountain made the first balloon ascent from a ship;
     the S.S. Fanny.
1880 the American Canoe Association was formed.
1914 Germany declared war on France and German troops entered
     Belgium.
1921 aerial crop dusting was carried out for the first time over a
     field in Ohio.
1958 the submarine U.S.S. Nautilus crossed under the North Pole
     ice cap.
1958 James R. Sordelet reenlisted in the U.S. Navy at the North
     Pole.
1960 the republic of Niger became independent.

1976 the "Viking I" beamed an image of the Martian landscape back
       to Earth.

The following people were born on August 3:

F. Sylvester "Silver" Flint in 1855.
Ernie Pyle in 1900.
Leon Uris in 1924.
Tony Bennett in 1926.

August 4   Lizzie Borden Liberation Day
                                    Coast Guard Day
                                    Cook Islands Constitution Day
                                    Malawian Public Holiday

1227 Genghis Khan died while on an expedition in northwest China.
1874 the Chautauqua Organization was formed.
1914 Great Britain declared war on Germany.
1914 Germany declared war on Belgium.
1917 Liberia declared war on Germany.
1940 Italian troops invaded British Somaliland.
1952 the first transatlantic helicopter flight was completed.
1953 A.C. Glassell, Jr. caught a 1,560 pound black marlin in Peru.
1956 Wilhelm Herz became the first person to ride a motorcycle
       in excess of 200 m.p.h.
1957 Juan Manuel Fangio, in the last race of his career, won the
       German Grand Prix and acquired his fifth consecutive world
       driving championship.

The following people were born on August 4:

Percy Shelley in 1792.
Sir Harry Lauder in 1870.
Maurice Richard in 1921.

August 5   Feast of the Dedication of the
                                    Basilica of St. Mary Major
                                    Iranian Constitution Day

1861 the federal income tax law was enacted.
1864 rallying his forces in the Battle of Mobile Bay, Admiral David

Glasgow Farragut commanded: "Damn the torpedoes, full speed ahead!"

1914 Montenegro declared war on Austria.

1914 America's first electric traffic lights were installed in Cleveland, Ohio.

1926 Don Juan, starring John Barrymore, the first motion picture with sound, made its premier.

1929 the Graf Zeppelin made its first flight to America.

1948 Charles S. Reed caught an eleven pound golden trout in Wyoming.

1960 the Republic of Upper Volta became an independent nation.

1961 Ice Harbor Dam, Washington registered a temperature of 118° F.

1963 the United States of America, the Union of Soviet Socialist Republics and the United Kingdom signed a nuclear test ban treaty.

1964 rebels in the Republic of the Congo (Leopoldville) captured Stanleyville and made it their capital.

The following people were born on August 5:

Conrad Aiken in 1889.
Neil Armstrong in 1930.

August 6   Bolivia Independence Day
                                      Judge Crater Day
                                      Founding of Bogota (Colombia)
                                      Hiroshima Day
                                      Jamaica Independence Day
                                      Peace Festival (Japan)

930 A.D., Northern Europe's first democracy and the world's oldest continuing surviving parliament, the Icelandic Althing, met at Thingvellir.

1727 an Ursuline convent was established in New Orleans.

1825 Bolivia became an independent nation.

1890 William Kemmler became the first person to be executed in an electric chair.

1890 Cy Young began a baseball career in which he would eventually win a total of 511 games as a pitcher.

1896 France proclaimed Madagascar to be a colonial possession.

1912 the Progressive Party held its convention in Chicago.

1914 Austria declared war on Russia.

1914 Serbia declared war on Germany.

1926 Gertrude Ederle swam the English Channel.

1945 a United States Air Force bomber, nicknamed the "Enola Gay," dropped an atomic bomb at 8:15 a.m. on Hiroshima, Japan.

1962 Jamaica became an independent nation.
1977 Larry Martin caught a 1,282 pound Atlantic blue marlin in the
      Virgin Islands.

The following people were born on August 6:

Alfred Tennyson in 1809.
Dutch Schultz (Arthur Flegenheimer) in 1902.
Clara Bow in 1905.
Lucille Ball in 1911.
Robert Mitchum in 1917.
Andy Warhol in 1927.

August 7   Colombian National Holiday (Battle
                                         of Boyaca)
                                       First Day of Crayfish Season (Swe-
                                         den)
                                       Ivory Coast Independence Day

1679 Le Griffon set out on its maiden voyage on Lake Erie.
1825 the locomotive was invented by George Stephenson.
1847 George Page patented the disk type plow.
1869 the first photograph of a total solar eclipse was made in Mt.
      Pleasant, Iowa.
1888 Theophilus Van Kannel patented the revolving door.
1888 Jack the Ripper killed the first of his six victims.
1897 the Navy submarine U.S.S. Plunger was launched.
1914 Spain declared itself neutral.
1942 U.S. troops landed on Guadalcanal.
1960 the republic of the Ivory Coast declared its independence.
1964 President Lyndon Johnson's Tonkin Gulf Resolution passed through
      Congress and the United States officially entered into the
      Vietnamese civil war.
1980 Ms. Lorena Zisk drove from Providence, Rhode Island to Virginia
      to visit a friend.

The following people were born on August 7:

Bill McKechnie in 1886.
Louis S.B. Leakey in 1903.
Ralph Bunche in 1904.
Stan Freberg in 1926.
Everett "Rocky" Bridges in 1927.
Don Larsen in 1929.
B.J. Thomas in 1942.
Lana Cantrell in 1943.

August 8   Fox Hill Day (second Tuesday in
                                          the Bahamas)
                                          International Character Day
                                          Jamat-ul-Wida (Bangladesh)
                                          Upper Volta Independence Day
                                          Victory Day (second Monday in
                                          Rhode Island)
                                          Youth Day (second Monday in Zam-
                                          bia)

   332 B.C., the Phoenician city of Tyre fell to Alexander the Great.
1540 Henry VIII married his fifth wife, Catherine Howard.
1576 Tycho Brahe's observatory in Uraniborg, Denmark was inaugu-
       rated.
1588 remnants of the Spanish Armada retreated from the English
       Navy in defeat.
1865 Samuel P. Calthorp patented a streamlined railroad train.
1876 Thomas Edison patented the mimeograph machine.
1899 Albert T. Marshall patented a household refrigerating machine.
1899 a hurricane caused the deaths of 3,369 Puerto Ricans.
1914 Montenegro declared war on Germany.
1945 the Soviet Union declared war on Japan.
1963 the Great Train Robbery took place in Cheddington, England.
1970 Larry Daunis caught a sixty-five pound lake trout in the North-
       west Territories.

The following people were born on August 8:

Rory Calhoun in 1922.
Esther Williams in 1923.
Mel Tillis in 1932.
Dustin Hoffman in 1937.
Connie Stevens in 1938.

August 9   Nagasaki Memorial Moment of
                                          Silence (Japan)
                                          Sanusi Army Day (Libya)
                                          Shab-e-Qadar (Bangladesh)
                                          Singapore's National Day

1607 Thanksgiving Day was celebrated in Phippsburg, Maine.
1829 the "Stourbridge Lion" was tested. Built in Stourbridge, England,
       it was the first railroad locomotive to operate in the U.S.
1848 the Free Soil Party held its convention in Buffalo, New York.
1851 the first significant discovery of Australian gold was made
       at Ballarat, Victoria.
1859 Nathan Ames obtained a patent for an escalator.

1892 Thomas Edison patented a duplex telegraph.
1910 Alva J. Fisher patented a complete, self-contained, electric washing machine.
1916 Lassen Volcanic National Park was established.
1930 Perryville, Tennessee registered a temperature of 113° F.
1936 Jesse Owens won his fourth Olympic gold medal.
1945 at 11:02 a.m., the U.S. exploded a second atomic bomb; this time over Nagasaki, Japan. The United States remains the only nation ever to use a nuclear device as a weapon.
1960 South Kasai province seceded from the Republic of the Congo (Léopoldville).
1965 Singapore became a separate and independent nation.
1969 Sharon Tate and her guests were murdered by the Manson "family."
1974 on the verge of impeachment, President Richard Nixon resigned from his office and Gerald Ford assumed the presidency.

The following people were born on August 9:

Jean Piaget in 1896.
Fred Sanford in 1919.
Bob Cousy in 1928.
Rod Laver in 1938.
David Steinberg in 1942.

August 10   Ecuador Independence Day
                                        Family Day
                                        Herbert Hoover's Birthday Celebra-
                                            tion
                                        Missouri Admission Day

1628 the glory of the Swedish Navy, the Vasa, capsized and sank on its maiden voyage.
1821 Missouri was admitted to the Union.
1846 the Smithsonian Institute was formally established.
1869 O.B. Brown patented a moving picture projector.
1886 Elihu Thomson patented an electric welding process.
1911 the first transcontinental automobile tour group arrived in Los Angeles.
1936 Ozark, Arkansas registered a temperature of 120° F.
1936 Plain Dealing, Louisiana registered a temperature of 114° F.
1938 Pendleton, Oregon registered a temperature of 119° F.
1944 U.S. troops reoccupied Guam.

The following people were born on August 10:

Herbert Hoover in 1874.

Jimmy Dean and Eddie Fisher in 1928.
Ian Anderson in 1948.

August 11   Chad Independence Day
                                 Zimbabwe Heroes Day

8242 B.C., the mesolithic period began in northern France, Denmark
     and Latvia.
 117 A.D., Hadrian became emperor of Rome.
1480 Turkish forces occupied Otranto in southern Italy.
1770 Captain James Cook navigated the Bering Strait.
1863 Cambodia became a French protectorate.
1874 Henry S. Parmelee patented the sprinkler head.
1896 Harvey Hubbell patented an electric light socket with a pull
     chain.
1906 Eugene Lauste of London patented a sound-on-film process.
1914 John Randolph Bray patented the present technique of making
     animated cartoons.
1914 Northwest River, Newfoundland registered a temperature of
     42° C.
1930 the American Lutheran Church was organized.
1943 the Allied powers opened the Quebec Conference.
1943 Benjamin F. White won the Hambletonian for the fourth time.
1960 the Republic of Chad became independent.
1965 virtual insurrection broke out in Watts.
1966 Indonesia and Malaysia officially ended a three year undeclared
     war.

The following people were born on August 11:

Alex Haley in 1921.
Mike Douglas in 1925.
Arlene Dahl in 1927.

August 12   Indian Day (Massachusetts)
                                 King Hussein's Accession (Jordan)
                                 Queen's Birthday (Thailand)

1658 a police force was established in New Amsterdam.
1676 King Philip was killed and "King Philip's War" came to an end.
1851 Isaac M. Singer patented a sewing machine with a rocking (double)
     treadle.
1891 King Jaja's body was returned to Opobo and was received by
     his people with unprecedented wailings.

1898 the United States formally took possession of Hawaii.
1914 France and Great Britain declared war on Austria.
1936 Seymour, Texas registered a temperature of 120° F.
1953 Ann Davidson arrived in Miami after sailing solo across the
     Atlantic Ocean.
1953 the Soviet Union exploded its first hydrogen bomb.
1960 the "Echo I" satellite was launched from Cape Canaveral.
1961 East Germany began construction of the Berlin Wall.
1972 the last U.S. ground troops pulled out of Vietnam.

The following people were born on August 12:

Christy Mathewson in 1880.
Cecil B. DeMille in 1881.
Erwin Schrödinger in 1887.
Ray Schalk in 1892.
Porter Wagoner in 1927.

August 13   Central African Republic Indepen-
                                        dence Day
                                     Show Day (Queensland, Australia)
                                     The Three Glorious Days begin (in
                                        the People's Republic of the
                                        Congo)
                                     Women's Day (Tunisia)

1039 Alhazen, an Arabian physicist, died in Cairo at the age of seventy-
     four.
1521 Hernando Cortés retook Tenochtitlan, imprisoned Cuauhtemoc,
     and soon solidified his control over Mexico.
1587 Manteo became the first native American to be baptized at
     Roanoke, Virginia.
1844 Willamette University opened in Salem, Oregon.
1889 William Gray patented the coin operated telephone.
1898 U.S. forces captured Manila.
1934 "Li'l Abner" made its first appearance as a syndicated comic
     strip.
1955 Glenn T. Simpson caught a seventy-nine and a half pound flathead
     catfish in Indiana.
1960 the Central African Empire proclaimed its independence.
1966 Chairman Mao Tse-tung endorsed the "proletarian cultural revolu-
     tion" of the Red Guards.

The following people were born on August 13:

Annie Oakley in 1860.
Bert Lahr in 1895.

Alfred Hitchcock in 1899.
Ben Hogan in 1912.
Frederick Sanger in 1918.
Neville Brand in 1921.
Wilmer D. "Vinegar Bend" Mizell in 1930.

August 14   Atlantic Charter Day
                                        Liberty Tree Day (Massachusetts)
                                        Pakistan Independence Day
                                        Summer Holiday (San Marino)

  893 A.D., Charles the Simple became emperor of the Western Franks.
1385 the Portuguese defeated the Castilians in the Battle of Aljubar-
     rota.
1811 Paraguay proclaimed its independence from Spain.
1834 England passed an improved poor law.
1912 the United States sent the Marines to Nicaragua because of
     its bad debts.
1917 China declared war on Germany and Austria.
1935 the Social Security Act took effect.
1936 the National Union for Social Justice held a national convention
     in Cleveland.
1945 Japan offered to surrender if Emperor Hirohito would be permit-
     ted to keep his throne.
1947 Pakistan became an independent nation.
1956 the development of the stroboradiograph was announced.
1971 Bahrain regained its independence.

The following people were born on August 14:

Cupid Charles in 1868.
Buddy Greco in 1926.
Dash Crofts in 1940.
David Crosby in 1941.
Mark Fidrych in 1954.

August 15   Congo Independence Day
                                        Discovery Day (third Monday in the
                                           Yukon)
                                        Feast of the Assumption of the Vir-
                                           gin Mary
                                        Founding of Asunción (Paraguay)
                                        Hawaii Admission Day (third Friday)
                                        India Independence Day

Korea Liberation Day
Mothers Day (Costa Rica)

1281 an invading Mongol army was stranded in Japan by a typhoon
     which destroyed their fleet, leaving them to be killed or en-
     slaved.
1294 Kublai Khan died at the age of eighty.
1456 Henry Cremer finished binding Gutenberg's Bible.
1635 a hurricane struck the Plymouth Colony.
1848 M. Waldo Hanchett patented the dental chair.
1863 after widespread native-foreigner friction, a British squadron
     bombarded Kagoshima, convincing the Japanese that expulsion
     of foreigners was impracticable.
1914 the Panama Canal opened to traffic.
1928 Bark Lake, Quebec registered a temperature of 40° C.
1936 the Union Party held its convention in Cleveland.
1944 the U.S. Seventh Army landed in the South of France.
1947 the independence of India was effected.
1948 Syngman Rhee proclaimed the Republic of (South) Korea.
1950 the United States of Indonesia and the Republic of Indonesia
     merged.
1960 the Congo Republic (Brazzaville) became a recognized indepen-
     dent nation.
1961 the Berlin Wall was completed.

The following people were born on August 15:

Napoleon Bonaparte in 1769.
Sir Walter Scott in 1771.
Charlie Comiskey in 1859.
Ethel Barrymore in 1879.
Edna Ferber in 1887.
T.E. Lawrence (of Arabia) in 1888.
Julia Child in 1912.
Phyllis Schlafly in 1924.

August 16   Bennington Battle Day (Vermont)
                                    Cyprus Independence Day
                                    Restoration of the Republic (Do-
                                        minican Republic)

1294 Roger Bacon died at Oxford at the age of eighty.
1777 the British were defeated in the Battle of Bennington.
1780 the Battle of Camden was fought.
1815 David Dodge organized the New York Peace Society.
1898 Edwin Prescott obtained a patent for a roller coaster.
1916 the International Migratory Bird Treaty was signed.

1918 Lothar Witzke was found guilty of spying for Germany and was
     sentenced to death.
1953 the Shah of Iran fled to Iraq.
1960 Captain Joseph W. Kittinger, Jr. free fell for four minutes and
     thirty-eight seconds from an altitude of 85,300 feet.
1960 the independent Republic of Cyprus was established.
1967 Jeanne P. Branson caught a five pound, fifteen ounce grayling
     in the Northwest Territories.
1977 Elvis Presley died.

The following people were born on August 16:

Amos Alonzo Stagg in 1862.
William "Baby Doll" Jacobson in 1890.
George Meany in 1894.
Al Hibbler in 1915.
Fess Parker in 1925.
Ann Blyth in 1928.
Robert Culp and Frank Gifford in 1930.
Eydie Gorme in 1931.

August 17   Anniversary of General San Martín's
                                      Death (Argentina)
                                   Gabon Independence Day
                                   Indonesia Independence Day

10,429 B.C., Daku, of the Kubian tribe of Armenia, became the first
     person to successfully domesticate a goat.
1743 the first elevator in Europe was installed by order of Louis
     XV.
1807 Robert Fulton's steamboat, the Clermont, steamed up the Hudson
     River.
1809 the Disciples of Christ were organized.
1835 Solyman Merrick patented the wrench.
1891 the "People's Bath," a public bath facility with showers, opened
     in New York City.
1915 Charles Franklin Kettering patented the automobile electric
     self-starter.
1938 already the world featherweight and welterweight boxing cham-
     pion, Henry Armstrong won the world lightweight championship
     from Lou Ambers.
1945 the Republic of Indonesia was proclaimed.
1959 a major earthquake literally shook the Rocky Mountains around
     Yellowstone Park.
1960 the Gabon Republic declared its independence.

The following people were born on August 17:

Davey Crockett in 1786.
Marcus Garvey in 1887.
Mae West in 1892.
Maureen O'Hara in 1921.
John W. "Boog" Powell in 1941.

August 18   Feast of St. Helen

 486 B.C., Darius I, emperor of Persia, died after a prosperous thirty-
     five year reign.
1587 Virginia Dare was born at Roanoke Island and became the first
     child of English parents to be born in America.
1840 the American Society of Dental Surgeons was organized.
1913 the Veterans of Foreign Wars was formed in Denver.
1919 the Anti-Cigarette League of America was formed in Chicago.
1922 Gene Sarazen won the Professional Golfers Tournament in Oak-
     mont, Pennsylvania.
1925 Chauve Souris, the first sound-on-film production, was shown
     in London.
1926 the first television picture was a weather map which was telecast
     from Arlington, Virginia to Washington, D.C.
1931 a patent was granted to Henry F. Bosenberg for a new strain
     of climbing rose.
1960 the first commercial oral contraceptive went on the market.
1963 James H. Meredith graduated from the University of Mississippi,
     the first black to earn a degree from this 115 year old institute.

The following people were born on August 18:

Virginia Dare in 1587.
Burleigh Grimes in 1893.
Roman Polanski in 1933.
Roberto Clemente in 1934.
Robert Redford in 1937.

August 19   Day of the Regaining of the Inde-
                                           pendence of Afghanistan
                                        National Aviation Day
                                        President Quezon Day (Philippines)
                                        Uprising of the 28th of Mordad (Iran)
                                        Freedom of Enterprise Week (begins
                                           Sunday of the last full week)

  14 A.D., Caesar Augustus died at the age of eighty-two.

1762 John Montagu IV, Earl of Sandwich, invented the sandwich.
1812 the U.S.S. Constitution engaged and defeated the British frigate Guerriere.
1855 the Y.M.C.A. World Alliance was formed.
1856 Gail Borden obtained a patent for the commercial production cf condensed milk.
1929 "Amos and Andy" debuted on Chicago WMAQ radio.
1935 Rexton, New Brunswick registered a temperature of 39° C.
1935 Collegeville, Nova Scotia registered a temperature of 38° C.
1935 Charlottetown, Prince Edward Island registered a temperature of 37° C.
1957 David G. Simons ascended to an altitude of 101,516 feet in a balloon.
1958 the submarine Triton set out on a submerged circumnavigation of the Earth.
1960 creatures from Earth (two dogs and six mice) survived a flight into space (and back) for the first time aboard Sputnik V.
1976 W.J. Long caught a fifty-six pound bigmouth buffalo in Missouri.

The following people were born on August 19:

Seth Thomas in 1785.
Orville Wright in 1871.
Ogden Nash in 1902.
Willie Shoemaker in 1931.
Jill St. John in 1940.

August 20   Anniversary of the Exile of King
                                 Muhammad V (Morocco)
                                 Hungarian Constitution Day

1680 ten days after the Indian revolt had begun, the Spanish garrison at Santa Fe surrendered to Pueblo and Apache warriors. The following day they evacuated to El Paso.
1887 the American Association of Public Accountants was incorporated.
1910 Jacob E. Fickel became the first aviator to fire a gun from an airplane.
1912 Congress empowered its federal agencies to impose a plant quarantine to exclude harmful pests from the United States.
1920 the first commercial radio station, 8MK (now WWJ, Detroit, Michigan) instituted its first daily scheduled broadcast.
1923 the United States' first dirigible was launched at Lakehurst, New Jersey.
1940 Leon Trotsky was assassinated.
1960 two dogs and six mice were recovered alive after having orbited Earth aboard Sputnik V.
1960 Senegal became an independent, autonomous nation upon its withdrawal from the Mali Federation.

1968 Soviet troops invaded Czechoslovakia.
1968 James D. McAdam, Jr. caught a 563½ pound giant sea bass in California.

The following people were born on August 20:

Jöns Jakob Berzelius in 1779.
Emily Brontë in 1818.
Benjamin Harrison in 1833.
Edgar Guest in 1881.
H.P. Lovecraft in 1890.
Isaac Hayes in 1942.

August 21   Feast of St. Jane Frances de Chantal

1808 the British defeated the French in a battle at Vimeiro in Portugal.
1841 John Hampson patented venetian blinds.
1878 the American Bar Association was organized.
1888 William Seward Burroughs patented his adding machine.
1911 Vicenzo Peruggia stole the "Mona Lisa."
1915 Italy declared war on Turkey.
1944 the Dumbarton Oaks Conference took place.
1959 Hawaii was admitted to the Union.
1968 Jeanne P. Branson caught a twenty-nine pound, eleven ounce Arctic char in the Northwest Territories.
1969 Greg Perez caught a 1,153 pound Pacific blue marlin near Guam.
1975 E. John O'Dell caught a twenty-one pound kawakawa in Hawaii.
1983 exiled Filipino opposition leader Benigno Aquino was assassinated as he stepped from an airplane that had just returned him to Manila.

The following people were born on August 21:

Ledell "Cannonball" Titcomb in 1865.
William "Count" Basie in 1904.
Wilt Chamberlain in 1936.

August 22   Feast of the Immaculate Heart of
                                 Mary

565 A.D., St. Columba recorded sighting the Loch Ness monster which he called a "fearsome beast."
1514 the Ottoman Turks defeated the Persians at Chaldiran.
1670 Hiacoomes, a Massachusetts Indian, became an ordained Christian preacher.

1762 Ann Franklin became the editor of the <u>Newport</u> (Rhode Island) Mercury.
1822 Peter Force patented a wall paper printing press.
1865 William Sheppard patented a liquid form of soap.
1902 Theodore Roosevelt became the first U.S. president to ride in an automobile.
1906 the Victor Talking Machine Company manufactured the first phonograph with a horn enclosed in the cabinet.
1910 Korea was formally annexed by Japan and was renamed Chosen.
1955 Israeli-Egyptian fighting broke out in the Gaza Strip.

The following people were born on August 22:

A. Claude Debussy in 1862.
Urban Shocker in 1890.
Ray Bradbury in 1920.
Carl Yastrzemski in 1939.
Valerie Harper in 1940.

August 23   Romania Liberation Day

the sun enters the house of Virgo.
1237 B.C., Rameses (II) the Great, the pharaoh from whom the flight of the Israelites was made, died after reigning for sixty-seven years.
 884 A.D., Charles the Fat became emperor of the Western Franks.
1305 Sir William Wallace was executed in London.
1516 the Battle of Marjdabik took place.
1609 Galileo demonstrated his spy-glass to the members of the Venetian Senate.
1904 Harry D. Weed patented the automobile tire chain.
1914 Japan declared war on Germany.
1921 Emir Faisal was proclaimed King of Iraq.
1927 Nicola Sacco and Bartolomeo Vanzetti were executed.
1944 German troops in Paris were forced to capitulate.
1944 Romania accepted terms for an armistice.
1958 Chinese artillery bombarded Quemoy.

The following people were born on August 23:

Georges Cuvier in 1769.
Albert E. "Cowboy" Jones in 1874.
Ernie Bushmiller in 1905.
Gene Kelly in 1912.
George Kell in 1922.

August 24   St. Bartholomew's Day
Liberian National Flag Day
Vesuvius Day

79 A.D., Mount Vesuvius erupted and buried Pompeii and Herculan-
eum.
1415 the Portuguese took Ceuta, in Africa, from the Moors.
1572 the St. Bartholomew's Day Massacre in France was carried
out.
1676 Quanpen, an Indian sachem also known as Sowagonish, was found
guilty of participating in King Philip's War by a jury of white
colonists and sentenced to die.
1814 British troops burned Washington, D.C.
1853 the Stockbridge (Massachusetts) Village Improvement Society
was organized. It was the first such society in the U.S.
1869 Cornelius Swarthout patented the waffle iron.
1939 the first successful flight of a jet aircraft was made in Germany.
1944 Romania surrendered to the Soviets.
1954 the Communist Party was outlawed in the United States.
1963 John Pennel became the first person to pole vault over seventeen
feet.

The following people were born on August 24:

Jim O'Rourke in 1852.
Mason Williams in 1938.

August 25   Hong Kong Liberation Day (last
Monday)
Paraguayan Constitution Day
Umhlanga Day or Reed Dance Day
(last Monday in Swaziland)
Uruguay Independence Day

1804 in York, England, Alicia Meynell became the first woman to
compete as a jockey in a horse race.
1825 Uruguay declared itself an independent republic.
1830 the Belgian Revolution began.
1840 Joseph Gibbons patented a seeding machine.
1875 Matthew Webb became the first person to swim the English
Channel.
1914 Japan declared war on Austria.
1941 British and Soviet forces invaded Iran.
1941 Ted Allen threw 130 consecutive ringers in horseshoe pitching
competition.
1944 Romania declared war on Germany.
1944 General Charles de Gaulle led the French liberation forces
into Paris.

1949 "Father Knows Best" was first broadcast on NBC radio.
1956 the South African government ordered 100,000 non-white people
     to leave their Johannesburg homes within a year to make
     room for whites.
1960 South Kasai and Katanga formed a confederacy.
1981 after a four year journey, "Voyager II" made its closest approach
     to the planet Saturn at 11:24 p.m.

The following people were born on August 25:

Ivan the Terrible in 1530.
Allan Pinkerton in 1819.
Bret Harte in 1836.
Hans Krebs in 1900.
Leonard Bernstein in 1918.
George Wallace in 1919.
Althea Gibson in 1927.
Sean Connery in 1930.
Gene Simmons in 1949.

August 26   Susan B. Anthony Day (Massachusetts)
                                        Krakatoa Day
                                        Namibia Day
                                        Women's Equality Day

1346 a group of English longbowmen defeated a detachment of French
     knights in the Battle of Crecy.
1676 in accordance with the order of Governor Walter Clarke of
     Rhode Island, Quanpen was executed for participating in
     King Philip's War.
1790 the Massachusetts Historical Society was organized.
1843 Charles Thurber patented the first successful typewriter.
1883 the island of Krakatoa erupted killing 36,000 people. The oceans
     and the atmosphere carried the effects of the blast for years.
1884 Ottmar Mergenthaler patented the linotype machine.
1914 the Battle of Tannenberg began.
1920 the women's suffrage (nineteenth) amendment took effect.
1957 the Soviet Union announced the successful firing of an intercon-
     tinental ballistic missile.
1977 Cecil Browne caught a $375\frac{1}{2}$ pound Atlantic bigeye tuna in Mary-
     land.

The following people were born on August 26:

Antoine Lavoisier in 1743.
John Wilkes Booth in 1838.
Elmer Klumpp and Albert B. Sabin in 1906.

August 27   Lyndon Johnson's Birthday (Texas)
                                       Sri Chinmoy Birthday Celebration
                                       Day

413 B.C., a solar eclipse occurred and was observed and recorded
    in Greece.
1576 Titian died in Venice.
1650 the Wood/Bland/Pennant/Brewster expedition left Fort Henry
    to cross the Allegheny Mountains.
1776 American forces were defeated in the Battle of Long Island.
1789 the French declaration of the rights of man was issued.
1828 Uruguay achieved its independence and was recognized by Brazil
    and Argentina.
1832 Black Hawk surrendered at Prairie du Chien.
1859 Edward Drake drilled a successful oil well at Titusville, Pennsyl-
    vania.
1883 the eruption of Krakatoa finally subsided.
1889 Charles G. Conn patented the all metal clarinet.
1894 Congress passed a federal income tax law that was later declared
    unconstitutional.
1912 Edgar Rice Burroughs' Tarzan of the Apes was published.
1916 Romania declared war on Austria-Hungary.
1928 the United States signed the Pact of Paris (Kellogg-Briand Pact).
1962 "Mariner II" was launched. It was the first interplanetary space
    shot.
1979 agents of the Irish Republican Army murdered Lord Louis Mount-
    batten.

The following people were born on August 27:

Georg Wilhelm Friedrich Hegel in 1770.
Hannibal Hamlin in 1809.
Charles G. Dawes in 1865.
Samuel Goldwyn in 1882.
Everett "Dizzy" Nutter in 1892.
Lyndon B. Johnson in 1908.
Martha Raye in 1916.
Harry Lee "Peanuts" Lowrey in 1918.
Tuesday Weld in 1943.

August 28   Feast of St. Augustine

430 A.D., St. Augustine died and Vandals captured his African capital.
1784 the U.S.S. Empress of China arrived in Canton, China.
1798 John J. Dufour established a vineyard in Lexington, Kentucky.
1849 Venice surrendered and the Italian Revolution was suppressed.

1867 U.S. agents occupied the Midway Islands in the Pacific.
1904 the first person was thrown in jail for speeding in an automobile
     which had been operating at the blinding speed of fifteen
     to twenty m.p.h.
1910 Montenegro proclaimed itself an independent principality.
1914 Austria declared war on Belgium.
1916 Italy declared war on Germany.
1916 Germany declared war on Romania.
1919 the Associated Actors and Artists of America was incorporated.
1938 Edgar Bergen's partner, Charlie McCarthy, received a "Master
     of Innuendo and Snappy Comeback" degree from the School
     of Speech at Northwestern University.

The following people were born on August 28:

Johann Wolfgang von Goethe in 1749.
Charles Boyer in 1899.
Bruno Bettelheim in 1903.
Donald O'Connor in 1925.
Ben Gazzara in 1930.

August 29   Feast of the Beheading of St. John
                                        the Baptist

236,488,773 B.C., the first dinosaur hatched in what is now Wichita
     Falls, Texas.
1533 Atahualpa, the last Inca emperor, was executed by Francisco
     Pizarro.
1758 the first American Indian reservation was established at Indian
     Mills, New Jersey.
1820 a revolution began in Oporto, Portugal to drive out that nation's
     regency.
1842 the Treaty of Nanking opened several Chinese ports to the British
     and allowed opium traffic to continue. China also ceded Hong
     Kong to Great Britain.
1869 Major John Wesley Powell emerged from his first exploration
     of the Grand Canyon.
1871 an imperial decree abolishing fiefs and creating prefectures
     put Japan solidly on a road away from feudalism.
1892 Billy "Pop" Schriver caught a ball dropped from the Washington
     Monument in Washington, D.C.
1896 Li Hung-Chang's chef invented chop suey in New York.
1937 China and the Soviet Union concluded a treaty of friendship
     which aided China in meeting the invasion from Japan.

The following people were born on August 29:

John Locke in 1632.
Oliver Wendell Holmes in 1809.
Ingrid Bergman in 1916.
Charlie "Bird" Parker in 1920.
Dinah Washington in 1924.
Elliott Gould in 1938.
Michael Jackson in 1958.

August 30   Huey Long's Birthday (Louisiana)
                                        Feast of St. Rose of Lima (Peru)
                                        Victory Day (Turkey)

1637 the Congregational Church council met in Cambridge, Massachu-
     setts to condemn the preachings of Anne Hutchinson's party.
1721 the Treaty of Nystadt ended the Great Northern War. Russia
     won control of several Baltic ports from Sweden.
1813 Fort Mims fell to a group of Creek warriors.
1842 Congress prohibited "The importation of all indecent and obscene
     prints, paintings, lithographs, engravings and transparencies."
1842 Congress placed an import tariff of seventy-five cents a pound
     on opium.
1905 Ty Cobb played in his first major league baseball game and
     doubled his first time at bat.
1916 Turkey declared war on Romania.
1926 the first Hambletonian harness race was held.
1928 Jawaharlal Nehru founded the Independence of India League.
1960 Japan Stationery Company marketed the first felt-tipped pen.
1961 James B. Parsons became the first black judge to be confirmed
     as a judge in a U.S. District Court.

The following people were born on August 30:

Ernest Rutherford in 1871.
Huey P. Long in 1893.
Roy Wilkins in 1901.
Fred MacMurray in 1908.
Shirley Booth in 1909.
Joan Blondell in 1912.
Ted Williams in 1918.
Jean-Claude Killy in 1943.

August 31   Commemoration of the 1942 General
                                                   Strike (Luxembourg)
                                                   (British) Commonwealth Day (Ma-
                                                   laysia, Trinidad and Tobago)
                                                   Malaysia's National Day
                                                   Pushtoonistan Day (Afghanistan)
                                                   Summer Holiday (United Kingdom)
                                                   Trinidad and Tobago Independence
                                                   Day

1842 Micah Rugg patented a nut and bolt machine.
1881 the lawn tennis national championship matches were held at
     Newport, Rhode Island.
1886 about 100 lives were lost and extensive damage was done by
     an earthquake in Charleston, South Carolina.
1907 Great Britain and Russia settled their conflicting interests
     in Persia and Afghanistan.
1920 radio station 8MK (WWJ), Detroit, broadcast the first radio
     news program.
1926 a second non-aggression pact was concluded between Afghanistan
     and the Soviet Union.
1941 "The Great Gildersleeve" began appearing as an independent
     show.
1955 General Motors demonstrated a fifteen inch solar powered auto-
     mobile in Chicago.
1955 Nashua defeated Swaps at Arlington Park race track.
1957 Malaysia became an independent nation.
1962 Trinidad and Tobago became an independent nation.
1964 Rocky Marciano was killed in a plane crash near Newton, Iowa.
1972 Olga Korbut won two gold medals at the Munich Olympic Games.

The following people were born on August 31:

Eddie Plank in 1875.
Charles "Buster" Brown in 1881.
Arthur Godfrey in 1903.
Sir Alfred Lovell in 1913.
Richard Basehart in 1914.
Buddy Hackett in 1924.
James Coburn in 1928.
Jean Beliveau in 1931.
Eldridge Cleaver and Frank Robinson in 1935.

September

The first day of September marks the following commemorations:

Braderie (Luxembourg)
Labor Day (first Monday)
Libyan Arab Jamahiriya (1969) Independence Day
Qatar Independence Day
Settler's Day (first Monday in South Africa)

Cable Television Month
Philatelic Publications Month

National Spanish Green Olive Week (begins the first Thursday)

September 1

1557 Jacques Cartier died at St. Malo.
1819 John J. Wood patented a plow with interchangeable parts.
1862 the federal government began taxing tobacco.
1878 Emma M. Nutt became the first woman telephone operator.
1880 the first U.S. national lawn tennis tournament was held on Staten Island.
1897 the municipal subway in Boston opened for traffic.
1905 Alberta and Saskatchewan were formed into provinces within the Canadian Dominion.
1914 the last known passenger pigeon died at the Cincinnati Zoo.
1916 the federal child labor law was enacted.
1916 the international migratory bird treaty was ratified.
1916 Bulgaria declared war on Romania.
1919 the Communist Labor Party of America held its first convention in Chicago.
1920 Lebanon was administratively separated from Syria by the French administration on the basis of religion.
1923 an estimated 200,000 died in an earthquake in Tokyo.
1925 Benjamin D. Chamberlin patented a glass light bulb machine.
1939 World War II began when Germany invaded Poland.
1939 Switzerland proclaimed its neutrality which it was able to maintain throughout World War II.

189

1971 Qatar became an independent state.
1983 a Soviet aircraft shot down Korean Air Lines flight 007, killing
       269 passengers and crew.

The following people were born on September 1:

Engelbert Humperdinck in 1854.
Edgar Rice Burroughs in 1875.
Walter Reuther in 1907.
Melvin Laird in 1922.
Rocky Marciano (Rocco Marchegiano) in 1923.
Yvonne DeCarlo in 1924.
Conway Twitty (Harold Jenkins) in 1935.
Lily Tomlin in 1936.
Barry Gibb in 1946.
Brian Bellows in 1964.

September 2   Vietnam Independence Day

  31 B.C., Mark Anthony was defeated in the Battle of Actium.
1666 the great Pudding Lane Fire in London began, eventually destroy-
       ing 13,000 houses.
1789 the United States Treasury Department was organized.
1858 Cyrus W. Field was honored at a dinner at the Metropolitan
       Hotel in New York with the first commemorative cigar band.
1898 Horatio H. Kitchener retook the Sudan for Britain at the Battle
       of Omdurman.
1919 the Communist Party of America was officially formed.
1930 the first Europe to U.S. transatlantic flight was completed
       by Captain Dieudonne Coste and Maurice Bellonte.
1940 the Great Smoky Mountains National Park was dedicated.
1944 Brussels was liberated from German occupation.
1945 Japan formally surrendered and World War II came to an end.
1945 Ho Chi Minh proclaimed the Democratic Republic of Vietnam.
1952 Dr. Floyd J. Lewis performed the first heart operation in which
       the deep freezing technique was used.
1979 Sir Ranulph Fiennes and Charles Burton set out to circle the
       globe via the South and North poles.

The following people were born on September 2:

John Henry in 1864.
Laurindo Almeida and Cleveland Amory in 1917.
Martha Mitchell in 1918.
Jimmy Clanton in 1940.
Jimmy Connors in 1952.

September 3   Liberation of Monaco
                                         St. Marinus Day (San Marino)

 296 B.C., Euclid completed <u>Elements</u>, his book on mathematics
     which became the standard for the study of geometry.
1650 Oliver Cromwell defeated the Scots at the Battle of Dunbar.
1651 Oliver Cromwell defeated Charles II at the Battle of Worcester.
1654 Oliver Cromwell disputed parliament on the issue of whether
     the office of Protector should be elective or hereditary.
1658 Oliver Cromwell died.
1783 the Treaty of Paris ended the American Revolutionary War.
1833 the <u>New York Sun</u> began publishing a daily newspaper.
1838 Frederick Douglass escaped from slavery.
1895 the first professional football game was played between Latrobe,
     Pennsylvania and Jeanette, Pennsylvania.
1900 the Union Reform Party held its first convention.
1935 Sir Malcolm Campbell became the first person to drive a car
     in excess of 300 m.p.h.
1939 Great Britain and France declared war on Germany.
1943 Allied forces landed in Southern Italy.
1950 Nino Farina clinched the World Diving Championship in the
     Italian Grand Prix at Monza.
1951 "Search for Tomorrow" debuted on CBS television.
1957 Governor Orval Faubus blocked the integration of the schools
     of Little Rock, Arkansas.

The following people were born on September 3:

Edward Stanky in 1917.
Valerie Perrine in 1943.

September 4   Newspaper Carrier Day

 476 A.D., Romulus Augustus, the last emperor of the west, was
     deposed and the Roman Empire came to an end.
1609 Henry Hudson came upon Manhattan Island.
1645 the first Lutheran church building in America was dedicated.
1781 El Pueblo de Nuestra Señora la Reina de los Angeles de Porciun-
     cula was founded.
1833 Barney Flaherty, of the <u>New York Sun</u>, became America's first
     newspaper carrier.
1885 the first self-service restaurant opened in New York City.
1886 Geronimo finally surrendered.
1888 George Eastman patented the roll film camera.
1906 Wisconsin held the first state wide primary election.
1934 Argentina proclaimed its neutrality in world affairs.
1935 the National Labor Relations Board held its first meeting.

1941 German forces began the Siege of Leningrad.
1944 British troops liberated Antwerp.
1967 Ford Motor Company introduced the Edsel.
1980 Dr. Alec Rodgers announced the discovery of a heretofore un-
     known class of stars.
1980 Dr. Stephen Synott announced the discovery of Jupiter's sixteenth
     moon, tentatively designated 1980-J3.

The following people were born on September 4:

Henry Ford II in 1917.
Paul Harvey in 1918.
Mitzi Gaynor in 1931.

September 5   Be Late for Something Day

94,789 B.C., the Early Würm period of glaciation ended and the glacial
     interstadial began.
1666 the great London Fire burned out.
1774 the First Continental Congress convened in Philadelphia. Peyton
     Randolph was elected president.
1836 Sam Houston was elected President of Texas.
1881 a forest fire devastated over 1,000,000 acres in Michigan's thumb.
1905 the Russo-Japanese War ended.
1914 the Battle of the Marne began.
1922 the London Daily News reported that small toads fell from
     the sky for two days at Chalon-sur-Saône, France.
1923 Thomas B. Hines demonstrated the smoke screen.
1925 Centerville, Alabama registered a temperature of 112° F.
1933 Fulgencio Batista led a coup in Cuba and became a behind-the-
     scenes dictator without official position.
1939 the United States declared its neutrality in the "European War."
1960 Leopold S. Senghor became the first president of the Republic
     of Senegal.
1979 with clear weather, at 10:45 a.m., five people sighted a UFO
     hovering over a field near Dresser, Wisconsin.

The following people were born on September 5:

Jesse James in 1847.
Nap Lajoie in 1875.
Darryl Zanuck in 1902.
Bob Newhart in 1929.
Raquel Welch in 1942.

September 6   Defense of Pakistan Day
São Tomé and Príncipe Dia dos
Martires da Liberdade (Liberation
of Martyrs)
Swaziland Independence Day or
Somhlolo

1104 B.C., Nebuchadnezzar I of Babylonia, died after reigning for
twenty-one years.
1622 the Spanish galleon Atocha sank off the coast of Florida with
perhaps $100,000,000 worth of gold and silver aboard.
1819 Thomas Blanchard patented his lathe.
1901 President William McKinley was shot. The wound caused his
death on September fourteenth.
1914 the Battle of Masurian Lakes began.
1939 the Union of South Africa declared war on Germany.
1948 Juliana became Queen of the Netherlands.
1950 the Congress of the United States recommended a $62,500,000
Marshall Plan loan to Generalissimo Franco's Spanish government.
1968 Swaziland became an independent nation.
1970 Arab terrorists hijacked four jet airliners.
1972 Arab terrorists killed eleven Israeli athletes at the Olympic
games in Munich.

The following people were born on September 6:

Marquis de Lafayette in 1757.
John Dalton in 1766.
Jane Addams in 1860.
Thomas P. "Oyster" Burns in 1862.
Urban C. "Red" Faber in 1888.
Jo Anne Worley in 1937.
Jane Curtin in 1947.

September 7   Brazil Independence Day
Grandparents Day (first Sunday
after Labor Day)

70 A.D., Jerusalem fell under the Roman siege and the revolt in
Judaea was put down.
1522 Juan de Elcano completed a circumnavigation of the Earth
with the expedition that had begun under the command of
Ferdinand Magellan.
1630 the first settlement was established at Boston.
1776 Ezra Lee, aboard the one man submarine American Turtle,
unsuccessfully attacked H.M.S. Eagle.

1812 Russian troops retreated from the French at the Battle of Borodino.
1822 the independence of Brazil was proclaimed.
1860 Garibaldi took Naples.
1876 John McTammany patented a piano player.
1908 the Esperanto Club was organized.
1921 fifteen year old Margaret Gorman won the first Miss America contest.
1954 Weldon, North Carolina registered a temperature of 109° F.

The following people were born on September 7:

Queen Elizabeth I in 1533.
Thomas A. Hendricks in 1819.
Friedrich Kekule in 1829.
Grandma Moses (Anna Mary Robertson) in 1860.
James Van Allen in 1914.
Peter Lawford in 1923.
Buddy Holly (Charles Hardin Holley) in 1936.

September 8   International Literacy Day
                                   Our Lady of Meritxell Day (Andorra)
                                   Two Sieges and Regatta Day (Malta)

1565 the first permanent European settlement in America was founded at St. Augustine.
1565 the first American Roman Catholic parish was established at St. Augustine.
1636 Harvard College was established.
1664 the Dutch surrendered New Amsterdam (soon to become New York) to the English.
1866 the Bushnell sextuplets were born in Chicago.
1879 the steam whaler Mary and Helen was built in Bath, Maine.
1914 German armies reached the point of their furthest advance.
1945 U.S. forces displaced the Japanese from Korea.
1946 the Bulgarian monarchy was abolished.
1953 direct no-change bus service from New York to San Francisco was established.
1964 Eric Tinworth caught a 110 pound, 5 ounce cobia in Kenya.
1974 a TWA 707 jetliner crashed in the Ionian Sea after a bomb exploded on board. Responsibility was claimed by an Arab terrorist group.
1974 President Gerald R. Ford granted Richard M. Nixon a full and complete pardon for any offenses committed while in office.

The following people were born on September 8:

Richard the Lion Hearted in 1157.
Antonín Dvořák in 1841.
Sid Caesar in 1922.
Peter Sellers in 1925.
Don Rickles in 1926.
Lem Barney in 1945.

September 9   Bulgaria National Liberation Day
California Admission Day
Founding of the Democratic People's
    Republic of (North) Korea
Luxembourg Liberation Day
People of the Istria, Trieste and the
    Slovene Littoral Uprising Day
    (Yugoslavia)

1087 William the Conqueror died at sixty years of age in Rouen.
1513 James IV was defeated by Henry VIII in the Battle of Flodden
     Field.
1850 California was admitted to the Union.
1898 the national birling championship was held in Omaha, Nebraska.
1929 Dr. Erwin Foster Lowry announced the development of Konel,
     a new metal alloy.
1942 a bomb crater was found at Mount Emily, Oregon, possibly caused
     by a Japanese pilotless balloon.
1943 Italy surrendered to the Allies.
1943 Iran declared war on Germany.
1944 Bulgaria surrendered to the Allies.
1948 the People's Democratic Republic of (North) Korea was pro-
     claimed under Kim Il Sung.
1951 "Love of Life" debuted on CBS television.
1957 the Civil Rights Commission was established.
1976 Mao Tse-tung died at the age of eighty-two.

The following people were born on September 9:

Leo Tolstoy in 1828.
Frank Chance in 1877.
Frankie Frisch in 1898.
Waite Hoyt in 1899.
Cliff Robertson in 1925.
Otis Redding in 1941.
Billy Preston in 1946.

September 10   Belize's National Day
                                         Yugoslav Navy Day

1794 Blount College in Knoxville, Tennessee was chartered.
1813 Oliver Hazard Perry, victorious in the Battle of Lake Erie,
      dispatched the message, "We have met the enemy and they
      are ours..."
1815 the keel was laid for the first double decker steamboat, the
      Washington, in Wheeling, Virginia.
1884 the American Historical Association was founded.
1897 George Smith was charged with drunk driving and went into
      the London legal records as the city's first drunk driver.
1913 America's first coast to coast paved road, the Lincoln Highway,
      was opened.
1951 Florence Chadwick swam the English Channel from Dover to
      Sangatte.
1955 "Gunsmoke" was first shown on CBS television.
1974 Guinea-Bissau became an independent nation.
1975 Elizabeth Bayley Seton was canonized and became the first
      saint to have been born in the United States.

The following people were born in September 10:

Jacques Boucher de Crevecoeur de Perthes in 1788.
Ted Kluszewski in 1924.
Arnold Palmer in 1929.
Roger Maris in 1934.
Jose Feliciano in 1945.

September 11   Anniversary of the Death of Qaid-i-
                                         Azam (Pakistan)
                                         Ethiopian New Year
                                         Reunion of Eritrea with Ethiopia

390,416,190 B.C., the first true amphibian was hatched near the present
      site of Chicago.
1777 American forces were defeated at the Battle of Brandywine.
1789 Tench Coxe began serving as the first Internal Revenue Service
      Commissioner.
1812 the Russian settlement at Cazadero, California was dedicated.
1841 John Rand patented a collapsible tube for oil paints.
1850 the first recorded ticket scalping occurred in connection with
      a Jenny Lind concert at Castle Garden in New York City.
1875 "Professor Tigwissel's Burglar Alarm," the first newspaper cartoon
      strip, was published in the New York Daily Graphic.
1915 the British Women's Institute was founded in Wales at Llan-
      fairpwllgwyngyllgogerychwyrndrobwllandysiliogogogoch.
1930 the Kurdish rebellion in Turkey spread into Iraq.

1944 Allied forces crossed the Belgian border into Germany.
1949 the New York Yankees drew eleven bases on balls in the third
     inning.
1952 an artificial aortic valve was surgically inserted in a patient
     for the first time by Dr. Charles A. Hufnagel.

The following people were born on September 11:

O. Henry (William S. Porter) in 1862.
D.H. Lawrence in 1885.
Paul "Bear" Bryant in 1913.
Charles Evers in 1923.
Tom Landry in 1924.
Lola Falana in 1943.
Kristy McNichol in 1962.

September 12   Cape Verde Nationality Day
                                  Defender's Day (Maryland)
                                  Ethiopian Popular Revolution Com-
                                      memoration Day
                                  Guinea-Bissau's National Holiday
                                  Mid-Autumn Festival (Macao)
                                  Occupation Day (Rhodesia)
                                  Saudi Arabia's National Day

620,026,483 B.C., the Paleozoic era began.
 490 B.C., an Athenian force was victorious over the Persians in
     the Battle of Marathon.
1624 the first submarine, designed by Cornelius Drebbel, was tested
     in the River Thames.
1649 Oliver Cromwell suppressed the Irish rebellion at the storming
     of Drogheda.
1848 Switzerland instituted a new constitution replacing the Pact
     of 1815.
1866 "The Black Crook," the first important burlesque show, opened
     at Niblo's Garden in New York.
1869 the Prohibition Party was organized.
1873 the manufacture of the first Sholes type-writer was completed.
1910 Ms. A.S. Wells of the Los Angeles police force, became the
     first policewoman in American history.
1938 the Great Czechoslovakian Crisis began in which Germany an-
     nexed the Sudetenland.

The following people were born on September 12:

H.L. Mencken in 1880.
Ben Shahn in 1898.

Jesse Owens in 1913.
Mickey Lolich in 1940.
Maria Muldaur in 1943.
Barry White in 1944.
Terry Bradshaw in 1948.

September 13   Barry Day

122 A.D., Romans in England decided to build "Hadrian's Wall" from the Tyne to the Solway to insulate themselves from the feared Scots.
1788 plans, dates and authorization for the first United States presidential election were finalized.
1826 a rhinoceros was first seen in New York City.
1849 Tom McCoy died as a result of injuries incurred in a prize fight. He became the first prize fighting fatality in America.
1898 Hannibal W. Goodwin patented celluloid photographic film.
1922 the world's record high temperature was registered in Libya at 136.4° F. in the shade.
1943 Chiang Kai-shek was named president of the Chinese Republic.
1949 the Ladies Professional Golfers Association was formed.
1953 Nikita Khrushchev was elected First Secretary of the Soviet Communist Party's Central Committee.
1956 the Reserve Mining Company's taconite works at Silver Bay, Minnesota began full production.
1971 the World Hockey Association was formed.

The following people were born on September 13:

Walter Reed in 1851.
General John J. Pershing in 1860.
Emile Francis in 1926.
Kate Millett in 1934.
Mel Torme in 1935.
David Clayton-Thomas in 1941.
Jacqueline Bisset in 1946.

September 14   Battle of San Jacinto (Nicaragua)
                                     National Anthem Day (Maryland)

1321 Dante Alighieri died at the age of fifty-six.
1716 the first American lighthouse was kindled on Little Brewster Island, Massachusetts.
1812 Napoleon's forces occupied Moscow.

1814 Francis Scott Key wrote "The Star Spangled Banner."
1829 the Treaty of Adrianople affirmed the independence of Greece.
1886 George K. Anderson patented typewriter ribbon.
1908 the University of Missouri School of Journalism opened.
1923 Jack Dempsey knocked out Luis Firpo in the second round.
1940 the United States enacted the draft for the first time without
     being at war.
1959 a Soviet rocket (Lunik II) made a hard landing on the moon.
1963 the Fischer quintuplets were born.

The following people were born on September 14:

Friedrich von Humboldt in 1769.
Ivan Pavlov in 1849.
Kid Nichols in 1869.
Margaret Sanger in 1883.
Joey Heatherton in 1944.

September 15   Battle of Britain Day (England)
                                     Costa Rica Independence Day
                                     Diez y Seis Celebration (Mexico)
                                     El Salvador Independence Day
                                     Guatemala Independence Day
                                     Honduras Independence Day
                                     Nicaragua Independence Day
                                     Old People's Day
                                     Thimphu Domchoe (Bhutan)

 627 B.C., Assurbanipal, the last great king of Assyria, died after
     a forty-two year reign.
1776 a British force occupied New York. Washington withdrew to
     Harlem.
1812 the Russians began burning Moscow.
1821 Spain granted independence to Costa Rica, El Salvador, Guate-
     mala, Honduras and Nicaragua.
1830 the first national "colored" convention was held at Bethel Church
     in Philadelphia.
1857 Timothy Alden patented a typesetting machine.
1862 General "Stonewall" Jackson captured Harper's Ferry, West
     Virginia.
1863 Abraham Lincoln suspended habeas corpus after receiving author-
     ity from Congress to do so.
1882 the British occupied Cairo.
1913 the first American goat show opened in Rochester, New York.
1930 the Collingwood Memorial co-operative mortuary opened in
     Toledo, Ohio.
1935 Germany's Nuremberg Laws deprived all Jews of German citizen-
     ship.

1940 Peter Dubuc caught a forty-six pound, two ounce northern pike
      in New York.
1946 the Bulgarian People's Republic was proclaimed.
1950 United Nations forces landed at Inchon, South Korea.
1975 Gerald Townsend caught a 113 pound black drum in Delaware.
1975 Charles Nappi caught a twenty-two pound, seven ounce summer
      flounder in New York.
1978 Muhammad Ali defeated Leon Spinks to regain the heavyweight
      boxing title a third time.

The following people were born on September 15:

James Fenimore Cooper in 1789.
William H. Taft in 1857.
Judd "Slow Joe" Doyle in 1881.
Agatha Christie in 1891.
Jackie Cooper in 1922.
Julian "Cannonball" Adderly in 1928.

September 16   Cherokee Strip Day
                                    Mexico Independence Day
                                    Papua New Guinea Independence
                                    Day

1620 the Mayflower left Plymouth, England with 102 passengers
      and a small crew, bound for America.
1833 New York and New Jersey signed an interstate crime pact.
1893 the third and most spectacular Oklahoma land rush took place.
1908 Clark University in Worcester, Massachusetts began offering
      courses in Esperanto.
1919 the American Legion was incorporated.
1923 the Society of the Divine Word at Bay St. Louis, Mississippi
      opened a seminary to educate negro priests.
1941 Syria was proclaimed a republic.
1941 Mohammed Reza Pahlavi succeeded his father as Shah of Iran.
1944 Soviet troops moved into Sofia as they occupied Bulgaria.
1947 John Cobb drove the Railton Mobil Special over 400 m.p.h.
1959 E.B. Elliott caught a ninety-seven pound blue catfish in South
      Dakota.
1963 Singapore became an autonomous entity within the British Com-
      monwealth.
1975 Papua New Guinea became an independent nation.
1980 Iraq abrogated a 1975 agreement with Iran about territorial
      sovereignty, setting the stage for war.
1980 an Arkansas nuclear power plant had to close because the water
      coolant pipes were clogged with clams.

The following people were born on September 16:

James "Bad News" Galloway in 1887.
Emil "Hill Billy" Bildilli in 1912.
Lauren Bacall in 1924.
Charlie Byrd and B.B. King in 1925.
Peter Falk in 1927.
Elgin Baylor in 1934.

September 17   United States' Constitution Day

1607 proceedings were instituted in regard to John Robinson's accusa-
     tion that he had been slandered by Edward M. Wingfield,
     governor of Jamestown.
1778 United States authorities signed a treaty with the Delaware
     Indians guaranteeing their territorial rights.
1787 the United States' Constitution was ratified by Congress.
1844 Thomas F. Adams patented a printing press for polychromatic
     printing.
1862 the Battle of Antietam took place.
1872 Philip W. Pratt patented a sprinkler system for putting out
     fires.
1895 the battleship U.S.S. Maine was commissioned.
1901 Peter C. Hewitt patented the mercury vapor lamp.
1939 Soviet troops invaded Poland. The Polish government went into
     exile.
1953 Carolyn and Catherine Mouton were the first siamese twins
     to be successfully separated by surgery.
1957 Malaysia joined the United Nations.
1961 Tim Brown of the Philadelphia Eagles ran back the first kick-off
     in the first game of the season 105 yards for a touchdown.
1980 Anastasio Somoza was killed by a team of assassins using a
     bazooka and automatic weapons.

The following people were born on September 17:

Warren Burger in 1907.
Hank Williams in 1923.
George Blanda in 1927.
Roddy McDowell in 1928.
Anne Bancroft in 1931.
Ken Kesey in 1935.
Orlando Cepeda in 1937.
John Ritter in 1948.

September 18   Chile Independence Day
                                                   Victory of Uprona (Burundi)

4554 B.C., the chalcolithic period began in western India.
1634 Anne Hutchinson arrived in Boston, Massachusetts.
1679 the Griffon sank in a gale off Manitoulin Island.
1769 John Harris introduced the first piano.
1793 President Washington laid the cornerstone for the U.S. Capitol.
1810 Chile set up its own independent government.
1851 the first issue of the New York Times came out.
1898 the Fashoda Crisis between Britain and France began.
1915 the first asphalt covered automobile race track was opened
     in Cranston, Rhode Island.
1927 CBS made its first broadcast.
1934 the Soviet Union joined the League of Nations.
1954 the S.E.A.T.O. pact was signed.
1962 Burundi, Jamaica, Rwanda and Trinidad and Tobago joined the
     United Nations.

The following people were born on September 18:

Jean Foucault in 1819.
John Diefenbaker in 1895.
Greta Garbo in 1905.
Scotty Bowman and Jimmie Rodgers in 1933.
Robert Blake in 1938.
Frankie Avalon in 1940.

September 19   Chilean Armed Forces Day
                                                   Feast of St. Januarius
                                                   Thimphu Tsechu begins (three day
                                                       festival in Bhutan)

1356 the French defeated the English in the Battle of Poitiers.
1468 Johann Gutenberg died in Mainz at the age of seventy.
1783 a hot-air balloon made a flight with passengers (a sheep, a rooster
     and a duck) for the first time.
1838 Ephraim Morris patented the railroad brake.
1854 Henry B. Meyer patented a railroad sleeping car.
1876 Melville R. Bissell patented the carpet sweeper.
1881 President James A. Garfield died as a result of a gunshot wound
     he received on July second.
1888 the first recognized beauty contest was won in Spa, Belgium
     by Bertha Soucaret, an eighteen year old black woman.
1890 the Turkish frigate Ertogrul foundered off Japan: 540 lives
     were lost.
1893 in New Zealand, women voted in a national election for the
     first time in history.

1898 the New York State College of Forestry was established at
     Cornell University.
1928 Mickey Mouse made his acting debut in <u>Steamboat Willie</u> at
     the Colony Theater in New York City.
1931 the Mukden Incident took place.
1955 Argentine President Juan Peron resigned and went into exile.
1961 Betty and Barney Hill were picked up and examined by five
     beings in a flying saucer.
1980 an accidental explosion blew a nuclear missile warhead out
     of its storage silo in Arkansas.

The following people were born on September 19:

Duke Snider and Lurleen Wallace in 1926.
Brook Benton in 1931.
David McCallum in 1933.
Paul Williams in 1940.
"Mama" Cass Elliott in 1943.
Jane Blalock and Freda Payne in 1945.

September 20   Feast of SS. Eustace and his Com-
                                    panions

1848 the American Association for the Advancement of Science
     was organized.
1850 the Homeopathic Hospital of Pennsylvania was incorporated.
1859 George B. Simpson patented the electric range.
1860 the Prince of Wales arrived in Detroit, Michigan.
1870 Italy retook Rome from France.
1884 the Equal Rights Party formed and nominated Belva Lockwood
     for president.
1892 Frank Schuman patented wire glass.
1913 Francis Ouimet became the first amateur in history to win
     the U.S. Open golf tournament.
1960 Cameroon, the Central African Republic, Chad, the Congo
     Republic (Brazzaville), the Republic of the Congo (Léopold-
     ville), Cyprus, Dahomey, Gabon, Ivory Coast, Malagasy, Niger,
     Somalia, Togo, and Upper Volta joined the United Nations.
1973 Billie Jean King defeated Bobby Riggs 6-4, 6-3, 6-3, in Houston.

The following people were born on September 20:

Upton Sinclair in 1878.
Ferdinand "Jelly Roll" Morton in 1885.
Arnold "Red" Auerback in 1917.
Sophia Loren in 1934.

September 21   Autumn Holiday (Scotland)
Blessed Rainy Day (Bhutan)
Maltese Independence Day

1782 the U.S. Congress authorized the printing of an English language
Bible.
1784 the Pennsylvania Packet and Daily Advertiser became the first
daily publication to be issued in the United States.
1792 the French monarchy was abolished and France was declared
a republic.
1872 James H. Conyers became the first black midshipman at the
U.S. Naval Academy.
1875 Thaddeus S.C. Lowe patented a process for water gas production
of "illuminating or heating gas."
1895 the Duryea Motor Wagon Company was incorporated in Springfield, Massachusetts.
1903 the first western movies, Kit Carson and The Pioneers, were
copyrighted.
1949 Eugene McPherson, the first bicyclist to ride across the United
States, arrived in New York City.
1954 the first atomic powered submarine, the Nautilus, was commissioned.
1958 Jim Heth and Bill Burkhart landed after having flown their
Cessna 172 for 1200 hours, 18 minutes and 30 seconds. They
had remained airborne for fifty continuous days.
1964 Malta became an independent nation.
1980 Richard Todd completed forty-two passes for the New York
Jets.
1982 Al McReynolds caught a 78½ pound striped bass near Atlantic
City, New Jersey.

The following people were born on September 21:

Louis Joliet in 1645.
Jack Horner in 1863.
H.G. Wells in 1866.
Larry Hagman in 1931.

September 22   Kid's Day (fourth Saturday)
Mali Independence Day
Native American Day (fourth Fri-
day)

the autumnal equinox occurs.
1656 history's first all-female jury was convened in Maryland.
1692 the last eight witches were hanged in Salem, Massachusetts.
1776 Nathan Hale was hanged by the British.

1862 Abraham Lincoln made a preliminary announcement of the Emancipation Proclamation.
1915 the Second Battle of Champagne began.
1927 slavery was abolished in Sierra Leone.
1940 Japanese troops occupied French Indochina.
1945 a record $5,000,000 was wagered in one day at Belmont Park.
1953 Red Skelton's first television show was broadcast.
1957 Arthur Lawton caught a sixty-nine pound, fifteen ounce muskellunge in New York.
1960 Mali became an independent nation.

The following people were born on September 22:

Michael Faraday in 1791.
Bob Lemon in 1920.
Tom LaSorda in 1927.
Debby Boone in 1956.

September 23   Autumnal Equinox Day (Japan)
                                          Saudi Arabia's Unification Day

the sun enters the house of Libra.
1552 Christ's Hospital opened in London.
1642 Harvard held its first commencement exercises.
1780 Benedict Arnold's plan to surrender his army to the British was foiled.
1806 the Lewis and Clark expedition returned to St. Louis.
1845 standardized rules were established for baseball.
1845 the New York Knickerbocker Club became the first organized baseball team.
1897 Frontier Day was celebrated for the first time in Cheyenne, Wyoming.
1912 the first Mack Sennett "Keystone Comedy" film was released.
1932 Joseph V. McCarthy became the first baseball manager to win a pennant in both leagues.
1949 President Truman announced to the nation that the Soviet Union was testing atomic weapons.
1952 Rocky Marciano knocked out Jersey Joe Walcott in the thirteenth round.
1954 Lt. Col. Harry Fleming was court martialed and convicted of collaborating with his Korean captors.

The following people were born on September 23:

Augustus Caesar in 63 B.C.
Johann Encke in 1791.
Armand Fizeau in 1819.

Alan Lomax in 1867.
Mickey Rooney in 1920.
Ray Charles in 1930.
Bruce Springsteen in 1949.

September 24   Establishment of the Republic
                                    (Guinea-Bissau)
                                    Feast of Our Lady of Mercy (Do-
                                    minican Republic)
                                    New Caledonia Territorial Day
                                    Schwenkenfelder Thanksgiving Day
                                    Third Republic Day (Ghana)
                                    Trinidadian and Tobagonian Repub-
                                    lic Day

420,377,019 B.C., an arthropod survived on land for a twenty-four
    hour period for the first time on the site of present day down-
    town Seattle.
1398 Tamerlane crossed the Indus River en route to his conquest
    of the kingdom of Delhi.
1789 the United States Supreme Court was created.
1789 John Jay became the first U.S. Supreme Court Chief Justice.
1869 Jay Gould and James Fisk attempted to corner the U.S. gold
    market on the day that became known as "Black Friday."
1889 Alexander Dey patented the dial time recorder.
1905 the Swedish Riksdag acquiesced to Norway's declaration dissolving
    their union.
1906 Devil's Tower Wyoming was established as a national monument.
1950 the Philadelphia Eagles intercepted eight passes thrown by
    Jim Hardy of the Chicago Cardinals.
1960 the U.S.S. Enterprise, the world's first nuclear powered aircraft
    carrier, was launched.
1967 Jim Bakken kicked seven field goals for the St. Louis Cardinals.
1976 Trinidad and Tobago became a republic.

The following people were born on September 24:

F. Scott Fitzgerald in 1896.
Anthony Newley in 1931.
Jim Henson in 1936.

September 25   Day of the Mozambican People's
                                    Army
                                    "Discovery of the Pacific Ocean"
                                    Day

Kamarampaka Day (Rwanda)
Show Day (Victoria, Australia)

948 B.C., the first Phoenician colony was established in Spain.
1493 Christopher Columbus sailed from Portugal on his second voyage
which led him to Dominica, Puerto Rico and Jamaica.
1513 Vasco Núñez de Balboa found the Pacific Ocean.
1555 the German nation agreed to the Peace of Augsburg.
1915 the Third Battle of Artois began.
1924 Columbia University began offering courses in paleontology.
1926 Ford Motor Company established the eight hour day/five day
work week.
1933 NBC debuted "The Tom Mix Ralston Straightshooters."
1943 Soviet troops reoccupied Smolensk.
1962 Sonny Liston won the world heavyweight championship from
Floyd Patterson.
1976 Manual Salazar caught an eighty-seven pound dolphin in the
Papagallo Gulf.
1981 Sandra Day O'Connor became the first woman Justice of the
Supreme Court of the United States.

The following people were born on September 25:

William Faulkner in 1897.
Dmitri Shostakovich in 1906.
Barbara Walters in 1931.
Mark Hamill in 1951.

September 26   Yemen Arab Republic's Proclamation of the Republic Day

1580 Sir Francis Drake completed his circumnavigation of the Earth
aboard the Golden Hind.
1831 the Anti-Masonic Party held its first convention.
1871 David O. Saylor patented cement.
1872 the Ancient Arabic Order of Nobles of the Mystic Shrine instituted a temple in New York City.
1903 Alabama passed a law making it illegal to conduct a boycott.
1907 New Zealand became a dominion within the British Commonwealth.
1918 the Battles of the Argonne and of Ypres began.
1950 United Nations forces captured Seoul.
1960 the first of the Kennedy-Nixon TV debates took place.
1962 the Yemen Arab Republic was proclaimed following the assassination of King Iman Ahmed.
802,701 A.D., the time traveller in H.G. Wells' The Time Machine
arrived among the Eloi.

The following people were born on September 26:

Joseph Louis Proust in 1754.
Johnny Appleseed (Chapman) in 1774.
George Gershwin in 1898.
Marty Robbins in 1925.
Julie London in 1926.
Olivia Newton-John in 1948.

September 27   Feast of the Finding of the True
                                      Cross (Ethiopia)

1290 an earthquake in Chihli, China killed 100,000 people.
1892 the Diamond Match Company was granted a patent for "book matches."
1918 British forces broke through the Hindenburg Line.
1928 a museum of Thomas Edison's inventions was set up in Dearborn, Michigan.
1930 Bobby Jones won the U.S. Amateur golf championship at Philadelphia, Pennsylvania, completing a sweep of all four major titles (along with the U.S. Open, the British Open and the British Amateur championship).
1937 a Santa Claus school was opened in Albion, New York.
1939 Poland surrendered and was divided up by Germany and the Soviet Union.
1940 a German-Italian-Japanese mutual assistance pact was signed.
1954 "The Tonight Show" debuted on NBC television.
1961 Sierra Leone joined the United Nations.
1964 the Warren Commission released its report on the Kennedy assassination.

The following people were born on September 27:

Thomas Nast in 1840.
George Raft in 1895.
Shaun Cassidy in 1959.

September 28   Birthday of Confucius/Teacher's
                                      Day (Republic of China-Taiwan)
                                      National Good Neighbor Day
                                      Frances Willard Day (Minnesota)

1542 Juan Rodriguez Cabrillo became the first European to land on the Pacific coast of North America at San Diego.

1678 Pilgrim's Progress was published.
1800 New York City imported America's first fireboat.
1912 the Japanese steamer Kichemaru sank. A thousand lives were
     lost.
1915 the Battle of Kut-El-Amara took place.
1945 Robert T. Duncan appeared as Tonio in "I Pagliacci" and became
     the first black man to sing a white operatic role with a white
     cast.
1950 Indonesia joined the United Nations.
1951 Norm Van Brocklin of the Los Angeles Rams gained 554 yards
     passing against the New York Yanks.
1955 the World Series was broadcast in color for the first time.
1960 Senegal and Mali joined the United Nations.

The following people were born on September 28:

Friedrich Engels in 1820.
Georges "The Tiger" Clemenceau in 1841.
Ed Sullivan in 1902.
Al Capp in 1909.
Marcello Mastroianni in 1924.
Brigitte Bardot in 1934.

September 29   Battle of Boquerón Day (Paraguay)
                                    Brunei Constitution Day
                                    Michaelmas

1892 the first night football game was played at Mansfield, Pennsyl-
     vania.
1906 U.S. forces put down a liberal Cuban revolution and established
     a provisional government.
1911 Italy declared war on Turkey.
1915 the first transcontinental radio telephone message was sent.
1918 Bulgaria surrendered to the Allies.
1930 New York City College offered the first course in radio advertis-
     ing.
1938 Columbia University offered the first courses designed to train
     students as archivists.
1951 a football game was carried in color over a TV network for
     the first time.
1953 Carson Pirie Scott and Company of Chicago began selling insur-
     ance; it was the first American department store to do so.
1962 Valeri Brumel high jumped over a bar set at seven feet, five
     inches.

The following people were born on September 29:

Enrico Fermi in 1901.
Gene Autry in 1907.
Jerry Lee Lewis in 1935.
Madeline Kahn in 1942.

September 30   Botswana Independence Day
                                        Dia das Nacionalizações das Emprê-
                                        sas Agricolas (São Tomé and
                                        Príncipe)
                                        Feast of St. Jerome

1502 Amerigo Vespucci's return to Portugal was marked when he
     published his opinion that Brazil was in fact a new land hitherto
     unknown to Europeans.
1630 John Billington, one of the original pilgrims, was hanged for
     murder at Plymouth, Massachusetts.
1841 Samuel Slocum patented a machine "for sticking pins into paper."
1908 Dr. Jacques Brandenberger of Zurich patented cellophane.
1938 the Sudetenland was ceded to Germany by Czechoslovakia.
1942 Adolf Hitler announced that "The occupation of Stalingrad...
     will be a gigantic success...and no human being shall ever
     push us away from that spot."
1946 the Nuremberg war crimes tribunal adjourned. Its verdicts were
     as follows: of the twenty-two Nazi leaders tried, twelve re-
     ceived the death penalty, seven received prison terms and
     three were acquitted.
1947 Pakistan and Yemen joined the United Nations.
1955 actor James Dean died in a car wreck at the age of twenty-four.
1966 Botswana became an independent nation.
1979 a UFO landed in a field near the home of Patricia Dooley in
     Wisconsin.

The following people were born on September 30:

Hans Geiger in 1882.
Deborah Kerr in 1921.
Truman Capote in 1924.
Johnny Mathis in 1935.
Marilyn McCoo in 1943.

October

The first day of October marks the following commemorations:

Captain Regents Day (San Marino)
Clerk's Holiday (Barbados)
Korean Armed Forces Day
Nigeria Independence Day
People's Republic of China's Foundation of the Republic
Unification Day (Cameroon)
Universal Children's Day (first Monday)

Festival of Penha (Brazil)
Newspaper Week (Japan)

Gourmet Adventures Month
International Marine Travel Month
Michigan Library Month
National Applejack Month
National Hobby Month
National Restaurant Month
National Wine Festival Month
Pizza Festival Time Month

October 1

331 B.C., Alexander the Great defeated the Persian army at Gaugamela.
1848 the Massachusetts School for Idiotic and Feeble-minded Youth was established in Boston.
1861 the U.S. Army Balloon Corps was organized.
1869 the first official prepaid postcards were issued in Austria.
1888 the first National Geographic magazine was issued.
1889 sex education was first offered at Abbotsholme School in England.
1895 the Armenian massacres became a key event in a series of outrages by which Turkish authorities aimed to suppress its Armenian population.
1903 the first game of the first World Series was played.

1908 Henry Ford built the first Model T.
1934 Olivet College in Olivet, Michigan, dispensed with the credit-hour-point-grade-etc. system for students.
1936 Generalissimo Franco became Chief of State in Spain.
1938 German troops moved into Czechoslovakia's Sudetenland.
1942 the first U.S. designed and built jet aircraft was flown.
1949 the People's Republic of China was officially proclaimed.
1960 Nigeria achieved its independence.
1961 Roger Maris hit his sixty-first home run of the season.
1962 James Meredith became the first black student to attend the University of Mississippi.
1962 Johnny Carson took over as host of "The Tonight Show."
1963 Nigeria was declared a republic.
1963 16,732 U.S. troops were in Vietnam despite ongoing "plans for withdrawal."
1966 the world's first known white gorilla was discovered in Rio Muni.
1978 Tuvalu became an independent nation.

The following people were born on October 1:

Vladimir Horowitz in 1904.
Walter Matthau in 1920.
James Whitmore in 1921.
James Earl "Jimmy" Carter in 1924.
Tom Bosley in 1927.
George Peppard in 1928.
Angie Dickinson in 1931.
Richard Harris in 1933.
Julie Andrews in 1935.
Michael Landon (Eugene M. Orowitz) in 1937.
Rod Carew in 1945.

October 2   Fire Prevention Week (begins Sun-
                                        day of the week with the eighth)
                                        Mahatma Gandhi's Birthday (India)
                                        Guinea Independence Day
                                        Id Al Adaha (Ethiopia)

1608 Hans Lippershey of the Netherlands first demonstrated the telescope.
1721 the Boston Gazette announced the arrival of an "African camel... seven feet high and twelve feet long."
1866 J. Osterhoudt patented the tin can with a key opener.
1872 Phileas Fogg wagered twenty thousand pounds that he could travel around the world in eighty days.
1937 Drs. William H. Stewart, William J. Hoffman and Francis H. Ghiselin exhibited the first successful X-ray motion pictures

of human organs at a convention of the American Roentgen
Ray Society.
1938 Polish troops occupied Teschen.
1942 the Curaçao collided with the Queen Mary causing 335 lives
to be lost.
1942 "The Cisco Kid" came to WOR-Mutual radio.
1952 Britain tested its first atomic bomb in the Monte Bello Islands.
1956 the Atomicron, the first atomic powered clock, was exhibited
at the Overseas Press Club in New York City.
1958 Guinea gained its independence.
1976 Peter Hyde caught a 437 pound blue shark in Australia.

The following people were born on October 2:

Nat Turner in 1800.
Paul von Hindenburg in 1847.
Marshal Ferdinand Foch in 1851.
Mahatma Gandhi (Mohandas Karamchand) in 1869.
Cordell Hull in 1871.
"Bud" Abbot and Julius "Groucho" Marx in 1895.
Don McLean in 1945.

October 3   Francisco Morazan Day (Honduras)
                                     Kaechonjol or (South) Korean Na-
                                     tional Foundation Day
                                     Leiden Ontzet or Leyden Day (Ne-
                                     therlands)
                                     Luxembourg Moselle Wine Festival
                                     in Steinsel

2320 B.C., Tangun founded the nation of Korea.
1698 the first Fredericksburg, Virginia "Dog Mart" auction was held.
1863 Abraham Lincoln proclaimed Thanksgiving Day.
1873 Captain Jack was hanged and the Modoc War came to an end.
1877 Chief Joseph of the Nez Percé capitulated to General Oliver
O. Howard, saying, "I will fight no more forever."
1899 John S. Thurman patented a motor-driven vacuum cleaner.
1910 an insurrection broke out in Portugal in opposition to King Manuel
II.
1922 Rebecca L. Felton of Georgia became the first woman U.S.
Senator.
1924 King Sherif Hussein was forced to abdicate the throne of the
Hejaz (Saudi Arabia) in favor of his son Ali.
1935 Italy invaded Ethiopia.
1938 German troops completed their occupation of the Sudetenland.
1947 "The Spike Jones Show" debuted on CBS radio.
1955 the first Captain Kangaroo show was broadcast on CBS.

1962 Walter M. Schirra orbited the Earth six times.
1963 Gambia, a British protectorate, became self-governing.

The following people were born on October 3:

Fred Clarke in 1873.
Gore Vidal in 1925.
Chubby Checker (Ernest Evans) in 1941.

October 4   Feast of St. Francis of Assisi
                                     Lesotho Independence Day
                                     Vanuata National Unity Day

985 A.D., Sven the Forked-Beard succeeded Harald Bluetooth as
     King of Denmark.
1830 Isaac Adams patented a power printing press capable of fine
     book work.
1853 the Ottoman Empire declared war on Russia and the Crimean
     War began.
1881 Carl G.P. deLaval patented a continuous flow centrifugal cream
     separator.
1890 construction was begun on a project designed to utilize Niagara
     Falls to generate power on a large scale.
1895 Horace Rawlins won the first official U.S. Open golf tournament
     at the Newport, Rhode Island Country Club.
1940 a quetzal bird arrived in New York City.
1957 Sputnik I was launched from the Soviet Union.
1959 Lunik III circled the moon and photographed the far side.
1966 Basutoland became the independent nation of Lesotho.

The following people were born on October 4:

St. Francis of Assisi in 1182.
Rutherford B. Hayes in 1822.
Joseph "Buster" Keaton in 1895.
Rip Repulski in 1927.

October 5   Indonesian Army Day
                                     Macanese Republic Day
                                     Madeiran Republic Day
                                     Portugal Independence Day
                                     Solomon Islands' Day
                                     United Nations Day (Barbados)

1762 the British occupied Manila during their war with Spain.
1853 Antioch College opened in Yellow Springs, Ohio.
1869 F.A. Spofford and Matthew G. Raffington were granted a patent for a water velocipede.
1892 Emmet Dalton excepted, the entire Dalton Gang was killed during an attempted bank robbery.
1908 Bulgaria declared its independence from the Ottoman Empire.
1910 the Portuguese Republic was proclaimed and a provisional government was organized under Dr. Theophilo Braga.
1925 the Locarno Conference opened.
1930 Father Charles E. Coughlin made his first broadcast on CBS radio.
1947 nine European nations formed the Cominform.
1953 the New York Yankees won their fifth consecutive World Series.
1974 C. Larry McKinney caught a four pound, two ounce silver redhorse in Missouri.

The following people were born on October 5:

Denis Diderot in 1713.
Chester Alan Arthur in 1830.
"Long" John Reilly in 1858.
Davey Crockett in 1875.
Robert Goddard in 1882.
Philip Berrigan in 1923.
Richard Street in 1942.

October 6   Chung Yeung Festival
                                 Egyptian Armed Forces Day
                                 Eight Hour Day (New South Wales)
                                 Labour Day (Australian Capital
                                   Territory)
                                 Lesotho's National Sports Day

1,057,495 B.C., the Mindel (Kansan) period of glaciation ended and the second interglacial period began.
1683 the first Mennonites arrived in North America.
1766 John Henry made his American debut in Philadelphia.
1783 Benjamin Hanks patented a self-winding clock.
1863 America's first Turkish bath opened in Brooklyn.
1868 William H. Remington patented a nickel plating process.
1884 the Naval War College was established at Newport, Rhode Island.
1917 Peru severed relations with Germany.
1927 The Jazz Singer helped begin the era of "talking" films.
1928 Chiang Kai-shek was elected President of China by the Kuomintang.
1971 Mike Fischer caught an eight and three-quarter pound sauger in North Dakota.

1973 Egypt and Syria launched a surprise attack on Israel.
1976 a Cuban DC-8 crashed near Barbados following a bomb explosion.
1978 Jerry D. Leonard caught a sixty-seven and a quarter pound spearfish in North Carolina.
1981 President Anwar Sadat was assassinated.

The following people were born on October 6:

Miguel Cervantes in 1547.
Jenny Lind in 1820.
Helen Moody in 1905.
Thor Heyerdahl in 1914.
Shana Alexander in 1925.

October 7   Founding of the German Democratic
                             Republic Holiday
                             Libya Evacuation Day (Fascist
                             Italians)
                             Yugoslav People's Army Artillery
                             Day
                             Libyan Constitution Day

64,227,418 B.C., the last dinosaur died peacefully near present day Billings, Montana.
1571 Spain defeated the Turkish Navy in the Battle of Lepanto.
1765 the "Stamp Act Congress" met in New York.
1769 Captain James Cook landed in New Zealand 127 years after Dutch Captain Abel Janszoon Tasman first landed there.
1806 Ralph Wedgwood secured a patent for carbon paper.
1856 Cyrus Chambers, Jr. patented a paper folding machine.
1870 Leon Gambetta escaped by balloon from a besieged Paris.
1879 the Austro-German Alliance was formed.
1916 the Georgia Tech. football team defeated Cumberland College by a score of 222 to 0.
1917 Uruguay severed relations with Germany.
1919 Wilhelmina, Queen of the Netherlands, blessed the founding of KLM airline.
1941 "The Red Skelton Show" started on NBC radio.
1949 "Tokyo Rose" was sentenced for her propaganda role in World War II.
1949 the German Democratic Republic (East Germany) was established.
1950 United Nations forces invaded North Korea.
1951 the Western Hills Hotel formally opened in Fort Worth, Texas. It was the first hotel with all foam rubber mattresses, pillows and furniture cushions.
1957 "American Bandstand" made its first telecast on ABC.
1960 Nigeria joined the United Nations.

The following people were born on October 7:

William "Brickyard" Kennedy in 1868.
Niels Bohr in 1885.
Henry Agard Wallace in 1888.
Vaughn Monroe in 1911.
Al Martino in 1927.
Imamu Baraka (Leroi Jones) in 1934.

October 8   Discoverer's Day (second Monday
                                     in Hawaii)
                                 Feast of Cirio de Nazare (second
                                     Sunday in Brazil)
                                 Fiji Day (second Monday)
                                 Friendship Day (second Monday in
                                     Puerto Rico and the Virgin Is-
                                     lands)
                                 Hari Raya Haji (Singapore)
                                 Kurban Bayram (Cyprus)
                                 Thanksgiving Day (second Monday
                                     in Canada)
                                 White Sunday (second Sunday in
                                     American Samoa)
                                 National Y-Teen Week (begins the
                                     second Sunday)

1871 a forest fire began at Peshtigo, Wisconsin that burned across
     six counties and killed 1,100 people.
1904 the Vanderbilt Cup race was held in Hicksville, New York.
1906 the permanent wave was first demonstrated for the general
     public.
1918 Sergeant Alvin C. York captured 132 German soldiers by himself.
1929 the first in-flight movie was shown.
1935 Ozzie and Harriet Nelson were married.
1939 Andy Uram of the Green Bay Packers ran ninety-seven yards
     for a touchdown against the Chicago Cardinals.
1942 the first regular radio broadcast of "Abbot and Costello" was
     made.
1944 "The Adventures of Ozzie and Harriet" premiered on CBS radio.
1956 Don Larsen pitched a perfect game in the World Series.
1962 Algeria joined the United Nations.
1967 Che Guevara was killed in Bolivia.

The following people were born on October 8:

Frank S. "Ping" Bodie in 1887.
Eddie Rickenbacker in 1890.

George M. "Catfish" Metkovich in 1921.
David Carradine in 1937.
Jesse Jackson in 1941.
Chevy Chase (Cornelius Crane) in 1943.

October 9   Leif Ericsson Day (Iceland and the
                                 United States)
                                 Hangul or Korean Alphabet Day
                                 Independence of Guayaquil (Ecuador)
                                 Peruvian Day of National Dignity
                                 Uganda Independence Day
                                 Universal Postal Union Day

1000 Leif Ericsson reached Vinland (North America).
1855 Joshua C. Stoddard patented the calliope.
1855 Isaac M. Singer patented a sewing machine motor.
1871 the Great Chicago Fire started when Mrs. O'Leary's cow kicked
      over a lantern in the barn.
1877 the American Humane Association was organized.
1888 the Washington Monument in Washington, D.C. was opened
      to the public.
1890 Sherlock Holmes captured John Clay in a daring bank robbery
      attempt.
1914 the Battles of Warsaw and Ivangorod began.
1935 "The Cavalcade of America" was first heard on CBS radio.
1946 the Simmons Company started manufacturing electric blankets.
1950 General Douglas MacArthur ordered the United Nations forces
      to cross the thirty-eighth parallel in a drive that eventually
      reached the Yalu River.
1960 Eddie LeBaron of the Dallas Cowboys threw a two inch touchdown
      pass to Dick Bielski.
1962 Uganda became an independent nation.
1963 Uganda was proclaimed a republic.

The following people were born on October 9:

John Lennon in 1940.
Jackson Browne in 1950.

October 10   Beginning of the Wars for Indepen-
                                 dence (Cuba)
                                 Double Tenth Day (Taiwan)
                                 Health-Sports Day (Japan)
                                 Kruger Day (South Africa)

Oklahoma Historical Day
Republic of China's National Day
(Taiwan)

370 B.C., Hippocrates died at Larissa at the age of ninety.
1639 the first American apple harvest, in Boston, yielded "ten fair
     pippins."
1818 the Walk-in-the-Water made its maiden voyage.
1865 John W. Hyatt patented a billiard ball of composition material
     which resembled ivory.
1874 Great Britain annexed Fiji.
1886 the first formal dinner jacket was introduced by Griswold Loril-
     lard at the Tuxedo Park Country Club's Autumn Ball.
1904 John Chesbro won forty-one games as a pitcher for the New
     York Highlanders during the 1904 baseball season.
1911 the Chinese Revolution began.
1920 William Wambsganss executed an unassisted triple play in the
     World Series.
1933 Dreft began marketing the first synthetic detergent for home
     use.
1934 the Humanist Society held its first national assembly in New
     York City.
1935 Porgy and Bess opened in New York City.
1969 Edward J. Kirker caught a seventy-two pound striped bass in
     Massachusetts.
1970 Pierre Laporte, Quebec's Labor Minister, was kidnapped.
1970 Fiji became an independent parliamentary democracy.
1971 the New York Times produced a 972 page, seven and one half
     pound issue.
1973 Vice-President Spiro T. Agnew resigned. He later said he feared
     being assassinated on orders from the White House.
1980 an earthquake that registered 7.5 on the Richter Scale struck
     Al Asnam, Algeria, killing thousands.

The following people were born on October 10:

Henry Cavendish in 1731.
Giuseppe Verdi in 1813.
Helen Hayes in 1900.
Dorothy Lamour in 1914.
Adlai E. Stevenson III in 1930.
Tanya Tucker in 1958.

October 11   Anniversary of the Revolution
                                  (Panama)
                                  Day of Solidarity with South Afri-
                                  can Political Prisoners (United
                                  Nations)

People of Macedonia Uprising Day
(Yugoslavia)

1055 Ferdinand the Great of Leon and Castile drove the Moors from
Portugal and established Coimbra as the capital.
1737 an earthquake in Calcutta killed over 300,000.
1811 the first steam powered ferryboat began operating between
Hoboken and New York City.
1881 David H. Houston patented roll film for cameras.
1887 Dorr E. Felt patented the first adding machine which was "abso-
lutely accurate at all times."
1890 the Daughters of the American Revolution was organized.
1933 Delaware's state poorhouse was dedicated and officially opened.
1936 "Professor Quiz" was first broadcast over the radio.
1938 Games Slayter and John H. Thomas patented glass wool and
the machinery to make it.
1947 Mrs. L. Hallberg caught a thirty-one pound silver salmon in
British Columbia.
1955 Canada and the U.S.S.R. settled on some trade agreements
and established co-operative efforts in Arctic research.

The following people were born on October 11:

Franz Liszt in 1811.
Louis "Buttercup" Dickerson in 1858.
Eleanor Roosevelt in 1884.

October 12   Columbus Day (celebrated on the
second Monday in the United
States)
Day of the Polish Army
Day of the Race (Spain)
Día de la Raza (Mexico)
Discovery Day (Bahamas)
Equatorial Guinea's National Day
Hispanic Day (Canary Islands)
Pioneers Day (South Dakota)
Samoa's National Day
Somali Flag Day
Sudanese Republic Day

 539 B.C., Cyrus the Persian's army occupied Babylon.
1492 Columbus landed in the Bahamas.
1773 the Publick Hospital for Persons of Insane and Disordered Minds
was opened in Williamsburg, Virginia.
1920 Man O' War defeated Sir Barton at Kenilworth Park in his last
race.

1920 construction was begun on the Holland Tunnel between Jersey City and New York City.
1923 Casey Stengel's home run enabled the New York Giants to win that day's World Series game, 1 to 0, over the Yankees.
1925 William M. Brown, Episcopal Bishop of Arkansas, was deposed for heresy.
1928 Boston Children's Hospital staff accomplished the first successful use of an artificial respirator.
1937 Vern Huffman, of the Detroit Lions, ran an interception back 100 yards against the Brooklyn Dodgers.
1968 Fernando Po and Rio Muni combined into the independent nation of Equatorial Guinea.

The following people were born on October 12:

Aleister Crowley in 1875.
Joe Cronin in 1906.
Dick Gregory in 1932.
Melvin Franklin in 1942.

October 13   Assassination of the Hero of the
                                  Nation (Prince Louis Rwagasore
                                  in Burundi)
                                  St. Edward's Day
                                  Eight Hour Day (South Australia)
                                  Queen's Birthday (Western Australia)

1775 the United States authorized the U.S. Navy.
1778 the First Masonic Grand Lodge was organized at Williamsburg, Virginia.
1860 J.W. Black initiated aerial photography by taking a photograph from a balloon 1,200 feet over the city of Boston.
1860 at the Convention of London, the French convinced the Spanish and the British to join in on an invasion of Mexico.
1903 the Boston Red Sox won the first World Series.
1914 Christiaan De Wet led a rebellion in South Africa.
1921 Turkey formally recognized the Armenian Soviet Republic.
1943 Italy, under the leadership of Marshal Pietro Badoglio, declared war on Germany.
1951 a rubber covered football was used for the first time in a major collegiate game in Atlanta, Georgia.
1953 Samuel Bagno patented a burglar alarm operated by ultrasonic or radio waves.

The following people were born on October 13:

Virgil in 70 B.C.

Molly Pitcher in 1754.
Lillie Langtry in 1853.
George E. "Rube" Waddell in 1876.
Al Spalding in 1893.
William "Pickles" Dillhoefer in 1894.
Lenny Bruce in 1926.
Art Garfunkel in 1942.
Marie Osmond in 1959.

October 14   Quarrel Festival (Himeji, Japan)
                                     Yemen People's Republic's National
                                        Day
                                     Madagascar's National Day

610 A.D., the Grand Canal connection to Hangchow was opened.
815 A.D., Geber, an Arabian alchemist and author, died in Al-Kufah
    at the age of ninety-four.
1066 Normans conquered England at the Battle of Hastings.
1812 E.F. Vidocq became the first head of the French department
    of police detectives.
1840 the first general conference of the Second Advent Believers
    convened in Boston.
1884 George Eastman patented transparent paper strip photographic
    film.
1915 Bulgaria declared war on Serbia.
1922 Lester J. Maitland piloted an aircraft in excess of 200 m.p.h.
1947 the first faster than sound airplane flight was accomplished
    by pilot Charles E. Yeager.
1958 the Malagasy Republic was established.

The following people were born on October 14:

William Penn in 1644.
Dwight D. Eisenhower in 1890.
e e cummings (Edward Estlin Cummings) in 1894.
Lillian Gish in 1896.
Roger Moore in 1927.
John Dean in 1938.

October 15   Hurricane Thanksgiving Day (third
                                        Monday in the Virgin Islands)
                                     King's Birthday (Afghanistan)
                                     Sweetest Day (third Saturday)
                                     Tunisia Evacuation Day

White Cane Safety Day

1789 President George Washington began a tour of the New England states.
1878 the Edison Electric Light Company of New York City was incorporated to finance development of Thomas Edison's incandescent lamp.
1900 Billy Bolden is said to have formed the first jazz band.
1902 "Jelly Roll" Morton, self-proclaimed inventor of jazz, wrote "New Orleans Blues," his first jazz orchestration.
1915 Great Britain and Montenegro declared war on Bulgaria.
1917 the U.S. Army granted its first commissions to graduates of its camp for training negro officers in Des Moines, Iowa.
1939 Andy Farkas caught a ninety-nine yard touchdown pass from Frank Filchock for Washington.
1948 Frances L. Willoughby became the first woman doctor in the regular U.S. Navy.
1950 Aircall, Inc. instituted a radio-paging service in New York City.
1964 Alexei Kosygin succeeded Nikita Khrushchev as Soviet Premier.

The following people were born on October 15:

Friedrich W. Nietzsche in 1844.
John L. Sullivan in 1858.
Barry McGuire in 1935.
Richard Carpenter in 1946.

October 16   National Boss Day
                                World Food Day (United Nations)

 961 B.C., King David died after a thirty-nine year reign over the nation of Israel.
1676 the Treaty of Zuravno ended the war between Poland and the Turks.
1829 the Tremont House opened in Boston, Massachusetts and claimed the distinction of being the first hotel in the United States.
1846 anaesthesia was first used in major surgery.
1915 France declared war on Bulgaria.
1916 Fania Mindell, Ethel Byrne and Margaret Sanger opened a birth control clinic in Brooklyn.
1923 John Harwood patented the self-winding watch in Switzerland.
1934 Mao Tse-tung's army began its "Long March."
1946 Gordie Howe played in his first N.H.L. game for the Detroit Red Wings.
1949 civil war in Greece came to an end after more than three years of fighting.
1964 the People's Republic of China exploded its first nuclear device.

1973 the formation of OPEC was announced and the price of oil was raised.

The following people were born on October 16:

Noah Webster in 1758.
Oscar Wilde in 1856.
Eugene O'Neill in 1888.
William O. Douglas in 1898.
Leon "Goose" Goslin in 1900.
Walter "Boom-Boom" Beck in 1904.
Robert Ardrey in 1908.
Matt Batts in 1921.
Angela Lansbury in 1925.
Dave DeBusschere in 1940.

October 17   Dessalines Memorial Day (Haiti)
                                      Durga Puja begins (Bangladesh)
                                      Mother's Day (Malawi)

1777 the United States celebrated a national day of thanksgiving to commemorate the surrender of General John Burgoyne.
1834 James Bogardus patented a (dry) gas meter.
1888 the Capitol Savings Bank was organized. It was the first privately operated bank for blacks run by blacks.
1895 James Pullinger was ticketed for driving a "locomotive (automobile) during prohibited hours."
1941 the U.S.S. Kearny suffered a torpedo attack in the North Atlantic and became the first American warship to be torpedoed in World War II.
1943 the Detroit Lions set a record by rushing for a negative fifty-three yards against the Chicago Cardinals.
1948 "Pat" Harder of the Chicago Cardinals kicked nine "PAT's" against the New York Giants.
1954 Connie Mack sold his interest in the Philadelphia Athletics.
1956 the world's first full scale nuclear power plant opened in Calder Hall, England.
1957 Albert Camus was awarded the Nobel Prize for literature.
1973 Arab oil producing nations began a curtailment of oil shipments to the more industrialized nations.
1978 Michael MacDonald caught a 1,235 pound bluefin tuna near Prince Edward Island.

The following people were born on October 17:

Richard M. Johnson in 1781.
William "Candy" Cummings in 1848.

William "Buck" Ewing in 1859.
Rita Hayworth in 1918.
Tom Poston in 1927.
Cozy Cole in 1928.
Sterling Moss in 1929.
Jimmy Breslin in 1930.
Robert C. "Evel" Knievel in 1938.
James Seals in 1941.

October 18   Alaska Day
                                       Feast of St. Luke

4224 B.C., Al-Halli, the first recognized full-time scribe, invented
     writing in Mesopotamia.
1648 the "shoomakers of Boston" became the first group to have
     an authorized labor organization in the United States.
1685 the Edict of Nantes was revoked.
1870 Benjamin C. Tilghman patented a sand blasting process.
1892 the first telephone communications were opened between New
     York and Chicago.
1912 Turkey ended its war with Italy and embarked on another against
     Bulgaria, Serbia, Greece and Montenegro.
1930 Joseph Sylvester became the first jockey ever to win seven
     races in one day.
1942 Cecil Isbell, of the Green Bay Packers, threw a four inch touch-
     down pass to Don Huston against the Cleveland Rams.
1943 the U.S. Army crossed the Volturno River to capture Cancello.
1978 Gilbert Ponzi caught a fifty-three pound, ten ounce snook in
     Costa Rica.

The following people were born on October 18:

William "Boileryard" Clarke in 1868.
Pierre Elliott Trudeau in 1919.
Melina Mercouri in 1925.
George C. Scott in 1927.
Laura Nyro in 1947.

October 19   Robert H. Goddard's Anniversary
                                          Day
                                       Jamaica National Heroes Day
                                       Yorktown Day
                                       National Cleaner Air Week (begins
                                          Sunday of the last full week)

1198 Averröes, an Arabian philosopher, died in Morocco at the age
of seventy-two.
1466 after a successful war against the Teutonic Order, Poland acquired control of a number of Baltic ports in the Second Peace
of Thorn.
1781 General Charles Cornwallis surrendered at Yorktown.
1812 Napoleon began his disastrous retreat from Moscow.
1859 John Brown raided Harper's Ferry.
1874 Mary Walsh and Charles M. Colton were married in a balloon
over Cincinnati.
1879 Thomas Alva Edison successfully tested the first working incandescent electric light bulb.
1915 Italy and Russia declared war on Bulgaria.
1926 John C. Garand patented a semi-automatic rifle.
1936 Watertown (South Dakota) Senior High School began fingerprinting
all its students after listening to a lecture delivered by an
F.B.I. member.
1944 Marlon Brando made his stage debut.
1951 the United States formally ended the war with Germany.

The following people were born on October 19:

Cassius Marcellus Clay in 1810.
Mordecai "Three Finger" Brown in 1876.
Jack Anderson in 1922.
Peter Max in 1937.

October 20   Beograd Liberation Day (Yugoslavia)
                                       Kenyatta Day (Kenya)
                                       1944 Revolution Anniversary (Gua-
                                       temala)

1842 United States naval forces seized Monterrey, Mexico.
1903 an adjustment was made to the United States-Canada border
to the advantage of the United States.
1906 Dr. Lee deForest announced the development of a three element
vacuum tube: the triode.
1919 the Women's International Bowling Congress was organized.
1930 the Passfield White Paper suggested that some limitations on
Jewish immigration into Palestine might be beneficial.
1944 U.S. forces began an invasion of the Philippines.
1946 Frank Seno, of the Chicago Cardinals, returned a kick-off 105
yards against the New York Giants.
1950 United Nations forces took Pyongyang.
1951 Corporal Max Klinger was evaluated for a section eight discharge
by Divisional Psychiatrist Major Sidney Friedman.
1952 unrest among Mau Mau tribesmen prompted a declaration of
a state of emergency in Kenya.

1962 China and India got into a border war in the Himalaya Mountains.
1973 the Arab members of O.P.E.C. imposed an oil embargo on the United States.
1973 Attorney General Elliot Richardson resigned and President Richard Nixon fired William D. Ruckelshaus and Archibald Cox.

The following people were born on October 20:

Christopher Wren in 1632.
John Dewey in 1859.
Art Buchwald in 1925.
Mickey Mantle in 1931.

October 21   Anniversary of the Somali Revolution
                                       Honduran Armed Forces Day
                                       St. Ursula's Day (British Virgin Islands)
                                       Shah's Birthday (Iran)

1639 the State of Virginia passed an "act to compel physicians and surgeons to declare on oath the value of their medicines."
1805 Lord Horatio Nelson died victorious at the Battle of Trafalgar.
1842 United States naval forces restored Monterrey to Mexican control with apologies ("We thought we were at war!").
1849 James F. O'Connell appeared at the Franklin Theatre in New York as the "wonderful 'Tattooed Man'."
1917 the first American division to enter the World War I trenches did so near Nancy, France.
1923 the Deutsche Museum in Munich opened its planetarium.
1925 Westinghouse demonstrated a photoelectric cell at the Electrical Show in New York City.
1938 Canton fell to the Japanese.
1959 the Guggenheim Museum, designed by Frank Lloyd Wright, was formally opened.
1960 Great Britain's first nuclear powered submarine, H.M.S. Dreadnought, was launched.
1978 Daniel Vaccaro caught a ten and a quarter pound Atlantic bonito off Block Island.

The following people were born on October 21:

Alfred Nobel in 1833.
Whitey Ford in 1928.
Manfred Mann in 1941.
Carrie Fisher in 1956.

October 22   Labour Day (fourth Monday in New
                                              Zealand)
                                              World's End Day

 741 A.D., Charles the Hammer Martel died at the age of fifty-three.
1797 Andre-Jacques Garnerin made his first parachute jump.
1819 boat traffic began to use the first stretch of the Erie Canal
     from Rome to Utica.
1836 Sam Houston was sworn in as the President of Texas.
1844 according to William Miller, the world was to come to an end.
1883 the first opera was performed at the Metropolitan Opera House.
1915 the first intelligible wireless message was sent across the Atlantic
     Ocean.
1934 "Pretty Boy" Floyd was killed by F.B.I. agents in Ohio.
1953 France agreed to grant independence to Laos.
1962 President Kennedy publicized the Soviet/Cuban missile crisis
     and announced the imposition of a naval "quarantine" on Cuba.
1977 Eddie O'Daniel caught a thirty-two and a half pound smallmouth
     buffalo in Mississippi.

The following people were born on October 22:

Sarah Bernhardt in 1845.
Charles "Chick" Lathers in 1888.
Jimmie Foxx in 1907.
Annette Funicello in 1942.
Catherine Deneuve in 1943.

October 23   Chulalongkorn Day (Thailand)

the swallows leave San Juan Capistrano.
1814 the first modern plastic surgery operation was performed in
     Chelsea, England.
1850 a national convention of women advocating woman suffrage
     was held in Worcester, Massachusetts.
1885 Bryn Mawr College opened.
1911 the first wartime reconnaissance flight was made by the Italian
     Army Aviation Corps in Libya.
1915 the United States Horseshoe Pitchers' Association held its first
     national championship in Kellerton, Iowa.
1926 Stalin came out on top in his power struggle with Trotsky.
1936 Senator Arthur H. Moore dedicated the Millville, New Jersey
     "old age colony" at Roosevelt Park.
1944 the Battle of Leyte Gulf began.
1956 the Hungarian uprising began.
1977 David A. Hubbard caught an eight pound, three ounce redeye
     bass in Georgia.

1983 a suicide truck-bombing of Marine headquarters in Beirut killed 269 of the Marines stationed there as part of the multinational peace-keeping force.

The following people were born on October 23:

Adlai E. Stevenson in 1835.
Daniel "Jumping Jack" Jones in 1860.
Johnny Carson in 1925.
Jim Bunning in 1931.
Pele (Edson Arantes do Nascimento) in 1940.

October 24   Suez National Day (Egypt)
                                  United Nations Day
                                  World Development Information
                                      Day (United Nations)
                                  Zambia Independence Day
                                  Disarmament Week (United Nations)

the sun enters the house of Scorpio.
1648 the Treaties of Westphalia were concluded and Switzerland received formal recognition as an independent nation.
1836 Alonzo D. Phillips patented the match.
1882 Dr. Robert Koch discovered the tuberculosis germ.
1897 the New York Journal produced its first Sunday color supplement. It featured the "Yellow Kid" comic strip.
1901 Anna Edson Taylor went over the Niagara Falls in a barrel.
1917 the Caporetto campaign began in Italy.
1945 the United Nations formally came into existence.
1964 Zambia became an independent republic.
1970 Salvador Allende-Gossens, a marxist, was elected president of Chile.

The following people were born on October 24:

Anton van Leeuwenhoek in 1632.
Belva Lockwood in 1830.
James S. Sherman in 1855.
Yelberton A. Tittle in 1926.
David Nelson in 1936.
Juan Marichal in 1937.

October 25   St. Crispin's Day
                                  Sourest Day

Daylight Savings Time comes to an end at 2:00 a.m. (the last Sunday in October).
1400 Geoffrey Chaucer died at the age of sixty.
1415 the English defeated the French at the Battle of Agincourt.
1616 Dutchman Dirk Hartog was the first European to reach the vicinity of Australia when he landed on an island off the west coast of that continent.
1854 the "Charge of the Light Brigade" took place during the Battle of Balaclava.
1881 the Earps and the Clantons shot it out at the O.K. Corral in Tombstone, Arizona.
1881 Leslie L. Curtis patented an air brush.
1922 the Irish Dail Eireann adopted a constitution.
1929 President Warren G. Harding's Secretary of the Interior was convicted of accepting a $100,000 bribe.
1931 the George Washington Bridge between New York and New Jersey opened.
1938 Hankow fell to the Japanese.
1950 the People's Republic of China invaded Tibet.
1962 Uganda joined the United Nations.
1971 the People's Republic of China was admitted to the United Nations displacing Nationalist China.
1983 thousands of American troops landed on the small island nation of Grenada, occupied it, and replaced the existing Marxist government.

The following people were born on October 25:

Johann Strauss, Jr. in 1825.
Pablo Ruíz y Picasso in 1881.
Charles E. Coughlin in 1891.
Minnie Pearl (Sarah O.C. Cannon) in 1912.
Tony Franciosa in 1928.
Helen Reddy in 1941.

October 26   Austria's National Day
                                         Beninese Armed Forces Day
                                         Deepavali (Singapore)
                                         Gospel Day (Cook Islands)
                                         Rwandan Armed Forces Day
                                         South Vietnamese Republic Day

4004 B.C., the world, according to the painstaking calculations of the Bishop of Ussher, was created.
1006 Thorfinn Karlsefni and his expedition of about 160 Norse volunteers set up winter quarters in New Brunswick.
1785 the first mules to be imported into the United States arrived.

1825 the Erie Canal connected the Great Lakes with the Atlantic.
1858 Hamilton E. Smith patented a rotary motion washing machine.
1869 the American Jockey Club held a steeplechase at Jerome Park,
     Westchester County, New York; the first to be held in America.
1905 workers in St. Petersburg set up the first "soviet," or council.
1917 Brazil declared war on Germany.
1917 Felix the Cat was introduced to the public.
1955 Ngo Dinh Diem proclaimed South Vietnam to be a republic.
1959 Indian border police clashed with a Chinese force in Ladakh.

The following people were born on October 26:

Leon Trotsky in 1879.
Mahalia Jackson in 1911.
George H. "Snuffy" Stirnweiss in 1918.
Mohammad Reza Pahlavi in 1919.
Lynn Anderson in 1947.
Jaclyn Smith in 1948.

October 27   Angam Day (Nauru)
                                   Country's Change of Name Anniver-
                                     sary (Zaire)
                                   Deepawali (Fiji)
                                   Good Bear Day
                                   Navy Day
                                   Pakistani Revolution Day
                                   Saint Vincent Independence Day

1780 a Harvard College astronomical expedition made observations
     of a solar eclipse at Penobscot Bay.
1795 the Treaty of San Lorenzo between the United States and Spain
     fixed the boundary between the Mississippi Territory and
     West Florida.
1806 Napoleon occupied Berlin.
1869 the Vermont Dairymen's Association was organized.
1936 the Rome-Berlin Axis was initiated.
1938 DuPont announced the invention of nylon.
1947 Groucho Marx's "You Bet Your Life" debuted on ABC radio.
1949 N.L. Higgins caught a thirty-two pound Dolly Varden trout in
     Idaho.
1954 Walt Disney's hour long Sunday night TV program was first broad-
     cast.
1961 Mauritania and Mongolia joined the United Nations.
1962 President John F. Kennedy warned the Soviet Union that the
     United States would not tolerate the maintenance of Soviet
     offensive missiles in Cuba.
1964 Cher changed her last name from LaPierre to Bono.

1971 the Republic of the Congo changed its name to Zaire.

The following people were born on October 27:

Pierre Berthelot in 1827.
Theodore Roosevelt in 1858.
John J. "Egyptian" Healy in 1866.
Dylan Thomas in 1914.
Nanette Fabray in 1920.
Ralph Kiner in 1922.

October 28   Czechoslovakia Independence Day
                                  Folly Day
                                  Greece's National Day
                                  Greek National Day (Cyprus)

1776 following the Battle of White Plains, George Washington withdrew
     his troops to New Jersey.
1886 the Statue of Liberty was dedicated in New York Harbor.
1904 the St. Louis, Missouri police department adopted a finger-print-
     ing identification system.
1918 Czechoslovakia declared its independence.
1919 the Volstead Act was enacted.
1922 Mussolini's fascist "Black Shirts" occupied Rome.
1923 Wilbur "Fats" Henry kicked the officially recognized record
     punt of ninety-four yards for the Canton Bulldogs.
1929 the daughter of Mr. T.W. and Mrs. Evans was born in an airplane
     over Miami, Florida.
1940 Italy invaded Greece but the Greek army successfully counter-
     attacked.
1959 the Papacy of John XXIII, the 262nd Pope, began.
1962 Nikita Khrushchev announced that all Soviet offensive missiles
     would be removed from Cuba.

The following people were born on October 28:

Erasmus in 1466.
Captain James Cook in 1728.
Tommy Tucker in 1863.
Elias C. "Liz" Funk in 1904.
Jonas Salk in 1914.
Cleo Laine in 1928.
Jane Alexander in 1939.

October 29   Turkish National Day (Cyprus)
                                  Turkish Republic Days begin

1618 Sir Walter Raleigh was beheaded.
1766 the Gloucester Fox Hunting Club of Pennsylvania and New Jersey
     held their preliminary organizational meeting.
1911 the United States Supreme Court invoked the Sherman Anti-Trust
     Act and dissolved the American Tobacco Company.
1916 Sherif Hussein was proclaimed King of the Arabs in the Hejaz
     (Saudi Arabia).
1923 Turkey was proclaimed a republic with Kemal Ataturk as its
     president.
1929 the great depression was set off by the N.Y. stock market crash.
1940 conscription numbers were drawn for the upcoming draft.
1947 rain was successfully generated by seeding dry ice into some
     cumulus clouds, and, as a result, rain fell on a forest fire
     at Concord, New Hampshire.
1948 Sandy Saddler upset Willie Pep to win the world boxing feather-
     weight championship.
1956 Israeli forces invaded Egypt in co-operation with France and
     Great Britain, driving to the Suez Canal.
1973 O.J. Simpson gained enough yardage to go over the 1,000 yard
     mark after only seven N.F.L. games.

The following people were born on October 29:

John Keats in 1795.
Bela Lugosi in 1884.
Fannie Brice in 1891.
Joseph Goebbels in 1897.
Melba Moore in 1945.
Kate Jackson in 1949.

October 30   Descending Day of Lord Buddha
                                  from Heaven (Bhutan)

1888 John J. Loud patented a ball point pen.
1894 Daniel M. Cooper patented a time-card time recorder.
1905 the October Manifesto gave Russia a constitution.
1930 the Greeks and Turks concluded the Treaty of Ankara.
1938 Orson Welles' radio broadcast of War of the Worlds frightened
     a lot of people.
1941 the U.S.S. Reuben James was torpedoed and sunk while on convoy
     duty in the North Atlantic. It was the first American destroyer
     to be sunk by a torpedo in World War II.
1956 Soviet forces ended their occupation of Budapest.
1961 the U.S.S.R. exploded a fifty megaton nuclear bomb, the largest
     ever detonated.

1971 Ed Marinaro of Cornell gained 272 yards against Columbia and reached a total of 4,132 yards in his three year career.
1974 Muhammad Ali knocked out George Foreman in the eighth round in Zaire.

The following people were born on October 30:

John Adams in 1735.
Ed Delahanty in 1867.
Emily Post in 1873.
Ezra Pound in 1885.
Charles Atlas in 1894.
Ruth Gordon in 1896.
Bill Terry in 1898.
Grace Slick in 1939.
Henry Winkler in 1945.
Otis Williams in 1949.

October 31   Halloween
                                  National Magic Day
                                  National UNICEF Day
                                  Nevada Day
                                  Reformation Day
                                  Youth Honor Day (Iowa and Massa-
                                      chusetts)

1517 Martin Luther nailed his ninety-five theses to the Wittenberg church door.
1835 the Manufacturers' Mutual Fire Insurance Company of Rhode Island was incorporated. It was the first mutual fire insurance company in the United States.
1864 Nevada was admitted to the Union.
1868 the United States Postal Service approved uniforms for letter-carriers.
1883 the World Woman's Christian Temperance Union was organized.
1892 printed street car transfers went into use for the first time in Rochester, New York.
1926 Harry Houdini died in Detroit after promising his wife that he would try to reappear to her after his death.
1945 heavy fighting had resumed in the Chinese civil war.
1952 the United States detonated the first hydrogen bomb at Eniwetok.
1956 George J. Dufek landed an airplane at the South Pole.

The following people were born on October 31:

Chiang Kai-shek in 1886.
Dale Evans in 1912.
Lee Grant in 1927.

November

The first day of November marks the following commemorations:

All Saints' Day
Anniversary of the Algerian Revolution
Day of the Dead (Mexico, People's Republic of the Congo, Socialist
Republic of Slovenia, Yugoslavia)
Hawke's Bay Provincial Anniversary (New Zealand)
Marlborough Provincial Anniversary (New Zealand)

National Double Talk Week

National Accordion Month

November 1

1755 the great Lisbon earthquake took place.
1836 the Seminoles, under the leadership of Osceola, began resisting
forced removal from their homeland.
1848 the Boston Female Medical School was organized.
1873 Joseph F. Glidden of DeKalb, Illinois, invented barbed wire.
1879 Beadle and Adams, famed publishers of dime novels, published
the literary classic, Mustang Sam, the King of the Plains
by Joseph E. Badger, Jr.
1899 driving licenses issued in the Paris area reached a total of 1,795.
1906 the first forward pass was thrown during a Yale versus Harvard
football game.
1911 the Italian Air Corps conducted history's first airborne bombing
raid.
1939 the "Human Torch" and the "Submariner" first appeared in Marvel
Comics.
1950 the Pope proclaimed the dogma of the Assumption of the Virgin.
1959 Jacques Plante started a trend among N.H.L. goaltenders by
donning a protective mask during a regular season game.
1961 the Interstate Commerce Commission ordered all interstate
bus and rail terminals desegregated.
1964 George Blanda completed a record thirty-seven passes for Houston.

235

1975 Otavio C. Reboucas caught a 174 pound, 3 ounce white marlin in Brazil.

The following people were born on November 1:

Stephen Crane in 1871.
Gary Player in 1936.

November 2   All Souls' Day
                                        Commemoration of Dead (San Ma-
                                            rino)
                                        Election Day (the first Tuesday af-
                                            ter the first Monday in the U.S.)
                                        Memorial Day (Brazil, El Salvador)
                                        North Dakota Admission Day
                                        South Dakota Admission Day

1889 North Dakota and South Dakota were admitted to the Union.
1904 the federal penitentiary at Leavenworth began keeping fingerprint files.
1917 the Balfour Declaration, expressing British support, became a key factor in the establishment of the state of Israel.
1921 the American Birth Control League was founded.
1931 the DuPont Company became the first commercial scale producer of synthetic rubber.
1933 Ras Tafari ascended the throne of Ethiopia as Haile Selassie I.
1938 Germany awarded southern Slovakia to Hungary.
1940 the Luftwaffe bombed London for the fifty-seventh consecutive night.
1942 Field Marshall Montgomery defeated a German army at El Alamein.
1963 South Vietnamese President Ngo Dinh Diem was killed in a coup.

The following people were born on November 2:

Daniel Boone in 1734.
Marie Antoinette in 1755.
James K. Polk in 1795.
Warren G. Harding in 1865.
Burt Lancaster in 1913.

November 3   Culture Day (Japan)
                                  Dominica Independence Day
                                  Grand Festival of St. Hubert (Bel-
                                      gium)
                                  Independence of Cuenca (Ecuador)
                                  Panama Independence from Colom-
                                      bia Day

7729 B.C., Barzur announced his newly developed cloth making tech-
     nique called "weaving" at a news conference in eastern Turkey.
1837 prices of eight cents a pound for butter, three cents a pound
     for beef and twenty cents a pound for coffee, prompted Illinois
     housewives to stage a protest.
1863 J.T. Alden patented his yeast preparation.
1903 Panama declared its independence from Colombia.
1918 Austria-Hungary surrendered.
1918 the Polish Republic was proclaimed.
1930 the Detroit-Windsor Tunnel for cars and trucks opened.
1936 Ireland established a new constitution which abrogated its rela-
     tionship with Great Britain.
1946 the new Japanese constitution went into effect.
1954 Linus Pauling won a Nobel Prize for chemistry.
1957 the Soviet Union announced the launching of its second satellite,
     this one with a live dog aboard.
1978 Dominica became an independent nation.

The following people were born on November 3:

Bronco Nagurski in 1908.
Bob Feller in 1918.
Charles Bronson in 1922.
Larry Holmes in 1949.

November 4   Melbourne Cup Day (Victoria,
                                      Australia)
                                  Mischief Night (England)
                                  Panamanian Flag Day
                                  Will Rogers Day (Oklahoma)
                                  Tongan Constitution Day

1846 Benjamin F. Palmer patented an artificial leg.
1862 Richard J. Gatling patented his Gatling (machine) gun.
1873 Anthony Iske patented a slicing machine for dried beef.
1879 James J. Ritty patented the cash register.
1914 Russia and Serbia declared war on Turkey.
1922 the entrance to King Tutankhamen's tomb was discovered.
1923 George Halas, of the Chicago Bears, picked up an Oorang Indians
     fumble and ran it back ninety-eight yards for a touchdown.

1924 Mrs. Nellie Ross was elected Governor of Wyoming.
1934 the Detroit Lions set a record by rushing for 426 yards against Pittsburgh.
1956 Soviet troops mobilized to suppress the Hungarian insurrection.
1979 sixty hostages and the American Embassy in Tehran were seized by Iranian "students."

The following people were born on November 4:

Bobby Wallace in 1873.
Will Rogers in 1879.
Walter Cronkite in 1916.
Art Carney in 1918.
Martin Balsam in 1919.
Forrest "Spook" Jacobs in 1925.

November 5   Guy Fawkes' Day (England)
                                  First Cry of Independence (El Salvador)

1605 Guy Fawkes tried to blow up King James I and the Parliament.
1607 Guy Fawkes' Day was observed for the first time.
1639 the first colonial post office was established in Massachusetts.
1733 John P. Zenger began publishing the New York Weekly Journal; the first political newspaper in the United States.
1875 Susan B. Anthony was arrested for attempting to vote.
1895 George B. Selden received a patent for the automobile.
1911 the first transamerican flight took eighty-two hours and four minutes.
1914 France and Great Britain declared war on Turkey.
1930 the first commercial television broadcast was aired.
1972 M.R. Webster caught a nineteen and three quarter pound bowfin in South Carolina.
1974 Ella Grasso was elected governor of Connecticut.

The following people were born on November 5:

Eugene V. Debs in 1855.
Alfred "Greasy" Neale in 1891.
Orlin "Buck" Rogers and Roy Rogers in 1912.
Vivien Leigh in 1913.
Ike Turner in 1931.
Elke Sommer in 1941.
Nancy Green in 1943.
Tatum O'Neal in 1963.

November 6   Al-Massira Celebration Day (Moroc-
co)
Arbor Day (Samoa)
Gustavus Adolphus Day (Sweden)

355 A.D., Julian was chosen to be Caesar.
1869 the first college football game was played between Princeton
and Rutgers.
1884 Great Britain annexed the southeastern portion of New Guinea.
1906 a reorganization of the Chinese governmental system began
the suppression of the opium trade that eventually reached
a point where British importation of opium into China was
reduced to 4,136 chests in the year of 1915.
1917 the Bolshevik revolution in Russia began.
1933 Adolf Hitler said, "Your child belongs to us already."
1934 General Electric made the first installation of a "talking headlight" for the Union Pacific Railroad.
1943 Soviet troops recaptured Kiev.
1962 Richard M. Nixon held his "last" press conference and told the
press, "You won't have Dick Nixon to kick around anymore."
1966 Timmy Brown, of the Philadelphia Eagles, ran back two kick-offs
for touchdowns in the same game against the Dallas Cowboys.

The following people were born on November 6:

Absalom Jones in 1746.
John Philip Sousa in 1854.
Walter Johnson in 1887.
Ray Conniff in 1916.

November 7   Al Hijra (Oman)
Bangladesh Revolution Day
October Revolution Day (U.S.S.R.)

1519 Hernan Cortés' band of Conquistadors were dazzled at their
first sight of Tenochtitlan.
1659 the Treaty of the Pyrenees between France and Spain was signed.
1805 Lewis and Clark first sighted the Pacific Ocean.
1811 the Battle of Tippecanoe was fought.
1872 the Mary Celeste sailed from New York, bound for Genoa. The
ship was found adrift and abandoned in the Atlantic four
weeks later. The fate of those aboard is still unknown.
1874 the Republican Party was first represented by an elephant in
a political cartoon.
1876 Albert H. Hook patented a cigarette manufacturing machine.
1917 the Bolsheviks, led by Lenin, established the Council of People's
Commissars.

1932 "Buck Rogers in the Twenty-Fifth Century" was first heard
     on CBS radio.
1932 Stalin's second wife, Nadya, committed suicide after he had
     ordered the execution of an exiled friend of hers to whom
     she had recently written.
1940 the Tacoma Narrows Bridge collapsed into Puget Sound.
1973 Elvin Hooper caught a ninety pound red drum in North Carolina.

The following people were born on November 7:

Edward S. "The Only" Nolan in 1857.
Marie Curie in 1867.
Heinrich Himmler in 1900.
Konrad Lorenz in 1903.
Billy Graham in 1918.
Al Hirt in 1922.
Mary Travers in 1937.
Johnny Rivers in 1942.
Joni Mitchell in 1943.

November 8   Abet and Aid Punsters Day
                                  Dunce Day
                                  Montana Admission Day
                                  Youth Appreciation Week (begins
                                    the second Monday)

 432 A.D., Patrick arrived in Ireland to begin his ministry.
1519 Hernan Cortés was received by Montezuma in Tenochtitlan.
1731 Benjamin Franklin organized the first circulating library in
     Philadelphia.
1793 the Louvre opened as a museum.
1889 Montana was admitted to the Union.
1895 Wilhelm Roentgen discovered X-rays.
1910 William M. Frost patented an insect electrocutor.
1920 White Russian troops evacuated the Crimea and the Russian
     civil war came to an end.
1923 Adolf Hitler proclaimed the "Beer Hall Putsch" in Munich. Luden-
     dorff and Hitler were jailed. It was during this imprisonment
     that Hitler wrote Mein Kampf.
1942 Allied troops landed on the coast of North Africa.
1978 Arboukoba Volcano erupted for the first time in some 3,000
     years.

The following people were born on November 8:

Edmund Halley in 1656.
Beauty McGowan in 1901.

Katharine Hepburn in 1909.
Patti Page in 1927.
Minnie Riperton in 1948.

November 9   Cambodia Independence Day (Kam-
                                      puchea)
                                  Feast of the Dedication of the
                                      Basilica of St. John Lateran
                                  Peacemakers Day (Barbados)

1756 stage coach service between New York and Philadelphia was
     inaugurated.
1820 the Mercantile Library Association of the City of New York
     was organized.
1835 G.W. Davis received authorization to recruit twenty more men
     for the Texas Rangers.
1889 free mail delivery was established in cities with 5,000 or more
     inhabitants.
1911 George Claude applied for a patent for a neon tube advertising
     sign.
1918 Kaiser Wilhelm II abdicated and a German republic was pro-
     claimed.
1936 the giant panda was discovered in China.
1938 thousands of German Jews were sent to concentration camps
     in two days of pogroms.
1961 Major R.M. White piloted the X-15 rocket plane to a speed
     of 4,093 m.p.h.
1965 a power failure at the Niagara Falls generating plant resulted
     in a blackout of the eastern seaboard of the United States.

The following people were born on November 9:

Benjamin Banneker in 1731.
Ed Wynn in 1886.
Hedy Lamarr in 1915.
Spiro T. Agnew in 1918.
Carl Sagan in 1934.
Bob Gibson in 1935.

November 10   Hero Day (Indonesia)
                                  Kasmandlfahren (Lungau, Austria)
                                  Marine Corps Birthday
                                  St. Martin's Eve

4029 B.C., entombment of the first chieftain took place at the stone
     tombs at Ile Carn in Brittany.
1206 a solar eclipse occurred.
1635 Saybrook, the first English settlement in Connecticut, was estab-
     lished.
1775 the first United States Marines were organized.
1801 the state of Kentucky outlawed dueling.
1856 the Odontological Society of London was founded.
1872 Sir Henry Morgan Stanley found Dr. David Livingstone.
1891 the World Woman's Christian Temperance Union held its first
     convention in Boston.
1919 the American Legion held its first national convention.
1951 coast to coast dial telephone service, unaided by an operator,
     became available.

The following people were born on November 10:

Martin Luther in 1483.
Ray Bolger in 1904.
Tommy Dorsey in 1905.
Richard Burton in 1925.
Norm Cash in 1934.
Donna Fargo in 1945.
Dave Loggins in 1947.

November 11   Angola Independence Day
                                       Armistice Day for World War I
                                          (Belgium, France)
                                       Birthday of His Majesty the King
                                          (Bhutan)
                                       Cartagena Day (Colombia)
                                       Concordia Day
                                       Maldivian Republic Day
                                       Martinmas (St. Martin's Day)
                                       Remembrance Day (Bermuda,
                                          Canada, Turks and Caicos Islands)
                                       Rhodesia Independence Day
                                       Tazaungdaing (Burma)
                                       Veterans' Day
                                       Washington Admission Day

11,092 B.C., the Main Würm (Wisconsin) period of glaciation came
     to an end.
1817 Senaa Samma demonstrated the art of sword swallowing at
     St. John's Hall in New York City.
1851 Alvan Clark patented his telescope.
1865 Great Britain concluded a treaty of peace with the government
     of Bhutan settling various territorial disputes.

1889 Washington was admitted to the Union.
1917 the state of New York granted women the right to vote.
1918 World War I came to an end.
1921 the "Unknown Soldier" was buried at Arlington National Cemetery.
1925 Robert A. Millikan announced the detection of cosmic rays.
1945 Marshal Tito's National Front won a substantial majority in the election in Yugoslavia.
1965 Rhodesia unilaterally declared its independence but the rest of the world withheld recognition.
1968 the Maldives declared itself a republic.
1975 Angola (with Cabinda) became an independent nation.
1977 Siegried Dickemann caught an eighty-eight pound, two ounce albacore in the Canary Islands.

The following people were born on November 11:

Fyodor M. Dostoyevsky in 1821.
General George S. Patton in 1885.
Walter J. "Rabbit" Maranville in 1891.
Harold J. "Pie" Traynor in 1899.
Alger Hiss in 1904.
Kurt Vonnegut in 1922.
Jonathan Winters in 1925.
La Vern Baker in 1929.

November 12   Birthday of Sun Yat-sen (Republic
of China-Taiwan)
Elizabeth Cady Stanton Day

1859 a flying trapeze act was first performed in a circus.
1861 a cargo of oil was exported from the United States to Europe.
1903 the American Humane Association was incorporated.
1921 the Washington Conference opened. It was attended by representatives from Belgium, China, France, Great Britain, Italy, Japan, the Netherlands, Portugal, and the United States.
1941 Alma Heflin made her first flight as a test pilot.
1948 the Allies' war crimes tribunal sentenced Tojo and six other Japanese leaders to death. Sixteen others were sentenced to life imprisonment.
1956 Morocco, Sudan and Tunisia joined the United Nations.
1967 the Detroit Lions set an N.F.L. record by fumbling the ball eleven times, losing it five of those times.
1970 the worst cyclone/tidal wave of the century hit East Pakistan: 500,000 were killed.
1974 women were first added to the United Nations' Security Force.

1978 Luke J. Samaras caught a 189 pound, 2 ounce dog-tooth tuna
     in Tanzania.
1980 "Voyager I" flew within 77,000 miles of Saturn, sending back
     a great deal of surprising and inexplicable information.
1981 the space shuttle <u>Columbia</u> made its second flight into space.

The following people were born on November 12:

Elizabeth Cady Stanton in 1815.
Baha'u'llah in 1817.
Alexander Borodin in 1834.
Auguste Rodin in 1840.
Sun Yat-sen in 1867.
Carl Mays in 1891.
Grace Kelly in 1929.
Booker T. (Jones) in 1944.
Neil Young in 1945.

November 13   Feast of St. Homobonus

72,446,218 B.C., the first true primate was born to proud semi-primate
     parents.
1635 Thomas Parr, of Shropshire, England, died at the age of 152.
1839 the Liberty (anti-slavery) Party held its first convention.
1868 the National Philological Association was organized.
1918 the Austrian Republic was proclaimed.
1927 the Holland Tunnel opened.
1938 Mother Frances Xavier Cabrini was beatified.
1946 cloud seeding in Massachusetts produced the first artificially
     caused snowfall.
1955 Jose Fenykövi, on finding the largest elephant on record when
     he flew into Angola, shot and killed it.
1966 Detroit Lion Garo Yepremenian kicked six field goals against
     the Minnesota Vikings.
1974 Karen Silkwood died in an auto crash.
1981 the "Double Eagle V" completed the first manned transpacific
     balloon flight.

The following people were born on November 13:

St. Augustine in 354 A.D.
James C. Maxwell in 1831.
Edwin Booth in 1833.
Robert Louis Stevenson in 1850.
Paul Simon in 1942.

November 14   King Hussein's Birthday (Jordan)

1832 the world's first streetcar was introduced in New York City.
1851 Moby Dick was published.
1889 Nellie Bly set out to circle the world.
1910 an aircraft was launched from a naval vessel for the first time
     in history off the coast of Virginia.
1915 Booker T. Washington died in Tuskegee, Alabama at the age
     of fifty-seven.
1920 Joe Guyon, of the Canton Bulldogs, kicked a ninety-five yard
     punt against the Chicago Tigers.
1943 Sid Luckman, of the Chicago Bears, threw seven touchdown
     passes in one game against the New York Giants.
1956 the last of the rebels in Hungary capitulated. The estimated
     death toll in the Hungarian insurrection was 25,000 Hungarians
     and 7,000 Soviets.
1959 a major eruption of Kilauea began.
1972 the Dow-Jones average closed at over a thousand points.

The following people were born on November 14:

Maurice of Nassau in 1567.
Robert Fulton in 1765.
Sir Charles Lyell in 1797.
Claude Monet in 1840.
Jawaharlal Nehru in 1889.
Brian Keith in 1941.

November 15   Brazilian Republic Day
                                   Children's Shrine Visiting Day (Ja-
                                       pan)
                                   Dynasty Day (Belgium)

1315 the Swiss defeated Leopold of Austria in the Battle of Morgarten.
1777 the Articles of Confederation were adopted by the United States
     of America.
1881 the Federation of Organized Trades and Labor Unions (later
     known as the American Federation of Labor) was formed.
1887 the British steamer Wah Yeung burned at sea. Four hundred
     lives were lost.
1889 Dom Pedro II of Brazil, the last emperor in the western hemi-
     sphere, was dethroned.
1896 the Niagara Falls waterpower electricity generating station
     began transmitting power to Buffalo, New York.
1919 the U.S. Senate invoked cloture for the first time.
1926 NBC began operations.
1935 the Philippine commonwealth government was formally estab-
     blished under the United States' supervision.

1941 the German army began the Siege of Sevastopol.
1950 Arthur Dorrington became the first black player in major organized hockey.
1953 "Buddy" Young, of the Baltimore Colts, returned a kick-off 104 yards for a touchdown against the Philadelphia Eagles.
1969 President Richard Nixon watched football on TV inside, while outside, thousands were protesting the Vietnam War.

The following people were born on November 15:

Sir William Herschel in 1738.
Field Marshal Erwin Rommel in 1891.
Curtis Lemay in 1906.
Kit Carson in 1912.
Howard Baker in 1925.
Ed Asner in 1929.
Petula Clark in 1934.

November 16   First day of Ashura (Oman)
                                   Oklahoma Admission Day
                                   Statia and America Day
                                   National Farm-City Week (Friday
                                   before Thanksgiving)

1532 Francisco Pizarro seized Atahualpa, the Great Inca, and paralyzed the Incan governmental machinery.
1632 the Battle of Lützen took place.
1776 the British took Fort Washington.
1811 an earthquake in Missouri caused the Mississippi River to flow backwards.
1875 William Gibson Arlington Bonwill patented the dental mallet.
1907 Oklahoma was admitted to the Union.
1914 the Battles of Lodz and Lowicz began.
1918 the Hungarian Republic was proclaimed.
1945 the discovery of americium was announced.
1945 the discovery of curium was announced.
1945 Charles de Gaulle was elected president of the French provisional government.
1955 a dugong arrived in San Francisco.
1969 a report of the Mylai massacre was released.

The following people were born on November 16:

W.C. Handy in 1873.
Burgess Meredith in 1909.
Donna McKechnie in 1942.

November 17   Zairian National Army Day

1637 Anne Hutchinson was brought to trial for her activities in, and
      as founder of, the Antinomian Party. She was banished to
      the wilds of Rhode Island in March of 1638, where, in 1639,
      she founded Newport.
1797 Eli Terry patented his clock which told both "real time" and
      "apparent time."
1800 Congress had its first meeting in the new capitol building.
1831 New Grenada (Colombia) was declared an independent state.
1869 the Suez Canal was officially opened.
1875 the American Theosophical Society was founded by Helena
      Petrovna Blavatsky and Colonel Henry Steele Olcott.
1886 the American Newspaper Publishers Association was organized.
1933 the United States recognized the Soviet government.
1937 Lord Halifax visited with Adolf Hitler at Berchtesgaden.
1966 46,000 meteoroids fell over Arizona within a twenty minute
      time span.

The following people were born on November 17:

Field Marshal B.L. Montgomery of Alamein in 1887.
Rock Hudson in 1925.
Gordon Lightfoot in 1938.
Tom Seaver in 1944.

November 18   Haitian Army Day
                                       Oman's National Day
                                       Return of the King (Morocco)
                                       Vertieres Day (Haiti)

1805 the Lewis and Clark expedition finally reached the Pacific Ocean.
1820 the first historic discovery of Antarctica was made by Captain
      Nathaniel Palmer.
1874 the National Woman's Christian Temperance Union was organized.
1883 the United States adopted a standard time.
1890 the U.S.S. Maine was launched.
1894 the first comic strip, "The Origin of a New Species," by Richard
      Outcault, was printed in the New York Sunday World.
1913 Lincoln Deachey became the first person to do a loop-the-loop
      in an airplane.
1918 Latvia proclaimed its independence.
1935 the League of Nations voted economic sanctions against Italy.
1950 Fairchild Camera and Instrument Corporation announced the
      development of a fluoro-record reflector camera.
1978 Mount Etna erupted on its southeast flank.
1978 Representative Leo J. Ryan and four others were killed by Peo-
      ple's Temple Commune members in Guyana.

The following people were born on November 18:

Louis Daguerre in 1789.
Ignace Jan Paderewski in 1860.
Eugene Ormandy in 1899.
Imogene Coca in 1908.
Mickey Mouse in 1928.
Karl Schranz in 1938.
Brenda Vaccaro in 1939.

November 19   Brazilian Flag Day
                                   Discovery Day (Puerto Rico)
                                   Garifuna Settlement Day (Belize)
                                   Fête National (Monaco)

1493 Christopher Columbus found his way to Puerto Rico.
1794 the United States and Great Britain agreed to an extradition treaty.
1850 Frederick Langenheim patented glass plate magic lantern slides.
1863 Abraham Lincoln delivered his Gettysburg address.
1869 Canada purchased the Northwest Territories from the Hudson's Bay Company.
1872 Edmund D. Barbour patented an adding machine capable of printing sub-totals and totals.
1891 in Goppingen, Germany, the first model train set went on the market.
1941 Linda Darnell became the first woman to sell securities on the floor of the New York Curb Exchange.
1946 Afghanistan, Iceland and Sweden joined the United Nations.
1950 the Los Angeles Rams and the New York Yanks played a football game in which they gained a record combined total of 1,133 yards.
1978 911 people died in a mass suicide led by Reverend Jim Jones at the People's Temple Commune in Guyana.

The following people were born on November 19:

James A. Garfield in 1831.
Billy Sunday in 1862.
Roy Campanella in 1921.
Bob Mathias in 1930.
Dick Cavett in 1936.

November 20   Mexican Revolution Anniversary

1351 B.C., Egyptian Pharaoh Tutankhamen was entombed.
1776 the British took Fort Lee.
1817 Seminole Indians invaded Georgia.
1866 Howard University was founded.
1866 Pierre Lallemont patented a bicycle with a rotary crank.
1929 "The Goldbergs" debuted.
1940 Hungary joined the Axis.
1945 the Nuremberg trials started.
1947 "Meet the Press" debuted on NBC television.
1950 the U.S. Army's Seventh Division reached Manchuria.
1975 the U.S. Senate reported that the Central Intelligence Agency
     had plotted the killings of Fidel Castro, Patrice Lumumba,
     Ngo Dinh Diem, Rafael Trujillo and General Rene Schneider.
1975 the death of Generalissimo Francisco Franco ended his thirty-six
     year dictatorship in Spain.

The following people were born on November 20:

Otto von Guericke in 1602.
Chester Gould in 1900.
Robert F. Kennedy in 1925.
Kaye Ballard in 1926.
Dick Smothers in 1939.

November 21   Burma's National Day
                                   North Carolina Ratification Day
                                   Proclamation Day (Libya)

 479 B.C., Confucius died at the age of seventy-two.
1620 the Mayflower reached Provincetown, Massachusetts.
1766 the Southwark Theater, the first permanent theater building
     in America, opened with Lewis Hallam in The Gamester.
1789 North Carolina ratified the constitution of the United States.
1810 noted English actor George F. Cooke made his American debut
     in New York.
1871 Moses F. Gale patented the cigar lighter.
1922 the Laconia set out to circumnavigate the world.
1933 William C. Bullitt became the first ambassador from the United
     States to the Union of Soviet Socialist Republics.
1943 U.S. forces invaded the Gilbert Islands.
1946 President Harry Truman went for a ride in a captured German
     submarine.
1952 the United States Federal Bureau of Engraving and Printing
     printed its first two-color postage stamps.

The following people were born on November 21:

Socrates in 470 B.C.
Voltaire (François-Marie Arouet) in 1694.
"Handy" Andy High in 1897.
Foster Hewitt in 1903.
Stan Musial in 1920.
Marlo Thomas in 1943.
Goldie Hawn in 1945.

November 22   Feast of St. Cecelia
Guinea's National Day
Lebanon Independence Day
Thanksgiving (fourth Thursday)

1809 Peregrine Williamson patented the steel pen.
1822 El Salvador petitioned the United States to become a participant state in the Union.
1842 Lassen Peak in California erupted.
1910 Arthur F. Knight patented the steel shafted golf club.
1915 the Battle of Ctesiphon began.
1916 Jack London committed suicide.
1923 Lothar Witzke, convicted German spy, was pardoned and deported by President Calvin Coolidge.
1930 the Yale-Harvard football game was broadcast to Great Britain over the BBC.
1932 Robert J. Jauch, Ivan R. Farnham and Ross H. Arnold received a patent for their computer pump.
1963 John F. Kennedy was assassinated in Dallas.
1975 Prince Juan Carlos became King of Spain.

The following people were born on November 22:

René Robert de La Salle in 1643.
George Eliot (Marian Evans) in 1819.
John Nance Garner in 1868.
Charles de Gaulle in 1890.
Wiley Post in 1898.
Hoagy Carmichael in 1899.
Robert Vaughan in 1932.
Billie Jean King in 1943.

November 23   Labor Thanksgiving Day (Japan)
Repudiation Day (Maryland)
Yourwelcomegiving Day (Friday after Thanksgiving)

the sun enters the house of Sagittarius.

5251 B.C., Khav-por discovered that copper could be smelted from malachite in western Afghanistan.

1765 the Court of Frederick County, Maryland repudiated the British Stamp Act.

1835 Henry Burden patented a horseshoe manufacturing machine.

1848 the Female Medical Educational Society of Boston was organized.

1876 Columbia, Harvard and Princeton organized the Intercollegiate Football Association.

1889 the first juke box was installed at the Palais Royal Saloon in San Francisco.

1940 Romania joined the Axis.

1945 food rationing in the United States was ended.

1948 Frank Gerard Back patented a lens that provided zoom effects.

1980 a severe earthquake struck the Naples, Italy area. After a week of searching, 2,915 were found dead, 1,575 were still missing and 7,305 were injured.

The following people were born on November 23:

Franklin Pierce in 1804.
"Billy the Kid" Bonner in 1859.
Boris Karloff in 1887.

November 24   New Regime Day (Zaire)

1807 Thayendanagea (Joseph Brant) died.

1827 the Pennsylvania Horticultural Society was organized.

1863 the first official National Thanksgiving Day was celebrated.

1871 the National Rifle Association was incorporated.

1874 Joseph F. Glidden patented barbed wire.

1885 the Philomena Society was organized.

1896 Vermont enacted an absentee voting law. It was the first of the United States to do so.

1903 Clyde J. Coleman patented the electric self-starter for automobiles.

1949 Bob Smith, of the Detroit Lions, intercepted a pass and ran it back 102 yards for a touchdown against the Chicago Bears.

1971 D.B. Cooper pulled off a successful airplane hijacking by parachuting into the wilderness of the Cascade Mountains in Washington.

The following people were born on November 24:

Baruch Spinoza in 1632.
Zachary Taylor in 1784.
Bat Masterson in 1853.

Toulouse-Lautrec in 1864.
Scott Joplin in 1868.
Robert Sengstacke Abbot in 1870.
Alben W. Barkley in 1877.
Charles "Lucky" Luciano in 1897.
Joe Medwick in 1911.
William F. Buckley in 1925.

November 25   St. Catherine's Day
                                    Suriname Independence Day

1,420,070,968 B.C., the Proterozoic era began.
1542 James V was defeated at the Battle of Solway Moss.
1837 William Crompton patented a silk power loom.
1874 the Greenback Party was organized at Indianapolis, Indiana.
1875 Prime Minister Benjamin Disraeli engineered the purchase of
     the Khedive of Egypt's shares in the Suez Canal for Great
     Britain.
1884 John B. Meyenberg patented evaporated milk.
1912 the American College of Surgeons was incorporated.
1921 Crown Prince Hirohito became regent in Japan.
1922 Benito Mussolini was granted dictatorial powers over Italy.
1936 Germany and Japan signed an anti-Communist pact which was
     later negated by the German-Soviet non-agression pact.
1960 the federal research and development atomic reactor in Richland,
     Washington went into operation.
1965 General Mobutu took over the government of the Republic of
     the Congo (Leopoldville) in a military coup.
1975 Suriname attained independence.
1976 O.J. Simpson gained 273 yards for the Buffalo Bills in a Thanks-
     giving Day football game against the Detroit Lions.

The following people were born on November 25:

Andrew Carnegie in 1835.
Carry Nation in 1846.
Eddie Shore in 1902.
Joe DiMaggio in 1914.
Ricardo Montalban in 1920.
Tina Turner in 1941.

November 26   Acordo de Argelia (São Tomé and
                                       Príncipe)
                                    John Harvard Day

Sojourner Truth Day

885 A.D., Normans attacked Paris.
1716 an African lion was exhibited in America for the first time.
1825 the Kappa Alpha fraternity was established.
1832 the first street railway service in the United States began.
1865 Alice in Wonderland was published.
1867 J.B. Sutherland patented the refrigerated railroad car.
1883 Sojourner Truth died in Battle Creek, Michigan.
1896 the University of Chicago and the University of Michigan played
     a football game indoors at the Chicago Coliseum.
1941 Lebanon proclaimed itself an independent sovereign state.
1950 the Chinese entered the Korean War and drove the United Nations'
     forces back to the thirty-eighth parallel.

The following people were born on November 26:

Charles Schultz in 1922.
Robert Goulet in 1933.
Rich Little in 1938.

November 27   Battle of Tarapaca (Peru)
                                   First Sunday of Advent (four Sun-
                                   days before Christmas)

172,103,155 B.C., an archeopteryx in Yorkshire, England, made the
     first successful flight by a bird for a distance of 8.32 meters.
1095 Pope Urban II preached the First Crusade to a vast throng in
     Clermont-Ferrand.
1676 a major fire in Boston burned, "46 dwelling houses, besides other
     buildings, (the) meeting house, etc."
1779 the College of Philadelphia officially became the University
     of the State of Pennsylvania.
1826 John Walker invented the friction match in England.
1839 the American Statistical Association was organized.
1901 the Army War College in Washington, D.C. was authorized.
1938 Doug Russell, of the Chicago Cardinals, threw a ninety-eight
     yard touchdown pass to Gaynell Tinsley against the Cleveland
     Rams.
1951 a Nike missile, the United States' first ground-to-air missile,
     was successfully tested at the White Sands Proving Ground
     in New Mexico.
1966 the Washington Redskins and the New York Giants football
     teams scored a combined total of 113 points.

The following people were born on November 27:

Anders Celsius in 1701.
Jimi Hendrix in 1942.

November 28   Albania Independence Day
Chadian Republic Day
Mauritania Independence Day
Panama Independence from Spain
Day

1520 Ferdinand Magellan entered the Pacific Ocean.
1895 J. Frank Duryea won the Chicago to Waukegan auto race at
an average speed of 7.5 m.p.h.
1912 Albania became an independent nation.
1917 Estonia proclaimed its independence.
1925 the "Grand Old Opry" originated.
1929 Ernie Nevers, of the Chicago Cardinals, scored forty points
(six touchdowns and four "points after") against the Chicago
Bears.
1943 the Allied Powers opened the Tehran Conference.
1948 "Hopalong Cassidy" debuted on NBC television.
1948 the Polaroid Land Camera went on the market.
1958 Chad proclaimed itself a republic.
1958 the Middle Congo province of French Equatorial Africa voted
to proclaim itself independent as the Congo Republic (Brazzaville).
1958 the Gabon Republic was proclaimed.
1958 Mauritania was renamed the Mauritanian Islamic Republic.
1960 the Mauritanian Islamic Republic proclaimed its independence.
1966 the monarchy of Burundi was overthrown and a republican form
of government put in its place.

The following people were born on November 28:

William Blake in 1757.
Claude Lévi-Strauss in 1908.
Randy Newman in 1943.

November 29   Albania Liberation Day
International Day of Solidarity with
the Palestinian People
President Tubman's Birthday (Liberia)
Yugoslavian Republic Day

1775 the American colonial Committee of Secret Correspondence
was formed.

1825 America's first Italian opera performance took place at the Park Theater in New York City.
1890 the first Army-Navy football game ended with the score: Navy 24, Army 0.
1916 the United States set up a military government in the Dominican Republic.
1922 archeologist Howard Carter opened King Tutankhamen's tomb.
1929 Richard Byrd reached the South Pole by air.
1932 Laurens Hammond patented the electric bridge table.
1933 the state of Pennsylvania authorized state liquor stores.
1945 the Federal People's Republic of Yugoslavia was proclaimed.
1951 the United States conducted an underground atomic bomb test at Frenchman Flat, Nevada.
1953 American Airlines instituted the first regular commercial transcontinental air service from Los Angeles to New York.

The following people were born on November 29:

Christian Johann Doppler in 1803.
Louisa May Alcott in 1832.
Adam Clayton Powell in 1908.
John Mayall in 1933.
Chuck Mangione in 1940.

November 30   St. Andrew's Day
                                    Barbados Independence Day
                                    Benín's National Day
                                    Bonifacio Day (Philippines)
                                    People's Democratic Republic of
                                        Yemen's Independence Day
                                    Youth Day (Upper Volta)

  30 B.C., Cleopatra committed suicide.
1782 Great Britain recognized the United States. A preliminary treaty was signed in Paris.
1803 Spain ceded its claims to Louisiana to France.
1804 Supreme Court Justice Samuel Chase was impeached. He was acquitted.
1875 A.J. Errichson patented the oat-crushing machine.
1922 the Japanese Navy's Hosho began its sea trials. It was the first aircraft carrier to be specifically designed as such.
1936 the Crystal Palace in London was destroyed by fire.
1939 Dwight D. Eisenhower received his airplane pilot's license.
1939 the Russo-Finnish War began.
1950 concentrated milk went on the market for the first time in Wilmington, Delaware.
1954 a meteorite penetrated the roof of a house in Sylacauga, Alabama and struck Elizabeth Hodges.

1966 Barbados proclaimed its independence.
1967 the People's Democratic Republic of (South) Yemen was declared
       an independent nation.

The following people were born on November 30:

St. Gregory of Tours (Georgius Florentius) in 538 A.D.
Jonathan Swift in 1667.
Samuel Clemens (Mark Twain) in 1835.
Winston Churchill in 1874.
Efrem Zimbalist, Jr. in 1923.
Shirley Chisholm in 1924.
Dick Clark in 1929.
Abbie Hoffman in 1936.
Paul Stookey in 1937.

December

The first day of December marks the following commemorations:

Central African Republic Proclamation of the Republic
Macao Restoration of Independence
Madeira Independence Day
National Civil Air Patrol Day
Portugal Independence Restoration Day
University Students' Celebration (Iceland)
Westland Provincial Anniversary (New Zealand)

National Mimicry Week

Hi Nabor Month

December 1

1640 Portugal revolted to win its independence from Spain.
1783 the first hydrogen balloon voyage was made.
1816 gas lights were used commercially for the first time.
1887 China ceded Macao to Portugal.
1903 The Great Train Robbery was copyrighted. It was the first motion picture to employ a story line.
1904 Adon J. Hoffman applied for a patent for a steam operated pressing machine.
1913 the first drive-in automobile service station opened in Pittsburgh, Pennsylvania.
1917 Father Edward Joseph Flanagan founded Boys Town in Nebraska.
1924 the first National Corn Husking Championship Contest was held in Alleman, Iowa.
1940 "Davey" O'Brien, of the Philadelphia Eagles, completed thirty-three of sixty passes against the Washington Redskins.
1955 Rosa Parks refused to give her seat to a white man on a bus in Montgomery, Alabama.
1958 the Central African Republic was proclaimed.
1959 the International Antarctic Treaty was signed in Washington, D.C.

1970 the United States Senate passed the Consumer Protection Bill.

The following people were born on December 1:

Mary Martin in 1913.
Billy Paul in 1934.
Woody Allen and Lou Rawls in 1935.
Lee Trevino in 1939.
Richard Pryor in 1940.
Bette Midler in 1945.

December 2   Lao People's Democratic Republic's
                                  National Holiday
                                  United Arab Emirates Independence
                                  Day

1620 the first English language newspaper was published.
1716 Reverend Samuel Wesley began haunting the Epworth Rectory in Lincolnshire, England.
1805 the Battle of Austerlitz ended the Holy Roman Empire.
1823 the Monroe Doctrine was set forth by President James Monroe.
1859 John Brown was hanged.
1899 the United States acquired Tutuila and its harbor of Pago Pago.
1901 King Camp Gillette patented the disposable blade safety razor.
1909 the National Hockey Association was founded in Montreal.
1927 the Model A Ford was introduced at a cost of $385.
1932 "Charlie Chan" first came to NBC radio.
1942 Enrico Fermi and Arthur Compton achieved the world's first nuclear chain reaction.
1951 Bill Valverde caught a 279 pound alligator gar in Texas.
1954 Senator Joseph McCarthy was condemned by the United States Senate for making improper remarks.
1956 Fidel Castro landed in Cuba with an eighty-two man invasion group.
1967 the first human heart transplant was accomplished by Dr. Christian Barnard.
1971 the United Arab Emirates became independent.

The following people were born on December 2:

Georges Seurat in 1859.
Charles Ringling in 1863.
William Randolph Hearst, Jr. in 1915.
Maria Callas in 1923.

December 3   Feast of St. Francis Xavier
                                                  Illinois Admission Day

1818 Illinois was admitted to the Union.
1825 the Kappa Alpha fraternity held its first initiation.
1833 Oberlin Collegiate Institute opened as the first co-educational
     college in the United States. It later became the first U.S.
     college to accept negroes.
1834 the New York City Society of Surgeon-Dentists was formed.
1875 the Knickerbocker Club Coaching Club was formed to encourage
     the art of four in hand driving.
1910 the first neon lighting display was presented at the Paris Motor
     Show.
1922 Toll of the Sea, the first successful technicolor motion picture,
     was released.
1933 Gil LeFebvre, of the Cincinnati Reds, returned a punt ninety-eight
     yards for a touchdown against the Brooklyn Dodgers.
1934 Glenn Presnell, of the Detroit Lions, kicked a fifty-four yard
     field goal against the Green Bay Packers.
1948 Mary A. Hallaren received her commission and became the
     first woman officer in the regular Army of the United States.
1975 the Lao People's Democratic Republic was proclaimed.

The following people were born on December 3:

Gilbert Stuart in 1755.
Joseph Conrad in 1857.
Anna Freud in 1895.
Jean-Luc Godard and Andy Williams in 1930.

December 4   Day of the Artisans (Mexico)
                                                  Zweigsegen (Austria)

1839 the unit rule was adopted at the Whig Party convention in Harris-
     burg, Pennsylvania.
1843 John M. and Lyman Hollingsworth patented manila paper.
1867 the National Grange of the Patrons of Husbandry was organized.
1876 British trafficking of opium into China continued to increase
     to a rate of more than 82,000 chests per year.
1918 the Kingdom of the Serbs, Croats and Slovenes (Yugoslavia)
     was proclaimed.
1930 the Vatican gave its approval to the rhythm method of birth
     control devised by Dr. Harmann Knaus in 1928.
1935 St. Joseph's College in Philadelphia instituted anti-communist
     college classes.
1958 Dahomey proclaimed itself a republic.
1958 Ivory Coast proclaimed itself a republic.

1977 a hijacked Malay Boeing 737 exploded in mid-air and crashed into the Straits of Jahore.

The following people were born on December 4:

Lillian Russell in 1861.
Jesse Burkett in 1868.
Generalissimo Francisco Franco in 1892.
Harvey Kuenn in 1930.
Horst Buchholz in 1933.
Robert Vesco in 1935.
Max Baer in 1937.
Freddy Cannon in 1940.

December 5   Discovery Day (Haiti)
                                        King's Birthday (Thailand)
                                        St. Nicholas' Day (Austria, Nether-
                                            lands)
                                        Union of Soviet Socialist Repub-
                                            lics' Constitution Day

1,205,776 B.C., the first interglacial period ended and the Mindel (Kansan) period of glaciation began.
1776 the Phi Beta Kappa fraternity was founded.
1784 Phyllis Wheatley died in Boston.
1786 insurrectionists prevented the Massachusetts Supreme Court from holding session in what became known as Shays' Rebellion.
1846 C.F. Schoenbein patented cellulose nitrate.
1854 Aaron H. Allen patented the folding theater chair.
1876 Daniel C. Stillson patented his pipe wrench.
1906 the Young Women's Christian Association held its first national convention.
1914 the Battle of Limanova began.
1932 Albert Einstein was granted a visa to go to the United States.
1933 prohibition ended as the thirty-sixth state ratified the twenty-first amendment to the Constitution.
1936 the Soviet government adopted a new constitution.
1937 "Pat" Coffee threw a ninety-seven yard touchdown pass to Gaynell Tinsley for the Chicago Cardinals against the Bears.
1948 Charlie Conerly, of the New York Giants, completed thirty-six of fifty-three passes against the Pittsburgh Steelers.
1955 the Montgomery, Alabama bus boycott began.
1955 the A.F. of L. and the C.I.O. were reunited.
1979 a dozen "UFO's" performed aerobatics over Ansted, West Virginia.

The following people were born on December 5:

Martin Van Buren in 1782.
General George Armstrong Custer in 1839.
Walt Disney in 1901.
Strom Thurmond in 1902.
Otto Preminger in 1906.
Little Richard (Penniman) in 1935.
Jim Messina in 1947.

December 6   Day of Quito (Ecuador)
                                  Finland Independence Day

1492 Christopher Columbus reached the island of Hispaniola, home
     of the Arawak Indians.
1790 the United States Congress met in Philadelphia.
1877 Thomas Edison completed and tested the first phonograph.
1917 Finland proclaimed its independence.
1921 W.L. Mackenzie King was elected Canadian Prime Minister.
1921 a British-Irish treaty granted dominion status to the Irish Free
     State.
1941 the Soviet army counterattacked the Axis invasion.
1941 Great Britain declared war on Finland, Hungary and Romania.
1941 Franklin D. Roosevelt communicated with Hirohito in an attempt
     to avoid war.
1965 more than 125 people died when two trucks crashed into a crowd
     during a festival in Sotouboua, Togo.
1973 Gerald Ford was sworn in as the fortieth Vice-President of
     the United States.

The following people were born on December 6:

Nicholas Leblanc in 1742.
Joseph Louis Gay-Lussac in 1778.
Charles M. Hall in 1863.
Joyce Kilmer in 1886.
Ira Gershwin in 1896.
Dave Brubeck in 1920.

December 7   Cuba's Day of National Mourning
                                  Delaware Ratification Day
                                  Día de la Gritería (Nicaragua)
                                  Uhuru Day (Kenya)

  43 B.C., Mark Anthony had Cicero executed.
1787 Delaware became the first state to ratify the constitution of
     the United States.

1842 the New York Philharmonic Society gave its first public concert.
1891 the underwater railroad tunnel from Port Huron, Michigan to Sarnia, Ontario was opened for traffic.
1909 L.H. Bakeland patented thermosetting plastic.
1916 the Siege of Kut-El-Amara began.
1917 the United States declared war on Austria.
1926 the Electrolux Servel Corporation patented the gas refrigerator.
1941 U.S. manifest destiny and Japanese imperialism collided at Pearl Harbor, Hawaii.
1941 Japanese forces attacked the Philippines, Malaya, Hong Kong, Guam and the Midway Islands.
1945 Percy LeBaron Spencer patented the microwave oven.

The following people were born on December 7:

Mary Queen of Scots in 1542.
Eli Wallach in 1915.
Ted Knight in 1923.
Noam Chomsky in 1928.
Ellen Burstyn in 1932.
Harry Chapin in 1942.
Johnny Bench in 1947.

December 8   Beach Day (Uruguay)
                                  Conception Day (San Marino)
                                  Feast of the Immaculate Conception
                                  Lady of Camarin Day (Guam)
                                  Mothers Day (Panama)

1863 Abraham Lincoln issued the Proclamation of Amnesty and Reconstruction.
1886 the Federation of Organized Trades and Labor Unions adopted the name American Federation of Labor.
1908 Gustavus V became King of Sweden.
1909 the American Bird Banding Association was formed.
1914 the Battle of the Falkland Islands was fought.
1917 Ecuador severed relations with Germany.
1931 Lloyd Espenschied and Herman Affel received a patent for coaxial cable.
1941 Costa Rica, Cuba, the Dominican Republic, El Salvador, Guatemala, Haiti, Honduras, the Union of South Africa and the United States declared war on Japan.
1949 the Nationalist Chinese completed their withdrawal to Formosa, leaving mainland China under the control of Mao Tse-tung.
1963 Frank Sinatra, Jr. was kidnapped.
1980 John Lennon was shot and killed outside his New York apartment by a deranged assassin.

The following people were born on December 8:

Eli Whitney in 1765.
Diego Rivera in 1886.
James Thurber in 1894.
Sammy Davis, Jr. in 1925.
Maximilian Schell in 1930.
Flip Wilson in 1933.
Jim Morrison in 1943.
Greg Allman in 1947.

December 9   Battle of Ayacucho (Peru)
                                  Tanzania Independence and Repub-
                                  lic Day

 536 A.D., Belisarius retook Rome from the Ostrogoths in the name
     of Justinian.
1324 Marco Polo, world traveler, sinologist, successful administrator
     for Kublai Khan, and author of Book of Various Experiences,
     died in Venice at the age of seventy.
1869 the Noble Order of the Knights of Labor was founded.
1884 Levant M. Richardson patented ball-bearing roller skates.
1914 tear gas (xylyl-bromide) was demonstrated by Dr. von Tappen
     for the first time in Kumersdorf, Germany.
1917 the British took Jerusalem.
1934 the Italo-Ethiopian War began.
1938 a live coelacanth was caught off East London, South Africa.
1940 the British began their North African offensive.
1941 the United States commenced bombing in the Philippine Islands.
1961 Tanganyika became an independent nation which later combined
     with Zanzibar into the nation of Tanzania.

The following people were born on December 9:

John Milton in 1608.
Joel Chandler Harris in 1848.
Hermione Gingold in 1897.
Douglas Fairbanks, Jr. in 1909.
Lee J. Cobb and Broderick Crawford in 1911.
Kirk Douglas in 1918.
Redd Foxx (John Elroy Sanford) in 1922.
John Cassavetes in 1929.
Beau Bridges in 1941.
Donny Osmond in 1957.

December 10   Human Rights Day
                                         Mississippi Admission Day
                                         M.P.L.A. Foundation Day (Angola)
                                         Thai Constitution Day

1792 life insurance was first offered to the public by a U.S. company.
1817 Mississippi was admitted to the Union.
1845 Robert W. Thomson patented the pneumatic tyre.
1868 the use of traffic lights was initiated in London.
1869 the territorial legislature of Wyoming granted women the right
     to vote and hold public office.
1898 Spain ceded the Philippines, Puerto Rico and Guam to the United
     States.
1898 Cuba was granted its independence.
1901 the first Nobel Prizes were awarded.
1917 Panama declared war on Austria.
1931 Jane Addams and Dr. Nicholas Murray Butler jointly received
     the Nobel Prize for Peace.
1941 Japanese troops occupied Luzon in the Philippines.
1950 Dr. Ralph J. Bunche received a Nobel Prize.
1958 the first domestic jet airline passenger service began.
1962 the discovery of the molecular structure of DNA was recognized
     with a Nobel Prize.
1963 Zanzibar became an independent nation.

The following people were born on December 10:

Emily Dickinson in 1830.
Una Merkel in 1903.
Morton Gould in 1913.
Johnny Rodriquez in 1951.
Susan Dey in 1952.

December 11   Indiana Admission Day
                                         United Nations Children's Fund
                                         (UNICEF) Anniversary
                                         Upper Voltan Republic Day

1,752,009 B.C., Homo erectus attained the status of a species.
1816 Indiana was admitted to the Union.
1844 a dental extraction was performed with the patient under anaes-
     thesia for the first time.
1872 Pinckney B.S. Pinchback became the first black governor of
     one of the United States when he took over as the acting
     governor of Louisiana.
1919 the citizens of Enterprise, Alabama dedicated a monument
     to the boll weevil.

1936 King Edward VIII of England abdicated his throne for love.
1941 Japan occupied Guam.
1941 the United States declared war on Germany and Italy and vice-
     versa.
1941 Nicaragua declared war on Japan, Germany and Italy.
1946 the United Nations established UNICEF.
1958 the Voltaic Republic was proclaimed.

The following people were born on December 11:

Louis Hector Berlioz in 1803.
Robert Koch in 1843.
Charles "Old Hoss" Radbourn in 1854.
Max Born in 1882.
Carlo Ponti in 1913.
Rita Moreno in 1931.
Brenda Lee in 1944.

December 12   Azarbaijan Liberation Day (Iran)
                                   Nuestra Señora de Guadalupe or
                                     Guadalupe Day (Mexico)
                                   Kenya Independence Day
                                   National Ding-a-Ling Day
                                   Pennsylvania Ratification Day

1787 Pennsylvania ratified the constitution of the United States.
1796 George Chandler patented a nail cutting and heading machine.
1870 Representative Joseph H. Rainey, of South Carolina, was sworn
     in as the first black congressman to serve in the United States
     House of Representatives.
1897 "The Katzenjammer Kids" began appearing in the New York
     Journal.
1899 George F. Grant patented the golf tee.
1901 Guglielmo Marconi sent the first transatlantic wireless radio
     signal.
1916 Germany informed the Allied Powers (through the United States)
     that the Central Powers were prepared to negotiate a peace.
1935 the Egyptian constitution of 1923 was restored after having
     been suspended for seven years.
1936 the Sian Incident took place in which Chiang Kai-shek was kid-
     napped and forced to join various other Chinese factions
     in the fight against the Japanese.
1937 Japanese bombers attacked U.S. and British ships in the Yangtze
     River in what became known as the Panay Incident.
1958 Guinea joined the United Nations.
1963 Kenya became an independent nation.

The following people were born on December 12:

John F. "Phenomenal" Smith in 1864.
Edward G. Robinson in 1893.
Frank Sinatra in 1915.
Clyde Klutz in 1917.
Connie Francis in 1938.
Tom Hayden in 1940.
Dionne Warwick in 1941.

December 13

St. Lucia's Day (Sweden)
Maltese Republic Day

1631 a major eruption of Mount Vesuvius obliterated nearby towns
     and killed 3,000 people. The volcano's lava reached all the
     way to the sea.
1642 Abel Janszoon Tasman came upon New Zealand.
1766 the Gloucester (New Jersey) Fox Hunting Club held its first
     official meeting.
1769 Dartmouth College was chartered.
1853 the New York Infirmary was incorporated and staffed by woman
     physicians.
1903 Italo Marcioni patented the first ice cream cone mold.
1918 U.S. troops crossed the Rhine River into Germany.
1925 Reza Khan was proclaimed Reza Shah Pahlavi of Iran.
1926 the N.F.L. New York Giants beat the A.F.L. Philadelphia Quakers
     in the first interleague playoff, 31-0.
1928 "An American in Paris," by George Gershwin, premiered at
     the New York Philharmonic.
1937 Nanking fell to the Japanese.

The following people were born on December 13:

Drew Pearson in 1897.
Lillian Roth in 1910.
Dick Van Dyke in 1925.
Christopher Plummer in 1929.

December 14

Alabama Admission Day
Halcyon Days begin
Meeting of the Nine Evils (Bhutan)
Saint Lucia Day

1798 David Wilkinson patented the screw.

1798 David Wilkinson patented a nut and bolt machine.
1819 Alabama was admitted to the Union.
1889 the American Academy of Political and Social Science was
     organized.
1911 Roald Amundsen became the first person to reach the South
     Pole.
1924 the temperature dropped seventy-nine degrees in one day in
     Helena, Montana.
1934 New York Central Lines introduced the first streamlined steam
     locomotive.
1955 Albania, Austria, Bulgaria, Cambodia, Ceylon, Finland, Hungary,
     Ireland, Italy, Jordan, Laos, Libya, Nepal, Portugal, Romania
     and Spain joined the United Nations.
1961 Tanganyika joined the United Nations.
1962 "Mariner II" broadcast back thirty-five minutes' worth of informa-
     tion obtained by close-up monitoring of the planet Venus.

The following people were born on December 14:

Nostradamus in 1503.
Tycho Brahe in 1546.
Spike Jones in 1911.
Morey Amsterdam in 1914.
Charlie Rich in 1932.
Abbe Lane and Lee Remick in 1935.
Patty Duke in 1946.

December 15   Bill of Rights Day
                                   Holiday of the Dynasty of Burundi
                                   Mahendra Jayanti or Nepalese
                                     Constitution Day
                                   Statute Day (Netherlands Antilles)
                                   Underdog Day (third Friday)

1654 Luigi Antinori established a weather observation system, taking
     temperatures in four different cities on a daily basis.
1854 Philadelphia began using the first street cleaning machine.
1874 King David Kalakaua of Hawaii was formally received by Presi-
     dent Ulysses S. Grant.
1890 Sitting Bull was killed in a fight with the U.S. Army.
1891 James Naismith, a Canadian clergyman, invented basketball.
1906 the National Geographic Society presented its Hubbard Medal
     to Robert E. Peary.
1942 Massachusetts issued the first plastic license plate tabs.
1948 Alger Hiss was indicted for perjury.
1962 as leader of the victorious white supremacist Rhodesian Front
     Party, Winston Field became Rhodesia's prime minister.

1973 J. Paul Getty III was released by his kidnappers for a ransom of $2,800,000.
1976 the Argo Merchant spilled its oil off Nantucket Island.
1980 Sir Ranulph Fiennes and Charles Burton reached the South pole.

The following people were born on December 15:

Nero in 37 A.D.
Tim Conway in 1933.

December 16   Bahrain's National Day
Canterbury Provincial Anniversary
(New Zealand)
Day of the Covenant (South Africa)
Dingaan's Day (Swaziland)
First of the Nine Days of Posadas
Victory Day (Bangladesh)

1653 Oliver Cromwell became Lord Protector of the British Commonwealth.
1689 the British Parliament enacted a Bill of Rights.
1773 the Boston Tea Party took place.
1811 an earthquake caused the formation of Reelfoot Lake in Tennessee.
1917 Cuba declared war on Austria.
1920 an earthquake in Gansu, China caused 100,000 deaths.
1944 the Battle of the Bulge got underway.
1946 Thailand joined the United Nations.
1951 Jerry Williams, of the Los Angeles Rams, returned a missed field goal ninety-nine yards for a touchdown against the Green Bay Packers.
1952 Eugenio Cavaglia caught a thirty-five pound, fifteen ounce brown trout in Argentina.
1960 a United Airlines DC-8 and a TWA Super-Constellation collided over New York City.
1963 Kenya and Zanzibar joined the United Nations.

The following people were born on December 16:

Ludwig van Beethoven in 1770.
Jane Austen in 1775.
Noel Coward in 1899.
Margaret Mead in 1901.
Liv Ullman in 1939.

December 17   Anniversary of the Death of Simón
                                    Bolívar (Venezuela)
                                    Bhutan's National Day
                                    Wright Brothers Day

1398 Tamerlane sacked the city of Delhi.
1791 New York City instituted one-way traffic regulations.
1798 impeachment proceedings were instituted against United States
     Senator William Blount.
1880 the Edison Electric Illuminating Company was incorporated
     to supply electrical power to New York City.
1895 the Anti-Saloon League of America was formed.
1895 George Loomis Brownell patented machinery for making paper
     twine.
1903 Man's third powered flight was accomplished by the Wright
     Brothers when Orville Wright took off in their aeroplane
     on a twelve second flight at Kitty Hawk, North Carolina.
1917 the worst train wreck in history killed 543 people at Modane,
     France.
1939 the German battleship Graf Spee was scuttled outside the Monte-
     video harbor.
1969 Tiny Tim (Herbert Khaury) married Miss Vicki (Victoria Budinger)
     on "The Tonight Show."

The following people were born on December 17:

Paracelsus (Aureolus Philippus Theophrastus Bombastus von Hohenheim)
     in 1493.
Sir Humphry Davy in 1778.
John Greenleaf Whittier in 1807.
Arthur Fiedler in 1894.
Gene Rayburn in 1917.
Edward James Kendricks in 1939.

December 18   King Alfonso's Decision (Honduras)
                                    New Jersey Ratification Day
                                    Niger Republic Day

1787 New Jersey ratified the constitution of the United States.
1862 the New York Society for the Relief of the Ruptured and Crippled
     organized America's first orthopedic hospital.
1865 slavery was abolished in the United States when the thirty-fourth
     state approved the thirteenth amendment to the Constitution.
     The only state to reject the amendment was Mississippi.
1898 the Marquis de Chasseloup-Laubat achieved the speed of 39.24
     m.p.h. It was the first officially recognized automobile speed
     record.

1907 a Hotchkiss mounted Panhard was used in wartime for the first time in Casablanca.
1936 a giant panda named Su-Lin arrived in San Francisco.
1957 the first full-scale civilian commercial nuclear power plant in the United States began supplying electricity to Shippingport, Pennsylvania.
1961 India invaded Goa, Damao and Diu.
1966 a party of climbers reached the summit of Vinson Massif in Antarctica.

The following people were born on December 18:

Paul Klee in 1879.
Ty Cobb in 1886.
Abe Burrows in 1910.
Betty Grable in 1916.

December 19   Feast of SS. Nemesius and Other
                                   Martyrs
                                   Resistance Day (Vietnam)

 936 B.C., Hiram I of Tyre, King of Phoenicia, died after a highly successful thirty-three year reign.
1606 the Jamestown settlers left England for America.
1776 Thomas Paine's first "The American Crisis" essay appeared in The Pennsylvania Journal.
1842 the United States officially recognized the independence of Hawaii.
1854 Allen B. Wilson patented a sewing machine capable of sewing curved seams.
1871 Alvert L. Jones patented corrugated paper.
1910 the American Viscose Company began commercial production of rayon.
1920 the first American indoor curling rink opened in Brookline, Massachusetts.
1958 Niger proclaimed itself a republic.
1974 Nelson Rockefeller was sworn in as the forty-first Vice-President of the United States.

The following people were born on December 19:

Welcome Gaston in 1874.
Leonid Brezhnev in 1906.
David Susskind in 1920.
Al Kaline in 1934.

December 20   Louisiana Purchase Day
                                         Mudd Day

1590 Ambrose Pare, "the father of modern surgery," died in Paris
     at the age of eighty.
1790 Samuel Slater started the first successful cotton spinning mill
     in Pawtucket, Rhode Island.
1820 Missouri levied a tax on bachelors.
1860 the first steel shipping vessel, the Ma Robert (a.k.a. the Asthma-
     tic), sank in Africa.
1860 South Carolina seceded from the Union.
1870 impeachment proceedings were instituted against Governor
     William Woods Holden of North Carolina.
1879 Thomas Edison gave the first private demonstration of the incan-
     descent electric lamp.
1887 Benjamin F. Merritt patented an autograph time recorder.
1892 Alexander T. Brown and George F. Stillman patented the pneuma-
     tic automobile tire.
1922 Stanislas Wojciechowski became president of Poland.

The following people were born on December 20:

Harvey Firestone in 1868.
Branch Rickey in 1881.
Charles "Gabby" Hartnett in 1900.
Robert Van De Graff in 1901.
Irene Dunne in 1904.
Peter Criss in 1947.

December 21   Forefathers' Day
                                         Governo de Transicao or Transition
                                           of Government (São Tomé and
                                           Príncipe)
                                         Rauhnachte (Austria)
                                         Winter Solstice

1620 103 pilgrims from the Mayflower landed at Plymouth.
1849 the Philadelphia Skater's Club was formed.
1872 Phileas Fogg entered the Reform Club in London, seventy-nine
     days, twenty-three hours, fifty-nine minutes and fifty-nine
     seconds after his departure.
1898 Marie and Pierre Curie discovered radium.
1909 Berkely, California authorized the institution of a "junior high
     school."
1911 in Paris, the Jules Bonnot gang pulled off the first motorized
     bank hold-up.
1913 the New York Sunday World published the first crossword puzzle.

1914 Tillie's Punctured Romance, with Marie Dressler, Mabel Normand, Charles Chaplin and Mack Swain, was released.
1933 dried human blood serum was first prepared by Drs. Earl W. Flosdorf and Stuart Mudd in Philadelphia.
1937 Walt Disney's cartoon production of Snow White and the Seven Dwarfs was introduced in Los Angeles.
1958 Charles de Gaulle was elected President of the Fifth Republic of France.

The following people were born on December 21:

Benjamin Disraeli in 1804.
Joseph Stalin in 1879.
Walter Hagen in 1892.
Paul Winchell in 1922.
Jack Daniels in 1927.
Jane Fonda in 1937.
Frank Zappa in 1940.
Dave Kingman in 1948.
Chris Evert in 1954.

December 22   International Arbor Day
                                   Vietnamese People's Army Day
                                   Yugoslav People's Army Day

the sun enters the house of Capricorn.
1662 the first catamaran, the Experiment, was launched.
1775 the Continental Navy (of the United States) was organized.
1831 the New York and Harlem Railway (streetcar) Company received its franchise.
1877 Raoul Pictet produced liquid oxygen in Geneva.
1885 LaMarcus A. Thompson patented the railway switchback.
1894 Alfred Dreyfuss was convicted of treason.
1894 the United States Golf Association was formed.
1905 street fighting broke out in Moscow that lasted for about ten days.
1907 Adolph Topperwein completed ten days of exhibition shooting during which he shot at 72,500 small wooden cubes thrown into the air, hitting 72,491 of them.
1943 W.E.B. DuBois was elected to membership in the National Institute of Arts and Letters.

The following people were born on December 22:

Wilhelm Hisinger in 1766.
Matty Alou in 1938.

December 23   Feast of the Radishes (Mexico)

8733 B.C., the wheel was used for the first time in Beirut for the purpose of threshing.
1823 "A Visit from St. Nicholas" (" 'Twas the Night Before Christmas") was published.
1876 Midhat Pasha proclaimed the Ottoman Empire's constitution.
1907 the first all steel railroad passenger coach was completed.
1919 the hospital ship U.S.S. Relief was launched.
1920 Great Britain passed the Government of Ireland Act which divided the country into two administrative regions.
1941 U.S. Marines on Wake surrendered and Japanese troops occupied the island.
1947 John Bardeen, Walter Houser Brattain and William Shockley invented the transistor.
1948 Premier Hidecki Tojo was hanged in Tokyo as a war criminal.
1953 twenty-one American prisoners in North Korea refused to return to the United States.
1968 North Korea released the crew of the U.S.S. Pueblo following the United States' apology.

The following people were born on December 23:

Joseph Smith in 1805.
Connie Mack in 1862.
Albert "Bunny" Fabrique in 1887.
Henry "Hinkey" Haines in 1898.
Paul Hornung in 1935.

December 24   Christmas Eve
                    Libya (1951) Independence Day

1582 London Bridge Waterworks first began piping water into private homes.
1818 the music for "Silent Night" was composed by Franz Gruber for the original words by Josef Mohr.
1832 a charter was granted to the Georgia Infirmary "for the relief and protection of aged and afflicted Negroes" in Savannah, Georgia.
1889 Daniel C. Stover and William A. Hance patented a bicycle with a back pedal brake.
1906 the first general radio broadcast was made.
1908 New York City began exercising motion picture censorship.
1920 Enrico Caruso gave his last U.S. performance at the Metropolitan Opera House in New York.
1948 the first completely solar heated house was moved into, thanks to Amelia Peabody, Eleanor Raymond and Dr. Maria Telkes, in Dover, Massachusetts.

1951 the United Kingdom of Libya formally declared its independence as a constitutional monarchy.
1966 a U.S. Air Force CL-44 crashed in a South Vietnamese village killing 129 people.

The following people were born on December 24:

Jean Louis Pons in 1761.
Christopher "Kit" Carson in 1809.
James Joule in 1818.
Leadbelly (Huddie Ledbetter) in 1888.
Cab Calloway and I.F. Stone in 1907.
Ava Gardner in 1922.

December 25
Children's Day (People's Republic of the Congo)
Christmas
International Family Day
Republic of China's (Taiwan) Constitution Day
Sun's Birth Day

 496 B.C., Clovis, chief of the Frankish tribes in Gaul, was baptised.
 800 A.D., Charlemagne was crowned Emperor of the West by Pope Leo III.
1635 Samuel de Champlain died at the age of sixty-eight.
1741 the centigrade (Celsius) temperature scale was first used at Uppsala, Sweden.
1745 Prussia and Austria concluded the Treaty of Dresden.
1843 the first Christmas with Christmas cards was celebrated.
1882 the first Christmas with electric Christmas tree lights was celebrated.
1917 Fort Smith, Northwest Territories registered a temperature of -57° C.
1928 In Old Arizona, the first western talkie, was shown.
1934 A Christmas Carol was broadcast with Lionel Barrymore.
1941 Hong Kong surrendered to the Japanese.

The following people were born on December 25:

Jesus Christ in 5 B.C.
Sir Isaac Newton in 1642.
Clara Barton in 1821.
Mohammed Ali Jinnah in 1876.
Robert Ripley in 1893.
Rod Serling in 1924.
Barbara Mandrell in 1948.

December 26   Boxing Day
                                   Day of the Wren (Ireland)
                                   St. Stephen's Day

1776 Washington crossed the Delaware River and defeated the Hessians in the Battle of Trenton.
1805 the Pennsylvania Academy of Fine Arts was established.
1825 at the accession of Czar Nicholas I, the Decembrist Rising in Russia broke out and was suppressed all in the same day.
1833 Seth Fuller patented an annunciator.
1865 James H. Nason patented a coffee percolator.
1877 the Socialist Labor Party of North America held its first national convention.
1908 Jack Johnson won the world heavyweight title from Tommy Burns.
1917 the United States government took over the operation of American railroads for the duration of World War I.
1931 George Gershwin's musical comedy, Of Thee I Sing, opened at the Music Box Theater in New York.
1954 "The Shadow" radio show made its last regular broadcast.

The following people were born on December 26:

George E. "White Wings" Tebeau in 1862.
James "Queenie" O'Rourke in 1889.
Mao Tse-tung in 1893.
Richard Widmark in 1914.
Steve Allen in 1921.
Alan King in 1927.

December 27   Feast of St. John the Apostle
                                   Festival of Umuganuro (Burundi)

1831 H.M.S. Beagle sailed from England on a survey expedition to South America with Charles Darwin aboard as the ship's naturalist.
1845 Dr. Crawford Long introduced the use of ether as an anaesthetic in child birth.
1894 the Military Order of Foreign Wars was founded.
1906 the American Sociological Society held its first annual meeting in Providence, Rhode Island.
1907 the Dutch, having subdued the Achinese, completed the pacification of Sumatra.
1932 Radio City Music Hall opened.
1934 America's first youth hostel opened in Northfield, Massachusetts.
1945 the International Bank for Reconstruction and Development (the World Bank) was organized.

1947 the first "Howdy Doody" show was telecast.
1948 Cardinal Mindszenty was arrested in Hungary for protesting
     when Roman Catholic schools were nationalized.
1949 the United States of Indonesia became an independent nation.

The following people were born on December 27:

Johannes Kepler in 1571.
Louis Pasteur in 1822.
William "Ducky" Hemp in 1867.
Marlene Dietrich in 1904.

December 28   Childermas or Holy Innocents Day
                                    Iowa Admission Day
                                    Shri Panch Ko Janma Divas or
                                      Birthday of the King (Nepal)

1832 Vice-President of the United States J.C. Calhoun resigned.
1846 Iowa was admitted to the Union.
1869 Labor Day was inaugurated as a holiday by the Knights of Labor
     in Philadelphia.
1869 William F. Semple obtained a patent for chewing gum.
1877 John Stevens applied for a patent for a flour rolling mill.
1895 a motion picture was shown in public for the first time in Paris.
1928 Admiral Richard Evelyn Byrd reached the Antarctic ice barrier.
1935 the Works Project Administration (W.P.A.) Federal Art Project
     Gallery opened in New York City.
1942 R.O.D. Sullivan completed his 100th transatlantic flight.
1973 the comet Kohoutek reached perihelion.

The following people were born on December 28:

John Molson in 1763.
Count Sensenderfer in 1847.
Woodrow Wilson in 1856.
Ted Lyons in 1900.
Earl Fatha Hines in 1905.
Terry Sawchuck in 1929.
Edgar Winter in 1946.

December 29   Proclamation Day (South Australia)
                                    Texas Admission Day

1170 St. Thomas à Becket was murdered in the Canterbury Cathedral.

1837 J.A. Pitts patented a steam powered thresher.
1845 Texas was admitted to the Union.
1848 the first gas light was turned on in the White House.
1851 the Young Men's Christian Association was organized in Boston.
1890 the massacre that has become known as the "Battle of Wounded Knee" took place.
1891 Thomas Edison patented his radio.
1908 Otto Zachow and William Besserdich patented a four wheel brake system for automobiles.
1931 Harold C. Urey announced the discovery of heavy water (deuterium).
1952 transistorized hearing aids went on sale for the first time in Elmsford, New York.
1954 South Vietnam, Laos and Cambodia were granted independence.

The following people were born on December 29:

Charles Goodyear in 1800.
Pablo Casals in 1876.
General Billy Mitchell in 1879.
Mary Tyler Moore in 1937.
John Voight in 1938.

December 30   Anniversary of the Democratic
                                   Republic of Madagascar
                                   Day of the Proclamation of the
                                   Republic (Romania)
                                   Rizal Day (Philippines)

1730 an earthquake in Hokkaido, Japan killed 137,000 people.
1853 the Gadsden Purchase was completed.
1854 the Pennsylvania Rock Oil Company was incorporated.
1887 the American Physiological Society was formed.
1896 Philippine national hero Jose Rizal was executed by the Spanish Army and rebellion flared up again.
1903 the American Political Science Association was founded.
1913 W.D. Coolidge patented ductile tungsten.
1916 Gregory Rasputin was assassinated by a group led by Prince Felix Yusupov.
1917 Mountain City, Tennessee registered a temperature of -32° F.
1917 Lewisburg, West Virginia registered a temperature of -37° F.
1922 the Union of Soviet Socialist Republics was formally established.
1933 Bloomfield, Vermont registered a temperature of -50° F.
1947 the Socialist Republic of Romania was proclaimed.
1968 Mazama and Winthrop, Washington registered temperatures of -48° F.

The following people were born on December 30:

Joseph Rudyard Kipling in 1865.
Lester Patrick in 1883.
Hidecki Tojo in 1884.
Bert Parks in 1914.
Bo Diddley (Ellas McDaniels) in 1928.
Skeeter Davis (Mary Francis Penick) in 1931.
Sandy Koufax and Russ Tamblyn in 1935.
Del Shannon in 1939.
Michael Nesmith in 1942.
Davy Jones in 1946.

December 31   Feed Yourself Day
                                   Foundation of Party and People's
                                     Republic of the Congo
                                   Hogmanay (Scotland)
                                   Namahage (Japan)
                                   New Year's Eve
                                   St. Sylvester's Day
                                   Fiesta Bancaria (Guatemala)

1776 Rhode Island enacted a price regulation law "to prevent monopo-
     lies and oppression by excessive and unreasonable prices."
1862 the U.S.S. Monitor sank in a storm off Cape Hatteras.
1879 Thomas Edison demonstrated his incandescent electric lamp
     for the public.
1925 J. Skimmerhorn's catch of a forty-one pound cutthroat trout
     in Nevada went into the record books.
1943 Frank Sinatra opened at the Paramount Theatre to a great deal
     of screaming, swooning and dancing in the aisles.
1943 Soviet troops reoccupied Zhitomir.
1948 Senator Russell Long was sworn into the office which had been
     held previously by his father, Huey P. Long, and his mother,
     Rose McConnell Long.
1951 the Marshall Plan ended.
1953 Willie Shoemaker won his 400th horse race of the year.
1965 the total count of U.S. troops in South Vietnam reached 184,314.
1977 the northernmost point reached by the hybrid "killer bees" was
     Ciudad Bolívar, Venezuela.

The following people were born on December 31:

Michael J. "King" Kelly in 1857.
Henri Matisse in 1869.
Odetta in 1930.
John Denver and Sarah Miles in 1943.
Donna Summer in 1948.

Index of Birthdays

Aaron, H. 2/5
Abbot, B. 10/2
Abbot, R.S. 11/24
Abernathy, R. 3/11
Abzug, B. 7/24
Adams, A. 2/20
Adams, D. 4/19
Adams, E. 4/16
Adams, J. 10/30
Adams, J.Q. 7/11
Addams, C. 1/7
Addams, J. 9/6
Adderly, J. 9/15
Adenauer, K. 1/5
Adler, A. 2/17
Agassiz, J.L. 5/28
Agricola, G. 3/24
Agnew, S.T. 11/9
Aiken, C. 8/5
Aiken, L. 3/19

Alberghetti, A.M. 5/15
Albert, E. 4/22
Albertson, J. 6/16
Alcott, L.M. 11/29
Alda, A. 1/28
Aldrin, E. 1/20
Alexander, G. 2/26
Alexander, J. 10/28
Alexander, S. 10/6
Alger, H. 1/13
Ali, M. 1/18
Allen, E. 1/10
Allen, F. 5/31
Allen, G. 4/29
Allen, G. 7/26
Allen, M. 2/14
Allen, R. 3/8
Allen, S. 12/26
Allen, W. 12/1
Allman, G. 12/8

Dayan, M. 5/20
Deal, J.W. 1/21
Dean, J.H. 1/16
Dean, J. 8/10
Dean, J. 10/14
Debs, E.V. 11/5
DeBusschere, D. 10/16
Debussy, A.C. 8/22
DeCarlo, Y. 9/1
Decatur, S. 1/5
Dee, S. 4/23
Degas, E. 7/19
Delahanty, E. 10/30
DeLuise, D. 8/1
DeMille, C.B. 8/12
Dempsey, J. 6/24
Deneuve, C. 10/22
Denver, J. 12/31
Dern, B. 6/4
Descartes, R. 3/31
Dewey, J. 10/20
Dewey, T.E. 3/24
Dey, S. 12/10
Diamond, N. 1/24
Dickens, C. 2/7
Dickerson, L. 10/11
Dickey, B. 6/6
Dickinson, A. 10/1
Dickinson, E. 12/10
Diddley, B. 12/30
Diderot, D. 10/5
Didrickson, M. 6/26
Diefenbaker, J. 9/18
Diesel, R. 3/18
Dietrich, M. 12/27
Diller, P. 7/17
Dillhoefer, W. 10/13
Dillinger, J. 6/28
DiMaggio, J. 11/25
DiMucci, D. 7/18
Dion 7/18
Disney, W. 12/5
Disraeli, B. 12/21
Dodgson, C. 1/27
Dolenz, M. 3/9
Domino, A. 2/26
Donegan, L. 4/29
Donahue, T. 1/27
Donovan 5/10
Doppler, C.J. 11/29
Dorsey, J. 2/29
Dorsey, T. 11/10
DosPassos, J. 1/14
Dostoyevsky, F.M. 11/11
Doubleday, A. 6/26
Douglas, K. 12/9

Douglas, W. 5/10
Douglas, M. 8/11
Douglas, S. 4/23
Douglas, W.O. 10/16
Douglass, F. 2/14
Downs, H. 2/14
Doyle, A.C. 5/22
Doyle, J. 9/15
Dru, J. 1/31
Drysdale, D. 7/23
DuBois, W.E.B. 2/23
Duchin, P. 7/28
Duke, P. 12/14
Dukenfield, W.C. 1/29
Dumas, A. 7/27
Dunant, J.H. 5/8
Dunaway, F. 1/14
Dunbar, P.L. 6/27
Duncan, I. 5/27
Duncan, S. 2/20
Dunne, I. 12/20
Durante, J. 2/10
Dürer, A. 5/21
Durkheim, E. 4/15
Durocher, L. 7/27
Durrell, L. 2/27
Duryea, D. 1/23
Dvořák, A. 9/8
Dylan, B. 5/24

Eakins, T. 7/25
Earhart, A. 7/24
Earp, W. 3/19
Eastman, G. 7/12
Eastwood, C. 5/31
Ebsen, B. 4/2
Eckstine, B. 7/8
Eddy, D. 4/26
Eddy, N. 6/29
Edison, T.A. 2/11
Edward 3/10
Eggar, S. 3/5
Egstrom, N.D. 5/26
Ehrlich, P. 3/14
Einstein, A. 3/14
Eisenhower, D. 10/14
Eliot, G. 11/22
Elizabeth 1 9/7
Elizabeth II 4/21
Ellington, D. 4/29
Elliott, C. 9/19
Emerson, R.W. 5/25
Encke, J. 9/23
Enders, J. 2/10

Sydow, M. von 4/10
Szilard, L. 2/11

T., Booker 11/12
Taft, W.H. 9/15
Tallchief, M. 1/24
Talleyrand 2/13
Tamblyn, R. 12/30
Tarkenton, F. 2/3
Taylor, E. 2/27
Taylor, J. 3/12
Taylor, Z. 11/24
Tchaikovsky, P.I. 5/7
Tebeau, G.E. 12/26
Teller, E. 1/15
Temple, S. 4/23
Tennille, T. 5/8
Tennyson, A. 8/6
Terry, B. 10/30
Thant, U 1/22
Thomas, B.J. 8/7
Thomas, D. 1/6
Thomas, D. 10/27
Thomas, L. 4/6
Thomas, M. 11/21
Thomas, S. 8/19
Thomas, T. 7/14
Thoreau, H. 7/12
Thorpe, J. 5/28
Thumb, T. 1/4
Thurber, J. 12/8
Thurmond, S. 12/5
Thurston, H. 6/2
Tilden, B. 2/10
Tillis, M. 8/8
Tim, T. 4/12
Tinker, J. 7/27
Titcomb, L. 8/21
Tito 5/25
Tittle, Y.A. 10/24
Tocqueville, A. de 7/29
Tojo, H. 12/30
Tolkien, J.R.R 1/4
Tolstoy, L. 9/9
Tomlin, L. 9/1
Tompkins, D.D. 6/21
Tork, P. 2/13
Torme, M. 9/13
Torn, R. 2/6
Toscanini, A. 3/25
Toulouse-Lautrec 11/24
Toynbee, A. 4/14
Tracy, S. 5/5

Travers, M. 11/7
Travolta, J. 2/18
Trevino, L. 12/1
Traynor, H.J. 11/11
Trotsky, L. 10/26
Trout, P.H. 6/29
Trudeau, P.E. 10/18
Truman, E. 2/13
Truman, H. 2/20
Truman, H.S 5/8
Tubb, E. 2/9
Tucker, F. 2/12
Tucker, S. 1/13
Tucker, T. 10/10
Tucker, T. 10/28
Tufts, S. 7/16
Tunney, G. 5/25
Turner, I. 11/5
Turner, L. 2/8
Turner, N. 10/2
Turner, T. 11/25
Twain, M. 11/30
Twitty, C. 9/1
Tyler, J. 3/29
Tyler, R.W. 3/18

Udall, M.K. 6/15
Udall, S. 1/31
Uecker, B. 1/26
Uggams, L. 5/25
Ullman, L. 12/16
Ulyanov, V.I. 4/22
Unitas, J. 5/7
Updike, J. 3/18
Uris, L. 8/3
Ustinov, P. 4/16

Vaccaro, B. 11/18
Vadim, R. 1/26
Vale, J. 7/8
Valens, R. 5/13
Valentino, R. 5/6
Vallee, R. 7/28
Valli, F. 5/3
Van Allen, J. 9/7
Van Buren, M. 12/5
Vance, O. 3/4
Vance, V. 7/26
Van De Graff, R. 12/20
Van Doren, M. 2/6
Van Dyck, A. 3/22

Index of Commemorations

All commemorations are listed on their earliest possible dates.
See list of abbreviations on page 279.

1/1, 7; 2/17; 5/2, 29; 6/2, 23; 7/2, 16, 21; 9/15, 19, 21; 10/30; 11/11; 12/14
Bibliotecario, Día del (Chile) 7/10
Bieuwa (Bhutan) 1/7
Bike Mo 5/1
Bike Safety Wk 4/15
Bill of Rights Day 12/15
Bird Day (Iowa) 3/21
Black Nazarene Fiesta 1/1
Blessed Rainy Day (Bhutan) 9/21
Blessing of the Animals at the Cathedral (Mexico) 1/17
Blood Donor Mo, Ntnl 1/1
Bloomsday (Dublin, Ireland) 6/16
Blueberry Festival, Ntnl 7/16
(Pres) Bogoda's Death, Ann of (Cent African Rep) 3/29
Bogota, Founding of (Colombia) 8/6
Bolívar, Simón, Ann of the Death of (Venezuela) 12/17
Bolívar, Simón Birthday (Latin Amer) 7/24
Bolivia Ind Day 8/6
Bolivia Martyrs' Day 7/21
Bolivia
    1/24; 2/10; 7/16
Bon Festival (Japan) 7/13
Bonifacio Day 11/30
Boquerón, Btl of Day (Paraguay) 9/29
Borden, Lizzie Liberation Day 8/4
Boss Day, Ntnl 10/16
Botswana Ind Day 9/30
Bourgiba, Habib Birthday (Tunisia) 8/3
Boxing Day 12/26
Boy Scouts of Amer Ann Mo 2/1
Braderie (Luxembourg) 9/1
Brazil Ind Day 9/7
Brazilian Flag Day 11/19
Brazilian Rep Day 11/15
Brazil
    1/20, 25; 2/2; 4/21; 10/1, 8; 11/2
(St) Brigid's Day 2/1
Britain, Btl of Day 9/15
British Virgin Islands
    3/9; 7/1; 10/21
Brunei Const Day 9/29
Brunei
    6/1; 7/15
Buddha Day (Hawaii) 4/8
Buddha Purnima (Bangladesh) 4/30
Buddha's Parinirvana (Bhutan) 5/29
Bulgaria Ntnl Liberation Day 9/9
Bulgaria
    2/14; 5/24; 6/2
Bullfinch Exchange Day (Japan) 1/7

Bunker Hill Day (Mass) 6/17
Burbank, Luther Day 3/7
Burma Ind Day 1/4
Burma Martyrs' Day 7/19
Burmese Ntnl Day 11/21
Burmese Union Day 2/12
Burma
    3/2, 27; 11/11
Burns, Robert Day 1/25
Burundi Ind Day 7/1
Burundi
    9/18; 10/13; 12/15, 27
Buzzard Day in Hinckley, Ohio 3/15

Cable TV Mo 9/1
California Adm Day 9/9
Cambodia Ind Day 11/9
Cambodia
    3/6
Cameroon Ind Day 1/1
Cameroonian Rep Day 5/20
Cameroon
    2/11; 10/1
Camoens and Portuguese Communities Day (Macao) 6/10
Camoes Memorial Day (Portugal) 6/10
Camp Fire Girls Founders Day 3/17
Camping Wk, Amer 3/1
Canada-US Goodwill Wk 4/21
Canada
    7/1; 10/8; 11/11
Canary Islands
    10/12
Canberra Day (Australian Capital Terr) 3/17
Cancer Control Mo 4/1
Candelaria, Día de la (Mexico) 2/2
Candlemas 2/2
Canterbury Prov Ann (New Zealand) 12/16
Cape Henry Day 4/26
Cape Verde Ind Day 7/5
Cape Verde Ntnl Heroes Day 1/20
Cape Verde Ntnlity Day 9/12
Cape Verde
    6/1
Captain Regents Day (San Marino) 4/1 and 10/1
Carabobo, Btl of (Venezuela) 6/24
Car Care Mo 5/1
Caribbean Day (Guyana) 7/1
Caricom Day (Barbados) 8/3
Caricom Day (St Vincent) 7/6
Cartagena Day (Colombia) 11/11

Tahiti's Ntnl Holiday 7/14
Tahiti
  3/5
Take Over Day (Nauru) 7/1
(St) Tamenend's Day 5/1
Tanabata (Japan) 7/7
Tanzania Ind Day 12/9
Tanzanian Union Day 4/26
Tanzania
  1/12; 2/5; 7/7
Taranaki Prov Ann (New Zealand)
  3/31
Tarapaca, Btl of (Peru) 11/27
Tasmania
  3/1
Tazaungdaing (Burma) 11/11
Teacher's Day (Rep of China) 9/28
Teachers' Day (Czechoslovakia) 3/28
Teacher's Day (El Salvador) 6/22
Teachers' Day (Mass) 6/1
Telecommunication Day, World 5/17
Tennessee Adm Day 6/1
Territory Day (British Virgin Is) 7/1
Texas Adm Day 12/29
Texas Ind Day 3/2
Tha Tamil Thai-Pongal Day (Sri Lanka)
  1/14
Thai Const Day 12/10
Thailand's Ntnl Day 6/24
Thailand
  2/19; 4/6, 13; 5/5, 7, 18; 7/16; 8/12;
  10/23; 12/5
Thanksgiving Day (Canada) 10/8
Thanksgiving Day (US) 11/22
Thimphu Domchoe (Bhutan) 9/15
Thimphu Tsechu (Bhutan) 9/19
Third Republic Day (Ghana) 9/24
(St) Thomas Aquinas, Fst of 3/7
Three Glorious Days (Congo) 8/13-15
Three Kings Day 1/6
Throne, Fst of the (Morocco) 3/3
Time Memorial Day (Japan) 6/11
Tiradentes Day (Brazil) 4/21
Togo Ind Day 4/27
Togo Lib Day 1/13
Togo
  1/24; 4/24; 6/21
Tongan Const Day 11/4
Tonga
  4/25; 6/4
Trades Holiday (Scotland) 7/4
Traditional Day of Offering (Bhutan)
  1/7
Transition of Government (São Tomé
  and Príncipe) 12/21
Tree Planting Day, Lesotho's Ntnl 3/23

(King) Tribhuvan's Birthday (Nepal)
  2/18
Tribhuvan Jayanti (Nepal) 2/18
Trifon Zarezan (Bulgaria) 2/14
Trinidad and Tobago Ind Day 8/31
Trinidadian and Tobagonian Rep Day
  9/24
Trinidad and Tobago
  8/3
Truman, H. Birthday (Mo) 5/8
Truth, Sojourner Day 11/26
Tubman, Harriet Day 3/10
(President) Tubman's Birthday (Liberia)
  11/29
Tuen Ng Festival (Hong Kong) 6/6
Tunisia Evacuation Day 10/15
Tunisia Ind Day 3/20
Tunisia Martyrs' Day 4/9
Tunisian Rep Day 7/25
Tunisian Rev Day 1/18
Tunisia
  6/1; 8/3, 13
Turkey's Ntnl Sovreignty Day 4/23
Turkish Const Day 5/27
Turkish Ntnl Day (Cyprus) 10/29
Turkish Rep Day 10/28
Turkey
  5/19; 8/30
Turks and Caicos Islands
  11/11
Turtles Intnl Awareness Wk 8/1
Twelfth, The (N Ireland) 7/12
Twenty-sixth of July Movement, Celb
  of the (Cuba) 7/26
Two Sieges and Regatta Day (Malta)
  9/8

Uganda Ind Day 10/9
Uganda Lib Day 4/11
Uganda's Ntnl Holiday 7/11
Uhuru Day (Kenya) 12/7
Umhlanga Day (Swaziland) 8/25
Umuganuro, Festival of (Burundi) 12/27
Umutomboko Ceremony (Zambia) 7/29
Underdog Day 12/15
UNICEF Day, Ntnl 10/31
Unification Day (Cameroon) 10/1
Union Day (Romania) 1/24
Union of Soviet Socialist Republics'
  Const Day 12/5
Union of Soviet Socialist Republics
  1/21; 4/22; 5/1, 9; 11/7
United Arab Emirates Ind Day 12/2
United Kingdom
  5/25; 8/31

Index of Events

See list of abbreviations on page 279.

320

Drum, freshwater 4/20
Drum, red 11/7
Drunk driving 9/10
Dublin, Ireland 4/18; 7/17
Du Bois, W.E.B. 12/22
Dubuc, P. 9/15
Dubuque, Iowa 5/12
Duburg, SS 2/17
Duck-billed platypus 7/15
Duckering, F.W. 6/22
Ductile tungsten 12/30
Dueling 11/10
Dufek, G.J. 10/31
Dufour, J.J. 8/28
Dugong 11/16
Dulty, G. 4/24
Dumas, C. 6/29
Dumbarton Oaks Conference 8/21
Dunbar, Btl of 9/3
Duncan, J.S. 4/28
Duncan, R.T. 9/28
Dunkirk 6/4
Dunlop Latex Development Laboratories 7/3
Du Pont Co 2/16, 24; 10/27; 11/2
Duplicating machine 2/14
Durham, NC 1/1
Duryea, J.F. 11/28
Duryea Motor Wagon Co 9/21
Dutch 1/20; 3/17; 4/7, 20; 5/3, 4, 10; 9/6, 8; 10/2, 7; 11/12; 12/27

E Pluribus Unum 6/20
Eagle, HMS 9/7
Eagles, Philadelphia 9/17, 24; 11/6, 15; 12/1
Earmuffs 3/13
Earhart, A. 1/11; 5/20; 6/17; 7/2
Early Würm 7/25; 9/5
Earps 10/25
Earthquake 1/24; 2/4; 3/27; 4/18; 5/20, 22; 6/1, 7; 7/28; 8/17, 31; 9/1, 27; 10/10, 11; 11/1, 16, 23; 12/16, 30
East Germany 8/12
East London, S Africa 12/9
East River 6/15
Easter Rebellion 4/18, 29
Eastman, G. 9/4; 10/14
Ebert, J. 4/24
Echo Farms Dairy 1/11; 4/8
Echo I 8/12
Eclipse 11/10
Ecuador 2/12; 5/13; 12/8
Ederle, G. 8/6

"Edge of Night" 4/2
Edict of Nantes 4/15; 10/18
Edinburgh Music Soc 3/29
Edirne 6/5
Edison Electric Illuminating Co 12/17
Edison Electric Light Co 10/15
Edison, T.A. 1/27; 2/19; 4/14; 6/1; 8/8, 9; 9/27; 10/15, 19; 12/6, 20, 29, 31
Edsel 9/4
"Ed Sullivan Show" 1/12
Education 2/7
Edward VIII 12/11
Edwards Air Force Base 4/14
Egg incubator 3/30
Egypt 1/17; 2/12, 28; 3/26; 4/17, 19, 28; 5/31; 6/5, 23; 7/15, 19, 23; 8/22, 23; 10/6, 29; 11/20, 25; 12/12
Ehrlichman, J. 4/30; 7/12
Eichmann, A. 4/11; 5/23, 31
Eickemeyer, R. 4/3
Eight hour work day 1/5; 9/25
Eighteenth amendment 4/10
8MK, radio 8/20, 31
Einstein, A. 4/18; 8/2; 12/5
Eireann, Dail 10/25
Eisenhower, D.D. 1/16; 11/30
Ejection seat, aircraft 1/13
El Alamein 11/2
Elba 4/11
Elcano, Juan de 9/7
Eldfell 1/23
Election 4/11
Election Day 1/23
Election law 5/22
Electric blanket 10/9
Electric bridge table 11/29
Electric chair 8/6
Electric eye camera 1/16
Electric Home and Farm Authority, Inc 1/17
Electric light 1/27; 8/11
Electric power 2/7; 3/6
Electric printing press 2/25
Electric range 9/20
Electric razor 3/18
Electric starter 11/24
Electric street car 7/13
Electric street lights 3/31
Electrical Show 10/21
Electricity 6/15
Electrobasograph 6/12
Electrolux Servel Corp 12/7
Electron microscope 4/20
Elements 9/3
Elephant 4/13; 11/13
Elevated railway 6/2

Hydrogen balloon 12/1
Hydrogen bomb 10/31

Ibn Saud 1/8
Ibo 5/31
Ice cream 5/30
Ice cream cone 7/23; 12/13
Ice cream cone rolling machine 1/29
Iceberg 1/19
Iceland 6/8; 7/7, 17; 8/6; 11/19
Idaho 1/4, 16; 4/24; 6/6; 7/3, 28; 10/27
Iguala, Plan of 2/24
Ile Carn 11/10
Illinois 1/22; 3/22; 5/28; 6/10; 7/14;
    11/3; 12/3
Illinois Inst of Technology 6/28
Illinois, Univ of 7/15
Illinoisan period 4/12
Immigration act 6/25
Immigration quota 6/3; 5/26
Immigration Quota Act 5/19
Impeachment 3/13, 22; 5/9; 12/17, 20
Inca 8/29; 11/16
Incandescent electric lamp 10/15;
    12/20, 31
Inchon, South Korea 9/15
Income tax 2/25; 4/15; 7/12; 8/5, 27
Independence of India Lg 8/30
India 1/1, 14, 19, 26; 2/2; 3/9, 12, 18,
    28, 31; 4/18; 5/28; 6/21, 23; 7/8;
    8/15; 9/19; 10/20, 26; 12/18
Indian Affairs Commissioner 4/21
Indian Mills, NJ 8/29
Indian removal 3/26
Indian reservation 8/29
Indian rights, South African 2/24
Indiana 2/2; 3/9, 27; 7/14; 8/13; 12/11
Indianapolis, Ind 3/25; 5/1, 17; 11/25
Indianapolis "500" 5/30
Indians 1/23; 2/20, 29; 3/19, 22; 5/27;
    6/2, 9; 7/8; 8/13, 24, 29; 9/17
Indians, Oorang 11/4
Indians' scalps 2/20
Indochina 9/22
Indonesia 3/11, 12; 8/11, 15, 17; 9/28;
    12/27
Indus River 9/24
Industrial Recovery Act 6/16
Inebriate Asylum 5/15
Infant School Soc of NY 5/23
Inflation 11/3
In-flight movie 10/8
Information Service, US 1/18
"In God We Trust" 7/30

Ingalls, L. 10/5
"Inner Sanctum Mysteries" 1/7
Innuendo and Snappy Comeback, Mas-
    ter of 8/28
In Old Arizona 12/25
Inquisition 4/12
Insect 8/3
Insect electrocutor 11/8
Instant soup 7/30
Insurance co 1/11; 2/20; 6/17
Integrated college 12/3
Integration 9/3
Intercollegiate Football Ass 11/23
Intercollegiate Lacrosse Ass 3/11
Intercontinental Ballistic Missile (ICBM)
    8/26
Interglacial 2/12; 3/4; 4/12; 7/25; 10/6;
    12/5
Internal combustion engine 4/1
Internal Revenue Act 3/3
Internal Revenue Service 9/11
International Antarctic Try 12/1
International Bank for Reconstruction
    and Development 12/27
International Bur of Amer Reps 4/14
International Congress of Soil Science
    6/13
International Court at the Hague 1/30
International Red Cross 2/17
Interracial hospital 5/4
Interstadial 6/5; 9/5
Interstate Commerce Act 2/4
Interstate Commerce Commission 1/10;
    11/1
Interstate crime prevention 9/16
Io 3/9, 12
Ionian Sea 9/8
Iowa 1/12; 4/11; 7/20; 12/28
Iowa State College 5/23
"I Pagliacci" 9/28
Ipswich, Mass 7/19
Iran 1/20; 3/21; 4/1, 27; 8/16, 25; 9/9,
    16; 11/4
Iraq 6/10, 18; 7/14; 8/16, 23; 9/11, 16
Ireland 1/22; 4/18, 29; 7/1; 9/12; 10/25;
    11/3, 8; 12/6, 14, 23
Irish Republic 1/21
Irish Republican Army 8/27
Iron 1/6
Iron Age 2/11
Iron-clad warship 2/14
Isbell, C. 10/18
Ishpeming, Mich 2/21
Iske, Anthony 11/4
Islam 4/9; 6/7
Isle of Man TT Race 5/7